After the TRC:
Reflections on Truth and Reconciliation in South Africa

After the TRC:
Reflections on Truth and
Reconciliation in South Africa

EDITED BY

WILMOT JAMES AND LINDA VAN DE VIJVER

OHIO UNIVERSITY PRESS
Athens

First published in 2000 in Africa by David Philip Publishers (Pty) Ltd,
208 Werdmuller Centre, Claremont 7708, South Africa

Published in 2001 in North America by Ohio University Press, Scott Quadrangler,
Athens, Ohio 45701, United States

ISBN 0-86486-374-8 (David Philip)
ISBN 0-8214-1385-6 (Ohio University Press)

US CIP data available upon request.

Contents

Contributors

Heribert Adam is Professor of Sociology at Simon Fraser University in Vancouver, Canada.

Kanya Adam received her D. Phil from Oxford University and is currently a post-doctoral research fellow at the University of British Columbia in Vancouver, Canada.

Alex Boraine is a Visiting Professor to the Global Law School, New York University, and was formerly Vice-Chairperson of the TRC.

Colin Bundy is Vice-Chancellor and Principal of the University of the Witwatersrand.

Mary Burton was formerly a TRC Commissioner.

John de Gruchy is the Robert Selby Taylor Professor of Christian Studies at the University of Cape Town, and Director of the Graduate School of Humanities, University of Cape Town.

Richard Goldstone is a Justice of the Constitutional Court of South Africa, and was formerly the Prosecutor for the International Criminal Tribunals for Rwanda and former Yugoslavia.

Willem Heath is Head of the Heath Special Investigating Unit mandated by government to investigate corruption on a national level.

Wilmot James is Professor of Diversity Studies at the Graduate Schools of Business and Humanities, University of Cape Town.

Jeffrey Lever is a sociologist and works for the Impumelelo Innovations Awards Programme in Cape Town.

Mahmood Mamdani is the Herbert Lehman Professor of Government and Director of the Institute of African Studies at Columbia University, New York.

Gary Minkley is Associate Professor in the Department of History, University of the Western Cape.

Njabulo Ndebele is Vice-Chancellor and Principal of the University of Cape Town.

Dumisa Ntsebeza is an Advocate in Cape Town, and formerly a TRC Commissioner.

Kaizer Nyatsumba is Editor of the Daily News in Durban.

Grace Naledi Pandor is Chairperson of the National Council of Provinces, Parliament of South Africa.

Mamphela Ramphele is Managing Director at the World Bank, Washington, D.C., with special responsibility for Human Development.

Ciraj Rassool is a senior lecturer in the Department of History, University of the Western Cape.

Albie Sachs is a Justice of the Constitutional Court of South Africa.

Patricia Valdez is an independent consultant in Argentina and was formerly Director of the Commission on the Truth for El Salvador.

Linda van de Vijver is a researcher in the Faculty of Law, University of Cape Town.

Jan van Eck is an independent consultant currently working in Burundi.

Frederik Van Zyl Slabbert is a businessman, political consultant, lecturer, and Chairperson of the Open Society Initiative for Southern Africa.

Charles Villa-Vicencio is Executive Director of the Institute for Justice and Reconciliation, and was formerly Director of Research at the TRC.

Francis Wilson is Professor of Economics and Director of the South African Labour and Development Research Unit at the University of Cape Town.

Leslie Witz is a senior lecturer in the Department of History, University of the Western Cape.

Abbreviations

ANC – African National Congress
APLA – Azanian People's Liberation Army
AZAPO – Azanian People's Organisation
CAMP – Citizens' Army for Multi-Party Politics (Uganda)
CCB – Civil Co-operation Bureau
CODESA – Convention for a Democratic South Africa
CONADEP – National Commission for Disappeared Persons (Argentina)
COSAS – Congress of South African Students
COSATU – Congress of South African Trade Unions
DACST – Department of Arts and Culture, Science and Technology
Ecomog – Economic Community of West African States Monitoring Group
(peace-keeping force in Sierra Leone)
Frelimo – Frente de Libertação Moçambique (Mozambique Liberation Front)
GNU – Government of National Unity
ICC – International Criminal Court
Idasa – Institute for Democracy in South Africa
IFP – Inkatha Freedom Party
MK – Umkhonto weSizwe, military wing of the ANC
NATO – North Atlantic Treaty Organisation
NGO – Non-governmental organisation
NIS – National Intelligence Service
NP – National Party
PAC – Pan-Africanist Congress
RDP – Reconstruction and Development Programme
Renamo – Resistência Nacional Moçambicana (Mozambique National Resistance)
SACP – South African Communist Party

SMMEs – Small, medium and micro-enterprises
SWAPO – South West African People's Organisation
TRC – South African Truth and Reconciliation Commission
TRC Act – Promotion of National Unity and Reconciliation Act, No. 34 of 1995
UCT – University of Cape Town
UWC – University of the Western Cape
Wits – University of the Witwatersrand

Introduction

Wilmot James and Linda van de Vijver

South Africa is in the throes of having to come to terms with the legacy of apartheid. This process has not been and is not easy. Apartheid's all-encompassing legacy pervades every aspect of our lives. It often seems to us as if the dead are coming back to haunt the opportunities of the living. In thinking about this phenomenon the metaphor of the biblical figure Lazarus comes to mind.[1] He represents the memories of the dead and persecuted of South Africa's apartheid past as they intrude on the life of the present. Lazarus represents the re-animation of South Africa's memory.

Memory enters the public domain through a variety of sources. Biography, fiction, non-fictional history, contemporary commentary and artistic expression bring into the public domain memories of hurt, pain and suffering wrought by a long history of apartheid and colonialism.[2] Of these, the Report of the South African Truth and Reconciliation Commission[3] probably represents the single largest contribution to the memories embodied in the image of Lazarus.

The testimonies that emerged during the TRC process do not, obviously, constitute all memory. The Commission had a brief that, constitutionally and legislatively, limited its work to a period of history from 1960 to 1994, and to 'gross violations' of human rights, which in ordinary language means murder, torture and serious harm to persons. The Commission therefore evoked the memories of some, but not all South Africans. The dead cannot speak. Only some of the individuals who were victimised testified. Only those perpetrators who applied for amnesty told their stories. Their narratives are part of a much larger story, the story of apartheid, of our racial history, colonial settlement, genocide and war.

Lazarus walks largely because of the TRC. But his journey is rooted in a history of conflict and reconciliation. As Jakes Gerwel remarks, the effort in the 1980s and early 1990s to find peaceful and negotiated solutions to South Africa's conflict was the political expression of a long-standing social and economic impulse that pulled South Africans together, however unequal or fraught with conflict their social relations.[4] In the twentieth century, South Africans developed as interdependent rather than separate. Co-existence was always materially imminent, as the historian Charles van Onselen shows in his remarkable story of the black sharecropper Kas Maine.[5] The TRC Report therefore reveals merely one important aspect of a much larger effort of democratic South Africa to show in all its ugliness the perverse attempts of apartheid to prevent a people from finding some acceptable form of cohesion.

The first part of this book places the TRC in a historical as well as a comparative perspective. Colin Bundy traces the roots of the TRC against the historical background of apartheid, and considers what contribution the TRC has made to the writing of South Africa's history. Charles Villa-Vicencio deals with the question of what kind of history the TRC produced through its various processes and in its Report. Heribert Adam and Kanya Adam examine the ways in which different countries have sought to address the crimes committed by previous regimes, placing the TRC in an international comparative perspective.[6] Together, these contributions place those aspects of Lazarus that derive from the TRC into perspective, giving the reasons for his existence, for the kind of representation of apartheid history he offers, and stating why he walks a different path from his equivalents in Chile or Argentina or El Salvador or the former East Germany.

For what purpose is Lazarus walking? From the point of view of the TRC, he walks in order to heal and reconcile. The second part of this book contains a series of reflections on the extent to which the objectives of truth and reconciliation were met. Neither of these objectives can be measured in a precise manner and, given that the process has taken place so recently, it might simply be too early to tell. On the one hand, Patricia Valdez, Alex Boraine, Jan van Eck, Albie Sachs and Dumisa Ntsebeza believe in the potential of the TRC to approximate the truth and to build reconciliation. Kaizer Nyatsumba argues that while the TRC assisted in uncovering the truth about the past, and thus provided some measure of catharsis, it failed dismally to reconcile our nation, which remains divided to this day. Frederik Van Zyl Slabbert argues that only a court of law can obtain the truth, while Mahmood Mamdani suggests that the TRC frees whites and the dominant elites of the old regime of any responsibility for the harm caused by apartheid, a structure conceived more broadly as a system of oppression built upon, but also going far beyond, human rights violations.[7]

In truth, we do not yet know to what extent the TRC has achieved reconciliation. It is a great pity that there was no test of public opinion before and after the release of the TRC Report. It would, of course, be naïve to think that reconciliation can be achieved by a single process. Much depends on how the project of reconciliation and truth telling is taken forward. The immediate challenge is the implementation of the recommendations contained in the TRC Report. There is much to be done in this area. The amnesty process has still not run its course. Furthermore, the government has yet to act on the recommendations on the payment of reparation and interim relief, the creation of a TRC archive, and the development and implementation of a policy on memorialisation.

The third part of the book, entitled 'Unfinished Business', deals with these unresolved issues. Mary Burton provides a recent account of matters still requiring attention. Her disappointment at the slow pace of progress is evident. Ciraj Rassool, Leslie Witz and Gary Minkley reflect on what the memorialisation of the victims of apartheid repression might or might not represent. Linda van de Vijver considers the legal and moral aspects of the amnesty provisions, and, as the process of amnesty is incomplete and therefore a study of the patterns and tendencies would be premature, looks at two divergent cases as a test of the veracity of the process.

It is clear to observers that the government has lost some of its initial enthusiasm for the TRC and is inexplicably slow in implementing its admittedly voluminous recommendations. The failure of the government to respond adequately to the issue of reparation obliges us to question the alacrity with which amnesty was granted to perpetrators, and whether the amnesty decisions can still be justified.[8] The TRC itself disbanded before its work was completed, leaving the final volume consisting of individual notations about the fate of victims still unpublished, among other things. With hindsight we can say that there ought to have been a vehicle that moved the unfinished business to conclusion, as governments by their very nature tend to be slow. The manner in which the TRC Report was received by political parties also left much to be desired, as their responses cast doubt on a national process that was a central part of the transition, having had the full support of former President Nelson Mandela.

Uneasy and uncertain from the time it set out on its journey, the TRC now falters between the Mandela and Mbeki governments. Internationally, the TRC is greatly admired. Locally, it is seen as a backward-looking relic of the past, unable to conclude its business. Yet its business is larger than life, for the TRC was also intended to assist in consolidating a new set of values and mores consistent with democracy, human rights and justice. The South African Constitution and Bill of Rights encapsulate those values, and the TRC, together with institutions like the Human Rights Commission and the Commission for Gender Equality – described in the Constitution as state institutions supporting democracy – were designed to promote, entrench and consolidate the values. The question remains how this much larger task will be accomplished.

The fourth section of the book, 'After the TRC', is devoted to teasing out the values that we should strive for as a nation, that define our moral character and ethos. Njabulo Ndebele prepares the ground for such a discussion, by exploring by way of allegory the values of responsibility, accountability and fairness. Richard Goldstone examines the rule of law as a democratic value and how rule by a constitution is to be understood by a people unfamiliar with its principles. Willem Heath writes about proactive efforts to deal with corruption as a matter of principle and practice. John de Gruchy considers the question of where humanity derives its values from in the first place, and argues that the debate about the building of a moral culture, which was opened up by the TRC process, still waits to be taken forward. Mamphela Ramphele concludes the section by noting the importance of vigilance in resisting injustice and the responsibility of both government and civil society in exercising such vigilance in a country that must continue to challenge the legacy of apartheid.

These matters go beyond the TRC to the character of Lazarus' heart. What kind of person is he? What kind of person does he want to be? Does he have the will to become these things? Will he champion these values? How do these values intersect with race, racism and multi-culturalism? How are these values to be embodied in the soul of a nation that emerges from such a divided and torn past? In other words, what contribution can Lazarus make to a debate about the core values of a nation in the process of transition? It seems to us that the TRC's contribution is in many respects unprecedented in the annals of human history, cutting new paths; for while it illustrates the folly of injustice, intolerance and the reign of a cold and bloody-minded heart,[9] it also demonstrates the extraordinary ability to forgive and to make the commitment to a new South Africa. We all want this new South Africa to be just, tolerant and warm-hearted in its newly rediscovered humanity. The TRC's greatest contribution was to give back to South Africa its heart.[10]

To take history forward, we need to ask Lazarus to shift his gaze decisively from the past to the future. Our vision for South Africa cannot remain trapped in the iniquities of the past. It must free itself by taking the assets of the past and converting them into a promise of tomorrow. As a country we face three hard realities that could sabotage our achievements. The first is poverty, heavily concentrated among the coloured and African population. The second is a desperately under-educated African population. And the third is AIDS, which will, if left unchecked, remove a significant section of our population both now and in the future. A social order of young, under-educated and poor people making up the core of our society is South Africa's imminent nightmare.

The final section of the book, 'Building the Assets of the Nation', confronts these issues as challenges for the nation. Francis Wilson provides an overview of the scale and depth of poverty and inequality. Grace Naledi Pandor considers the impact of apartheid on the education system, and addresses the issue of how these iniquities can be reversed. Jeffrey Lever and Wilmot James closely examine the relationship between race, inequality and democracy. The challenge for Lazarus is to confront the deficits of our inheritance with the assets that we have as a people. South Africans know how to accumulate wealth, build roads and bridges, run banks, establish good universities, construct deep underground mines and make something out of nothing. South Africans know how to live in conflict but also how to make peace, reconcile and negotiate solutions to difficult issues. South Africa has produced its fair share of intellectuals, politicians, entrepreneurs, artists and musicians. Hence our future lies in employing these assets to overcome our deficits with confidence.

This book is based on the conference 'After the TRC: Reconciliation in the New Millennium' held in Cape Town in August 1999. Most of the contributions contained in this volume were presented there. Additional contributions to complete the book came from Heribert Adam, Kanya Adam, Patricia Valdez, Mahmood Mamdani, Frederik Van Zyl Slabbert, Ciraj Rassool, Leslie Witz, Gary Minkley, Linda van de Vijver, Jeffrey Lever and Wilmot James. The photographic essay 'Unfinished Business' immediately following this Introduction is based on an exhibition hosted by the 1999 conference.

We are grateful to the UCT Charitable Trust, United Kingdom, for financing the conference as well as the publication of this book. The University Research Committee of UCT also provided support. Our thanks also go to Geoff Grundlingh, Pamela Reynolds and Fiona Ross for producing the photographic essay, and to Geoff Grundlingh for the cover art and concept. We also gratefully acknowledge the work of Russell Martin and Lisa Compton of David Philip Publishers who brought the manuscript to publication in their usual conscientious manner.

Cape Town, September 2000

Unfinished Business

Geoffrey Grundlingh, Pamela Reynolds and Fiona Ross (with Amos Khomba, Charity Nana Khohlokoane, Edwin Rasmani, Eric Ndoyisile Tshandu, Mawethu Bikane, Mzikhaya Mkhabile, Nokwanda Tani, Noluthando Qaba, Nomeite Mfengu, Nowi Khomba, Ntsoaki Phelane, Xolile Dyabooi and Zandesile Ntsomi)

'Unfinished Business' reflects the duration and effects of political struggle in Zwelethemba, a small town in the heart of the Boland, the fruit-growing region of the Western Cape. Zwelethemba was established to house people classified African who, in 1954, were moved there from nearby Worcester during the state's dislocation of residential areas. Political confrontation between the residents of Zwelethemba and state security forces began in the 1950s. By the 1980s, resistance was well organised. Eric Ndoyisile Tshandu, one of the leading activists among the youth of Zwelethemba, explains the context within which political activism was shaped:

> From 1960, there was significant political activity in Zwelethemba against the apartheid regime. In the 1980s, Zwelethemba became a centre of turmoil and deep trouble as the youth resisted oppression. Many were closely involved for many years in local organisations with links to national and underground organisations. The security forces that were sent in to counter our activities were powerful and cruel. The suffering of many was profound but the community is proud of its history of resistance.

Most of the people represented in the essay were involved in protest against apartheid state oppression throughout the 1980s. They were young when the State of Emergency was imposed in 1985: almost all of them were at school. Many others fought with them. Only one person, Mzikhaya Mkhabile, represents an older generation. A prisoner on Robben Island in the 1960s, his experiences there remind us that revolt occurred over many years, that retaliation was brutal and that its form changed over time.

Our attention is drawn to the fact that political consciousness was passed down the generations. When leaders were imprisoned, young people and women took on the responsibility for organising opposition to the state. Activists, most of whom were young, were detained, interrogated and tortured. Their kin and friends also became targets of harassment.

During the State of Emergency, the police established a barricade at the only entrance to Zwelethemba and arbitrarily searched and detained people. Between 1985 and 1986, eight people were killed in confrontations with the police. Their graves lie in a straight row in the dusty, treeless graveyard that marks one of Zwelethemba's boundaries. Funeral processions were limited by magisterial order and monitored by police who also imposed a dusk-to-dawn curfew and patrolled the township.

Residents organised marches to protest against rent increases, educational policies and the local authorities and councillors. Protesters burned the offices of the Advisory Board, the post office, the municipal bar and the rent office. A school boycott instituted in 1984 was intensified in 1985. Young people ceased sleeping at home in order to avoid being captured by the police during random 'door-to-door' searches. Many people kept the front and back doors of houses open at night so that those fleeing the police could slip through houses and hide. A boycott against white-owned businesses was instituted.

The Truth and Reconciliation Commission in Worcester

On 24 to 26 June 1996, the Human Rights Violations Committee held a public hearing in Worcester. Two-thirds of the twenty-four testimonies made there were about people who had been young when they began to be politically active in standing against the apartheid regime. Eight of those about whom testimony was made had been detained and tortured, five shot dead, another three shot and injured, and one was beaten so severely that he lost an eye.

Twelve of the testifiers came from Worcester and the others from the nearby areas of Ashton, Montagu and Robertson. Of those from Worcester, two were men who had been detained and tortured in the 1960s (one was imprisoned on Robben Island with Nelson Mandela), one was a woman active in the 1980s, and one was a woman whose son was killed in Zwelethemba. The other eight joined the conflict against the state in the late 1970s and the 1980s. Of the latter, six were from Zwelethemba.

The testimonies illustrate the weight of political engagement against the state. They describe the extremities of pain, torture, cruelty, abuse of children as young as eleven years, death, humiliation, and sexual violation. They depict the central role of funerals and the state's interference with mourning. Testifiers spoke of betrayal; innocence; the weight of state responsibility for violations; the failure of members of the medical profession to act in accord with the ethics of that profession (two exceptions were mentioned); the consequences of gross violations of human rights that reverberate through time, especially as they concern loss (of a loved one, of houses, of possessions, of education, of training); the inability to work (because of disability, distress or rejection by potential employers); interference with mobility and pleasure (as a result of physical harm or unhappiness or mental impairment or fear); absolute breakdown; and the destruction of life chances and freedoms that hinders the full expression of potential in so many of life's usual opportunities.

The testimonies describe the weight of political engagement against the state:
- Some of the people pictured in the essay were members of banned organisations.
- Some were members of Umkhonto weSizwe (MK).
- Some were leaders; some were followers.
- Some gave public testimony before the Truth and Reconciliation Commission.
- Some gave statements.
- Some gave statements to the Commission after the date for submissions had passed.
- Many would still like to have their stories heard.

The people depicted here now occupy a range of positions in society:
- Amos Khomba is a councillor in Worcester.
- Charity Nana Khohlokoane is completing a Master's degree at the University of Cape Town.
- Edwin Rasmani is unemployed.
- Eric Ndoyisile Tshandu is an entrepreneur.
- Mawethu Bikane works for the Worcester municipality.
- Mzikhaya Mkhabile is retired.
- Nokwanda Tani is unemployed.
- Noluthando Qaba works part-time for Ilitha laBantu.
- Nomeite Mfengu is unemployed.
- Nowi Khomba is unemployed.
- Ntsoaki Phelane is completing a teaching diploma.
- Xolile Dyabooi is completing a Bachelor's degree at the University of Cape Town.
- Zandesile Ntsomi is a prison warder.

The unemployed contribute to party and community organisations, including the Community Policing Forum, the Zwelethemba Peacemakers' Association and other development organisations. They do not have regular incomes.

The texts which accompany the photographic portraits first shown at the TRC conference in August 1999 suggest the range of people's experiences and the nature of the consequences of those experiences.

Noluthando Qaba

My brother, Nkosinathi, was active. At home we were not free – the police harassed us looking for my brother. The police said he made bombs and that he encouraged the community in the rent boycott. We called him 'Springbok' because they could not catch him.

The police used to chase us with dogs and tear gas and rubber bullets. If it was quiet in the location they would knock at the door and come and search without permission and then leave. This continued after my brother left. There was no time to sit. The last day, police buses, cars with searchlights, came to our house. You would think it was a wedding! That was the last day they came to look for my brother. There was no life for him here in Zwelethemba. If he was here there would be a van – someone had called the police. If [they] called, the police would pay, and people needed money.

They never got my brother, Springbok. My brother skipped in 1985. He went to Angola. He died in 1988. We heard in 1990. We received a letter from Angola and then three men from Johannesburg came to tell us. He was in MK.

Ma se hart was seer [Mother's heart was sore] so she stopped working in the struggle. She felt small. She carried on a little with the ANC Women's League.

Edwin Rasmani

At the age of sixteen, I was arrested by the police and put in a cell for three days. On the fourth day, they took me to a car. There were about seven policemen. They placed a hood over my head. They probably took me to Nekkies [near the Breede River]. We arrived. They asked me my name. I told them. I was told to sit on the ground. I was told to tell the truth and, if I did so, they would release me. I was asked who burnt the house and the man. I denied knowledge of it. They put steel behind my knees and handcuffed my arms beneath it. They placed nails on my neck, ankles and hips for electric shocks and a tube over my head to cut my breathing. They shocked me. There was terrible pain. For about one and a half hours they shocked and questioned me continuously. I pretended to faint. They left me. They tried to revive me. They took me to a car, they carried me as I was too weak. I was taken back to the cell … On Monday about thirty of us appeared in the Magistrate's Court, charged with murder and arson, with public violence. We were charged and held until December. I was bailed out by my brother.

The trial continued for two and a half years. Edwin was acquitted.

Ntsoaki Phelane

Ntsoaki was sixteen years old when she was detained. She was held with other detainees in a police station for three days before being taken for interrogation.

As we were living there [in the prison], we sang freedom songs, praying. There was also a time during singing when we were sprayed by tear gas to keep us quiet. Comrades were taken out individually for investigation and tortured privately. I was in the third group to be tortured and investigated by the authorities. They took us to a place I can't even remember or have an idea of. The van which was carrying us was covered in black plastic so we did not see where we were or how we got there. When we got there we were taken individually to be tortured and the ones left behind just heard the screaming and crying as if you are in or near because of the echoing. It was late and when it was nearly my turn, they stopped and sent us back to prison. We were free then to go home.

Nomeite Mfengu

I started joining the struggle when I was fifteen years old. Later, I decided to cross the border but then I started to think about my two children so then I changed my mind about leaving the country. I decided to hide in Cape Town. I stayed there for six months without contact from my family and my children and I was so worried because I left my young ones and they knew nothing about where I was. One time I tried to phone at my home because I wanted to know about the situation, because of homesickness. They said to me, 'You must not come back now because even last night the police were at home searching the whole house looking for you.' Sometimes I used to cry when I was thinking of my sons. When I phoned them they also cried and asked where I am and when I am coming back to be with them again … Like on Christmas Day, when I thought about what my sons were wearing, because I was the mother and father of them.

Nowi Khomba and Eric Ndoyisile Tshandu

Nowi Khomba and Eric Ndoyisile Tshandu were among a group of young political activists who decided to leave South Africa and join the ANC in exile. Seven of the group lived in Zwelethemba. They went to Cape Town, where they hid in a safe house.

There two others, a man and a woman, joined them. The man was unknown to them. The group travelled to Matatiele, from where they hoped to cross the border into Lesotho. One night the young man who had joined them in Cape Town disappeared. The next day, the others were ambushed. Six were caught by the police and detained but two men escaped and returned to Zwelethemba to tell people what had happened.

The two women in the group were separated from the men. They were held under section 29 of the Internal Security Act. Some members of the group were held in solitary confinement. They were tortured. They were detained for six months, then released.

Of detention, Nowi remembered: Each of us was interrogated separately and each of us had a different story. Even now we are not sure who told what.

Eric remembered that while being tortured: I was at some stage shown an attaché case full of medical equipment and powders/spray. I was sprayed with a powder that made me dizzy and I fell with my eyes burning. They promised to drown me in the Breede River. In fact, I was taken there at night.

Amos Khomba

Amos Khomba was a leading youth activist and is now a councillor in Worcester. He is pictured in the graveyard of Zwelethemba beside Ntando Mrubatha's grave. Mrubatha testified at the Worcester hearing. He died on 10 February 1999 as a consequence of injuries inflicted on him during protests in 1986.

Nokwanda Tani

I was detained many times. I was detained under section 50 of the Internal Security Act. I was in Pollsmoor for fourteen days. We enjoyed it – we were there with the comrades from the Boland. We were taken from Hex-Tex on Saturday morning. There was a roadblock at the entrance to Zwelethemba and three police came to the bus. We laughed at them, you know. They randomly selected us.

Mr Tani: We kept our doors open all day and at night so that when the police came, the children could run through the house, out the back and over the fence.

Mrs Tani: The children were strong. You could not understand your child, you had to keep quiet.

Mawethu Bikane

Mawethu, 'the Black Pimpernel' as his colleagues laughingly call him, was an activist for many years. He had a talent for evading arrest. He was a trickster or, in Xhosa, phuncuka bamphethe, *someone who slips away.*

Once he was captured on the way to school and taken to the police station. Many people had been detained that day and the offices were crowded. He slid quietly into an office where an official was sitting and said, very politely, that he had come to check his licence. He was told that he was in the wrong place and given directions to go elsewhere. The official pointed out the route, and with him as his shield, Mawethu left the police station. He was noticed by other policemen as he passed through the gate and they gave chase, but he ran, jumped a fence and disappeared.

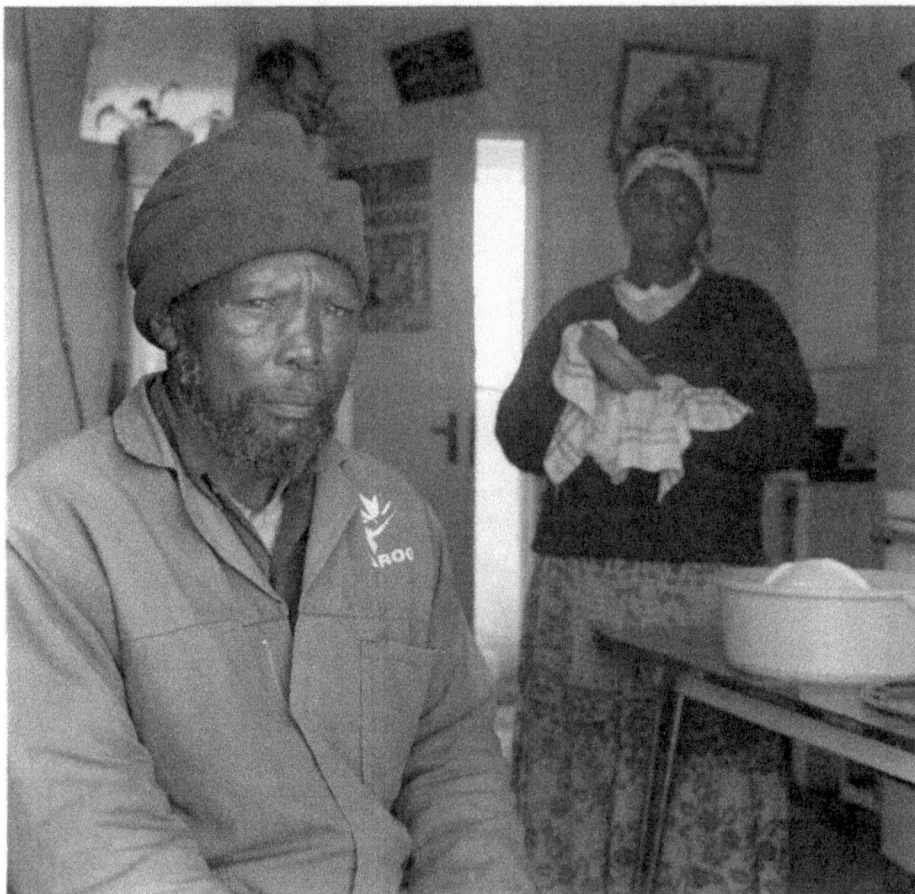

Mzikhaya Mkhabile

Mzikhaya Mkhabile has been a member of the ANC since the 1950s. In December 1962, he was arrested and tried on charges of terrorism. He spent twelve years on Robben Island with other political prisoners, including Nelson Mandela. He described an incident of torture to the Commission during his public testimony:

They beat me on my head with a big knobkierie, I fell on my mouth and when I tried to get up they beat me again, twice in the waist and my other leg felt numb. They told me to put the wheelbarrow aside which I tried to do and they told me to come with them. The supervisors then came along with spades. One hand-cuffed me. They dug a grave and with my hands behind my back they put me in this grave with only my head sticking out. They tried to close the grave. He took his knobkierie and pushed it into my penis, then he urinated into my mouth and I swallowed the urine.

GEOFFREY GRUNDLINGH, PAMELA REYNOLDS AND FIONA ROSS

Zandesile Ntsomi

Zandesile testified at the Commission's hearing on 24 June 1996. He described how the police shot him in the leg while visiting a friend. The police beat him up and, hours later, took him to hospital. His leg was amputated. The following day, he was discharged into the hands of the police, made to wait hours on a bench, driven back to Worcester and held in a police cell. The details of his treatment are horrific and can be read in the records of the Human Rights Violations Committee. Zandesile sued the state. The claim was dismissed and he was charged with the legal costs. Three letters of demand were sent to him.

And they stated that they estimated about R45 000 out of my own pocket and they also stated that the money can be taxed and I realised that this was going to be a serious matter. And I tried to get private lawyers because I wanted to have someone – a legal person – to help me do the affidavit. I tried to consult the lawyers … and I told them the whole situation and she [the lawyer] said, 'Okay, we'll make the affidavit but we must open a file'. And I had to pay R200. I've already paid R100, and I paid half of the amount. I told [the lawyer] that … I'm not prepared to pay anything because this is too much, even if it was not that because I am the loser, because I lost my leg. And then the next thing now, the state demands a lot of money from me. I am not prepared to pay it, and I don't have the means, and I can't even afford to pay that amount because it is a huge amount for me to pay. Because I felt that my human rights were violated and then at the end of the day I must pay the state some money. I don't think it's fair. So that's how the situation is.

Xolile Dyabooi

Xolile was severely tortured almost every day over a period of four months. He spent three years in solitary confinement. When he was indemnified and released from prison in 1991, he found it difficult to reconstruct his life. He returned to school and competed his Matric but he could not find a job nor did he have the money to continue his education. After five years, he said:

I saw myself as useless. Nothing I organised succeeded … In our society, if you don't manage to achieve, [to have] material goods, get married or whatsoever, then people start neglecting you … And another thing … the transition in South Africa was one of a special kind. It was another kind of transition. So many things just happened. So dramatically. So that resulted in people going without preparations, because most of us were not prepared for such a sudden change. We were thinking we were still fighting. As a result, I feel that we didn't become part, or I didn't become part, of the transition process. Due to that fact, I neglected it. I didn't see CODESA, I didn't see those things as a solution. I felt those boers are trying also to fuck our people around.

Xolile is now completing his Bachelor's degree at the University of Cape Town.

Charity Nana Khohlokoane

As revolutionaries, we encouraged the people to be all-rounders ... Now, our communities are changing their perceptions about politics. You have to redefine yourself. Redefine your role, redefine your character. Redefine your profile. The instrument to determine leadership has changed. In the eighties you were a leader in so far as you were defiant. Were you able to resist repression by the police? Were you able to come out of detention with your spirit undented? To emerge victorious because you did not tell them what they interrogated and tortured you for, and it is they who become frustrated because they did not achieve their goal? ... Yes, how many stones did you throw? When there was action – things to be burned, or violence to be meted out – how much upfront were you? You see? How articulate were you in terms of *toyi-toyiing*? How good were you in terms of memorising all the freedom songs? How good were you in terms of articulating all the positions of the Movement? That was the yardstick.

Now you are in the position in which you are supposed to be able to analyse the situation. You must be proactive. You must be able to formulate policy. You must be able to unpack transformation: critique it, provide alternatives, you see. And it's intellectual work. Besides that you must also be able to root yourself among the masses, understand their needs. Be where they need you. Be among them, suffer with them, advise them and so forth and so forth. So that's what makes you a leader. Besides that, in addition to that, you must acquire education, education is also important. So, if you have all those skills and in addition, education, then it puts you, yes, on a broad path, as the Xhosas say. *Ikubeka endleneni ebanzi.* So now, with education and all the other qualities and skills that all the comrades have, now you are one step ahead. That sets you on a broad path, free to manoeuvre without any hindrances.

Activists who died during the conflict in Zwelethemba, 1985–1990:
Nkosana Bahume
Thamsanqa van Staaden
Nondatsu Mazula
Nhunhu Simango
Thomas Kolo
Khotso Dyasi
Mawethu Nzima
Buzile Fadana

Activists who died in exile:
Nkosinathi Arthur Qaba
Mandlenkosi 'Cone' Bentele

*Several people who made written statements about human rights
violations to the Commission have died since 1996. They include:*
Ntando Mrubatha
Amos Dyantyi
George Nthetha
Tekana Williams
Rufus Oliphant

Part I:
Historical and Comparative Perspectives

Chapter One

The Beast of the Past: History and the TRC

Colin Bundy

One of the difficulties of discussing the Truth and Reconciliation Commission academically is that one can too easily fail to recognise its power. I am referring to its emotional, cultural and symbolic power, and, above all, to the potency and intensity of the testimony it elicited, especially in the public hearings. To revisit these in the five volumes of the TRC Report, or to have encountered them on radio or television during live broadcasts, is a confrontation with the human condition; it requires each of us to come to terms with the worst and best in our fellow citizens. There is horror in the testimonies, and grief and pain and anguish; there is courage, cowardice, resilience, self-knowledge and denial. The cumulative account provides an explicit and terrible record of violence, vindictiveness and brutalisation.

Similarly, if one is going to be critical of aspects of the TRC and its Report – as I am – it is important not to overlook its achievements or its political and moral substance. The Commissioners and staff lived through an emotionally demanding, litigious, and politically and intellectually contested thirty months. They traversed a political landscape of rock falls and quicksand, pitted with landmines – and it was scant consolation that this terrain was largely shaped by the TRC's own legal mandate. They marshalled vast amounts of data; they added important details to what was already known about human rights abuses; they produced a professionally competent published report. More than that: The hearings and the research conducted by the TRC 'had a dramatic impact on the popular psyche' of South Africans, and largely fulfilled one of its major goals: 'the public acknowledgment of the trauma experienced by victims'.[1] Above all, the TRC has made it impossible for South Africans ever to claim, 'but we didn't know' – and this is a considerable achievement.

My focus is on history and the TRC. I will try first to sketch the historical context in which the TRC was established. A second section will consider the

TRC Report as an exercise in the construction of historical knowledge; a third section reflects on the archival functions of the TRC; and a final section will pose some questions about the longer-term significance of the TRC for our historical understanding of our society and ourselves. The discipline of history and the TRC are in fact deeply implicated with each other. In a number of instances, the researchers and the compilers of the Report took questions typically asked by historians – questions about truth, causality, evidence and explanation – into the public and political domain. The TRC is a case study of how the past is constructed and presented, how it is contested, and what the role of history is in shaping values and institutions in civil society.

For their part, historians and other social scientists have already engaged deeply with the TRC as an object of enquiry. In June 1999, a conference entitled 'The TRC: Commissioning the Past' was jointly organised by the University of the Witwatersrand's History Workshop and the Centre for the Study of Violence and Reconciliation. The conference was enriched by exchanges between scholars analysing aspects of the TRC and researchers and staffers from the TRC who reflected critically on their experiences. This essay draws directly on some of the papers that dealt with issues around the TRC and history; and my own understanding of the Commission's operations and its Report was deepened by the scholarship on show at the conference.

The TRC in History

How does one begin to think historically about the TRC? How might one locate the Commission within a broader account of contemporary South African history? In particular, how might one characterise it in fairly conventional social science terms – as an item of legislation, as a political and social process, and in relation to other political and social processes? In other words, if analysis distances itself from the TRC as political drama or morality play, and eschews rhetorical celebration or denunciation of the Commission, what are we actually dealing with?

Basically, it is impossible to make much sense of the TRC unless one relates it to the political settlement arrived at between 1990 and 1993. The TRC was not merely a legal by-product of the political settlement, but in a more fundamental sense a crucial element of that settlement. And, to take one step further back in time, any account of the settlement necessarily depends upon the circumstances that led to it.

One of the earliest, most influential and most durable analyses of those circumstances was written by Harold Wolpe. In his *Race, Class and the Apartheid State*, published in 1988, Wolpe identified the prevailing conjuncture as one of unstable equilibrium in which the white bloc, while holding state power and having at its disposal the armed and security forces, was unable to suppress the mass opposition which, in turn, did not have the immediate capacity to overthrow the regime and the system. In this situation a space was opened up for initiatives suggesting a reformist solution to the country's crisis on the basis of a 'negotiated settlement'.[2]

This was prescient – and a far more useful starting point for understanding the negotiation process than many on offer. It is instructive to begin where Harold Wolpe pointed, which is also where the government and the ANC found themselves in 1989. The state was unable to re-impose order from above; the opposition forces were unable to seize power from below – and both had come to a reluctant recognition of this stalemate. Nelson Mandela's letter to P.W. Botha[3] in March 1989 (the crucial section of which proposed that 'The key to the whole situation is a negotiated settlement') and F.W. de Klerk's speech to Parliament on 2 February 1990 voiced the same logic. Although neither leader said so, their forces resembled the armies in Macbeth: 'As two spent swimmers, that do cling together.' Having both conceded, under enormous pressure, that a negotiated settlement was the only viable option, together they clung to the process.

To appreciate the tenacity of their grip, it is worth recalling the series of disclosures and disasters that threatened negotiations: Operation Vula, Inkathagate, Sebokeng, Boipatong, Bisho, and the seemingly endless killings on the East Rand and in Natal. Despite these, to a degree and at a pace that surprised many observers, the broad outlines of the settlement actually emerged quite rapidly. And they could do so because both the National Party and the African National Congress agreed on terms that deviated quite significantly from their initial negotiating positions. In particular, in November 1992 the ANC adopted its 'Strategic Perspectives' on negotiations. This committed a post-election government to a form of power-sharing for five years; entrenched the posts of white civil servants; and agreed to a form of amnesty that indemnified politicians, soldiers and security agents from civil or criminal prosecution in return for disclosure of their crimes.

Underpinning these explicitly political concessions – Hein Marais argues – was a retreat by the ANC with arguably longer-term implications. The ANC retreated from economic and social policy positions that would threaten, weaken or dismantle the structural foundations of a two-nation society.[4] Blade Nzimande, citing the Mexican sociologist Carlos Vilas, was one of the few to warn at the time that the most important thing about 'transitions' (initiated by previously repressive regimes) is that 'they do not project into the economic sphere, nor do they provide a framework for any substantial changes in the level of access of subordinate groups to socio-economic resources – by income redistribution, creating employment, improving living conditions, etc.'[5]

During CODESA, verily, the ANC sought first the political kingdom. The form of state (the balance between central and provincial powers), the terms of power-sharing (in the Government of National Unity), the details of entrenched legislation and veto powers, and the sustained efforts to bring the IFP and the Afrikaner right into electoral politics were the main focus of negotiations. There was an understandable concern with attaining, defending and reshaping state power – but concomitantly there was a tacit acceptance that negotiations would leave the structures of production, property, wealth and poverty virtually intact. From 1992 onwards, the ANC backed off from redistribution and state regulation, dropped demands like progressive taxation and a restructuring of the financial sector, and accepted a property rights clause sponsored by big business. In the process, it was assimilated into a web of institutional relations, systems and practices that historically had served white privilege and capital accumulation.

The ideology of the historic compromise dealt increasingly with the 'new' South Africa, and nation-building, 'the dominant discourse, came to orbit around postulated common interests and destinies – rather than difference, contradiction and antagonism – as the fundamental dynamics at work in society'.[6] Desmond Tutu's 'Rainbow Nation' metaphor translated this aptly into a popular register.

Viewed within this reading of the negotiated settlement, the TRC emerged as a crucial element of the historic compromise. More than that: Its own origins involved an attempt to balance demands for disclosure and justice with an existing commitment to a process of amnesty. The commitment to amnesty was a 'last minute compromise struck so late in the negotiation process that it had to be included in a "Postamble" tacked on to the end of the [Interim] Constitution';[7] the commitment to parallel processes of an official determination of the truth about past human rights abuses and some form of reparation came after the 1994 elections. 'This fusion of an amnesty process with a truth recovery and reparative process is without precedent among similar initiatives internationally.'[8]

This was an ambitious design; it was also an attempt to reconcile and accommodate fundamentally different and ultimately irreconcilable functions. As Graeme Simpson has written, 'most of the legal and jurisprudential dilemmas presented by the TRC process are actually rooted in its own almost bi-polar roles as both a "fact-finding" and quasi-judicial enterprise on the one hand, and as a psychologically sensitive mechanism for story telling and healing on the other.'[9]

This dualism shaped all the activities of the TRC, blurred its vision, and undermined the quality of its investigations. The truth and the reconciliation that it sought were not only the product of a compromise, but arguably were historically compromised.

The TRC Report as History

It goes without saying that the TRC was charged with writing an official history. It was required to establish as complete a picture as possible of the nature, causes and extent of the gross human rights violations that were committed between 1 March 1960 and 6 December 1993, including the antecedents, circumstances, factors and contexts of such violations, as well as the perspectives of the victims and the motives and perspectives of the persons responsible for committing these violations.[10]

This was an exceptionally demanding brief: The call for a catalogue of violations was complicated by the requirement also to grapple with causes, contexts, antecedents and motives. And, clearly, some of the authors of the Report recognised the epistemological and methodological issues inherent in the brief. As Deborah Posel has remarked, 'there can't be many official state commissions which ponder the question of the possibility of objective knowledge, explore the meaning of "truth", invoke historical sociologist Max Weber as a methodological role-model, and render their research process as a "dialectical encounter" with disparate sets of data.'[11]

Ultimately, I believe that, although the TRC wrestled with its brief, it failed to get a proper grip on it, let alone pin it to the floor. The result is a report that presents a structurally fragmented historical account, in which the contradictory pulls of the TRC's mandate exact a toll both epistemological and methodological. This case has been made more fully in a rigorous and penetrating paper by Deborah Posel, and at the real risk of over-simplifying her analysis, this section will draw directly upon her work.

Following Posel, one can identify internal tensions that run deeply through the TRC's report. First, the TRC embraced two very different notions of historical knowledge. It acknowledged the past as a site of contending constructions and perspectives, a realm of subjective, partial truths:

> The way its stories are told and the way they are heard change as the years go by. The spotlight gyrates, exposing old lies and illuminating new truths. As a fuller picture emerges, a new piece of the jigsaw puzzle of our past settles into place. Inevitably, evidence and information about our past will continue to emerge, as indeed they must. The Report of our Commission will now take its place in the historical landscape of which future generations will try to make sense – searching for the clues that lead, endlessly, to a truth that will, in the very nature of things, never be fully revealed.[12]

While this thoroughly modern historicism surfaces in the Report, it did not shape it. A quite different notion of historical knowledge arose from – perhaps was made necessary by – the TRC's desire to serve as an official, objective, impartial and authoritative source, one with legitimacy and credibility. This imperative gave rise to a series of truth claims of quite a different order. The Report claims, 'without fear of being contradicted, that we have contributed more to uncovering the truth about the past than all the court cases in the history of apartheid'. It believes 'we have provided enough of the truth about our past for there to be a consensus about it' and 'we should accept that truth has emerged'.[13] The TRC resolves the tension between these quite incompatible versions of truth by defining four kinds of truth: a factual or forensic truth – 'factual, corroborated ... accurate ... reliable [impartial objective]' – personal or narrative truth, social or 'dialogue' truth, and healing or restorative truth. While this is, as Posel demonstrates, 'a very wobbly, poorly constructed conceptual grid',[14] its real significance lies in the use made of it in the Report. Personal, social and healing truths are serviced in the hearings, the opportunities for victims and perpetrators to hear each other, and in the Commission's role as a vehicle for national reconciliation. But the Report itself adopts a conventionally positivist approach with respect to its findings, its historical judgements. 'The written text gives expression to an objectivity that is seemingly divested of subjective intrusions or contaminations. Findings on gross human rights violations are presented in quasi-judicial form, as impartial verdicts on the past.'[15]

A second major dilemma running through the Report was the issue of completeness. On the one hand, the Commission was obliged to accept statements from all South Africans who wished to make them; this held the possibility of an infinitely detailed, comprehensive and multi-vocal account of past traumas. On the other hand, the notion of reconciliation as writing closure to a divided past pulled in quite a different direction. It sought a single, national account – an overview, which could serve as the basis for a shared history, a common, collective understanding. This tension translated into an awkward methodological straddle. A great deal of time and effort seems to have gone into methods of data capturing and coding, which would allow the Report to quantify and categorise human rights violations – a conventional enough social science exercise. At the same time, the Commission selected for inclusion in the Report some of the individual cases: '[S]tories that illustrate particular events, trends and phenomena have been used as windows on the experiences of many people';[16] again a recognisable social science strategy, linking the particular to the general.

But in the Report, these two approaches are oddly dissociated. The quantification exercise has little or no relationship to the narration of individual cases – there is no explanatory link between the two kinds of evidence. So the task of understanding why individuals behaved as they did is made even more difficult by the decision to deal with the issue of 'motives and causes' in a separate article. So the Report contains quantitative surveys in one section; a general disembodied discussion of possible motives; a separate historical sketch of the apartheid past; and narratives of selected individual cases. As Posel notes, 'What the Report lacks is an attempt to integrate and synthesise these into a unified analysis. Instead, severing "motive" from "cause", and de-linking both from the narration of individual cases, the Report deprives itself of one of the essential tools of historical analysis.'[17]

The TRC and the Archive

I want to make three separate points about the TRC, the vast amount of evidence it accumulated, and the status of that evidence as part of a national archive. Firstly, as we have already seen, the TRC authors were involved in a process of selection, summary, distillation – which was also necessarily an exercise in exclusion, in silencing. This observation about the relations between power, knowledge, memory and the archive derives from Jacques Derrida. At the heart of Derrida's critique of the archive as practice and cultural construct is that it exercises power over knowledge. Archives confer authority on certain aspects of the past; they identify, classify and consign certain forms of knowledge into an apparent unity, and into a fixed, closed, artificially stabilised system. The archive becomes the official repository of memory, but is simultaneously a crucial site in the process of forgetting. The forgetfulness of the archive – of omitting that which 'operates in silence' and which 'never leaves its own archive'[18] – is systematic, not innocent; it is an act of repression, consigning its omissions to oblivion. Indeed, Derrida describes this repression as 'the violence of the archive'.

Brent Harris has given a Derridean reading of the TRC's archival function. He argues that the TRC's discursive statements appear to opt for the archive as closure, as fixing the past. Prototypically, Desmond Tutu's Foreword to the Report concludes: 'Having looked the beast of the past in the eye ... let us shut the door on the past.'[19] Harris argues that this is 'a mechanism for the fixing of knowledge and the ending of the instability of meanings'.[20] This impulse – to close the door on the past, to establish a version of the past that somehow transcends subjective and contesting views – comes from the TRC's commitment to nation-building rather than its commitment to an explanatory social science. The Report itself spells out this function quite dramatically, using a recurring 'healing' metaphor: 'However painful the experience, the wounds of the past must not be allowed to fester. They must be opened. They must be cleansed. And balm must be poured on them so they can heal. This is not to be obsessed with the past. It is to take care that the past is properly dealt with for the sake of the future.'[21]

A second, quite separate archival consideration is the section of the TRC Report that deals with the destruction of records. All of us knew that large-scale shredding and disposal of documents took place as the apartheid regime neared the end of its historical tether – but I wonder whether any of us grasped the extent of this. In forty-three devastating pages, the Report provides details of this process, and concludes that it 'probably did more to undermine the investigative work of the Commission than any other single factor'. There is, for example, for all practical purposes no documentary evidence that the CCB existed, let alone of who staffed it, how it was financed, and what it did. While some files of the State Security Council have survived, none appear to exist of its shadowy implementation structure, the National Security Management System. At the NIS headquarters, in six to eight months in 1993, the mass destruction of forty-four tons of paper and microfilm records took place. No shredding machines could have coped with this assault on evidence, and the NIS used instead the Iscor furnaces.[22]

There is a third archival issue: We know that a vast body of collected material will be deposited in the state archives, providing grist to the mill of a generation of scholars. But will the inner workings of the TRC itself form part of the accessible record? Will scholars be able to read not only the accumulated transcribed statements and the minutes of TRC meetings, but also the internal memos and e-mails? As André du Toit has noted, 'the visible public process was also the product of a largely invisible set of activities within the TRC. The critical anthropology of the bureaucratic production of "truths" by the TRC must complement further exploration of the vast archives generated.'[23] Some steps towards this critical anthropology have already been taken, notably through a paper by Lars Buur, which details some of the hidden mechanisms which shaped the Commission's knowledge production.[24]

The TRC and Historical Understanding

This section makes a basic point – and it does so in the knowledge that the point has been made by a number of others, perhaps most effectively by Mahmood Mamdani. It deals with the way in which the TRC has the potential to shape historical understanding, and in so doing to narrow, to constrain and even to distort such understanding. Once again, we must reflect on the Act that constituted the Commission, its mandate in terms of this legislation, and above all the ways in which this mandate demarcated the boundaries of the TRC's work. The TRC, as we have seen, was charged with the objective of promoting national unity and reconciliation by establishing as comprehensive an account as possible of gross human rights abuses over a period of thirty-four years.

Certainly, the Report is uncomfortably aware of the narrowness of this investigative mandate. It notes that the 'systemic and all-pervading character of apartheid' provided the background for its investigation. It speaks of the difficulty of concentrating only on those who had been killed, tortured or severely mistreated, as opposed to creating an awareness of 'systematic discrimination and dehumanisation'. It says that a strong case can be made that the violations of human rights by pass laws, migrant labour, forced removals, Bantu Education and so on had 'the most negative possible impact on the lives of the majority of South Africans'.[25] Yet despite these important caveats, the TRC Report is not in any important sense shaped by an intellectual or political critique of its mandate, nor by analysis that extends or transcends that mandate.

Deborah Posel acutely identified an ambiguity in the TRC's object of historical enquiry: The nature of apartheid was 'simultaneously merely the background to the Commission's investigations, yet absolutely central to its findings'.[26] The TRC's power of historical explanation would rest heavily upon its abilities to come to grips with apartheid, to relate the social and economic order to the human rights violations. Yet, as she demonstrates, the Report 'sheds remarkably little light on apartheid', fails to utilise existing research, does not theorise nor adequately conceptualise the apartheid state, and ultimately explains apartheid as a consequence of racism – a tautology that fails to explore the connections between racism and other social divides. One can look, for example, at the very beginning of the five-volume Report, at the Foreword that appears with Tutu's signature. In paragraph two, it accepts the time-frame of the Act uncritically. Contemporary history 'began in 1960 when the Sharpeville disaster took place' and 'it is this history with which we have had to come to terms'. It is arguable that the years from 1960 to the early 1990s constitute an identifiable historical period: one in which apartheid policies were most expansive and aggressively pursued; in which the state made a decisive shift towards more overtly authoritarian forms of social control and political repression; and in which mass transgressions of human rights in South Africa became internationally notorious.

But to treat this period as 'the history with which we have to come to terms' effectively frees us of the obligation to arrive at a similar reckoning with any other history. The high noon of human rights violations was preceded by a long dawn – a pre-history of dispossession, denial and subordination. Colonial conquest took two hundred years. Racial identities ascribed by colonial rule were rewritten – emphasised – by a distinctive form of industrialisation based upon the cheap labour of disenfranchised natives. Segregation policies, long before 1948, drew deeply discriminatory lines across housing, jobs, education and welfare.

What the TRC threatens to do is to uncouple these histories: to define three decades of the past in terms of perpetrators and victims and tightly defined categories of wrong, and to suggest that this is 'the beast of the past'. Let me illustrate the general point with a significant sub-theme. A substantial body of the testimony collected by the TRC dealt with torture at the hands of South African police officers. The Report provides a brief but chilling history of how torture was professionalised within the police, but especially in the Special Branch; how certain officers received training in torture techniques in France in the early sixties, and subsequently in Argentina, Chile and Taiwan. It details the legislation that drew new zones of penal licence – permitting solitary confinement and detention without trial. It quotes Joe Slovo: 'However firm the old type of policemen were ... they were not torturers ... In a sense, up to about 1960/1, the underground struggle was fought on a gentlemanly terrain. There was still a rule of law. You had a fair trial in their courts.' And while it demurs slightly – it received evidence on extensive forms of torture during the Pondoland Revolt of 1960, and it notes in a throwaway line that 'such methods were widely used in criminal investigations before the 1960s' – the Report essentially confines its account of violence at the hands of policemen to the years after Sharpeville.[27]

This is poor history. Without trying to make a full case for a different history, let me provide a couple of snapshots. In 1930, working in the locations of East London and Grahamstown, the anthropologist Monica Hunter noted: 'In collecting dreams, I found that by far the most frequent motif was a police raid.'[28] In 1937, a Police Commission of Inquiry appointed by Hertzog's government warned of the 'attitude of mutual distrust, suspicion and dislike' between police and black South Africans. This attitude was attributed to the 'unnecessary harshness, lack of sympathy, and even violence' used by police during the constant location raids to enforce tax, liquor and pass laws, which had 'a brutalising effect on the police'.[29] As Jack Simons drily noted in 1949, 'it is a short step from brutality to illegality' and, he added, 'in specific cases, policemen were shown to have flogged prisoners, beaten the soles of their feet, or ducked them in water until they were nearly unconscious.'[30]

The short memory span of the TRC in this specific instance is symptomatic of a more far-reaching incipient amnesia. Analytically, how helpful is it to focus on police torture and ignore bureaucratic terrorism? By bureaucratic terror I mean the use of state power against individuals and groups who are politically rightless, socially discriminated against, and economically subordinate. I refer to the routine denial of first-generation human rights; the everyday and unthinking dehumanisation of a social order that took root long before 1960. As Marks and Andersson put it, 'the counterpart of the state violence is the continued violence of unnecessary death, disease, degradation and disability' imposed by racially structured inequalities.[31] When Hannah Arendt coined the phrase 'the banality of evil' she concluded that 'the trouble with Eichmann was precisely that so many were like him, and the many were neither perverted nor sadistic, but they were, and still are, terribly and terrifyingly normal ... This normality was much more terrifying than all the atrocities put together.'[32]

It is this terror that escapes the TRC. By focusing so selectively on some of the horrors of the apartheid past, its hearings, paradoxically, have the effect of diminishing the full iniquity of that past. By highlighting the trauma of families of activists, the Commission unwittingly silences the lived realities of the multitude, the thousand unnatural shocks that apartheid flesh was heir to. It defines resistance by the active challenges of a heroic minority, but passes over the stoic endurance of the majority.

As Mahmood Mamdani puts it, '[t]he TRC's version of truth was established through narrow lenses, crafted to reflect the experience of a tiny minority' of victims and perpetrators. By individualising victimhood it surrendered the task of comprehending the social nature of dispossession. 'Perhaps the greatest moral compromise the TRC made was to embrace the legal fetishism of apartheid. In doing so, it made little distinction between what is legal and what is legitimate, between law and right.'[33]

This failure was memorably expressed by one of the foot soldiers of the TRC, Mahlubi Mabizela, a member of the research department. 'Farm labourers saw the TRC's coming as a sort of Messiah. But the policy decision was that their suffering was not covered by the Act, it was not a gross violation. The statement takers were the ones who had to say, sorry, we are not talking to you.'[34]

Conclusion

I want to end by referring to an incisive little book by Paul Connerton, called *How Societies Remember*. He begins with a general point about social memory:

> All beginnings contain an element of recollection. This is particularly so when a social group makes a concerted effort to begin with a wholly new start ... It is not just that it is very difficult to begin with a wholly new start, that too many old loyalties and habits inhibit the substitution of a novel enterprise for an old and established one. More fundamentally, it is that in all modes of experience we always base our particular experiences on a prior context in order to ensure that they are intelligible at all.[35]

In very specific cases, the 'concerted effort to begin with a wholly new start' takes place when a regime seeks to establish in a definitive manner a new social order. This was true for the regicides of Louis XVI, true for the Bolsheviks in 1917, and true for the Nuremberg trials. 'The settlement they seek is one in which the continuing struggle between the new order and the old will be definitively terminated, because the legitimacy of the victors will be validated once and for all … To pass judgement on the practices of the old regime is the constitutive act of the new order.'[36]

The TRC may appear to be passing judgement on the practices of the apartheid regime, but its remit and its reach are, in fact, very different. In its origins, in its mandate and in its procedures, it was incapable of that sort of judgement. It could not come to terms with the underlying structures and processes that have determined our identities and patterned our society. Because of its mandate, we may run the risk of defining a new order as one in which police may no longer enjoy impunity to torture opponents of the government, but fail to specify that ordinary citizens should not be poor and illiterate and powerless, or be pushed around by state officials and employers. Because of its analytical deficiencies, the TRC may not so much forge a new collective memory as facilitate social amnesia. And, parented by compromise, there is a final, ironic risk. The TRC and its charismatic chairperson committed themselves to nation-building. But will the Report help to build a single nation in the longer term, or will it legitimise a lopsided structure – two nations disguised as one, a hybrid social formation consisting of 'increasingly deracialised insiders and persistently black outsiders'?[37]

On the Limitations of Academic History: The Quest for Truth Demands Both More and Less

Charles Villa-Vicencio

The creative tension that exists between some academics and some who engage in 'hands-on' politics is well captured in an important conversation between the former President of the Czech Republic, Vaclav Havel, and Oxford historian Timothy Garton Ash.[1] Havel argues that if academics are indeed a breed 'with a heightened sense of responsibility and heightened understanding, then they undermine that claim if they refuse to take on themselves the burden of public office, on the grounds that it would mean dirtying their hands'. This statement comes in response to a comment by Garton Ash (in a public dispute with Vaclav Klaus, then Prime Minister of the Czech Republic) in which he suggests that the intellectual's job is to seek truth and the politician's 'to work with half truths'. Garton Ash still maintains that he is right. A healthy democracy, he argues, requires strict separation of the roles of the academic and the political players. The intellectual should be a 'mirror-holder', not an 'office holder'.

The Garton Ash view comes dangerously close to making an alarming distinction between academic and citizen. It hopefully does not mean that the academic cannot afford to engage in seeking to heal the messy past, if this means compromising on his or her academic distance and/or methodological correctness. In reviewing Garton Ash's latest book, *History of the Present: Essays, Sketches and Despatches from Europe in the 1990s*, Neal Ascherson asks whether the academic should not perhaps 'consent to let flecks of blood [and] stains of tears, spoil the whiteness of his shirt a little?'[2]

Colin Bundy has played many important roles in society, and has on more than a few occasions chosen to soil his shirt. On this occasion he chooses to be the Oxford don, or Wits academic, as promoted by Garton Ash, and has thus fomented an important debate.

As an academic critique of the published report of the Truth and Reconciliation Commission, his paper is difficult to fault. However, by way of a rejoinder, I think he is wrong in suggesting that the Commission was charged with 'writing an official history'. The Commission saw itself as offering no more than a historical comment from its perspective on a given period of history. To have dared more would have been most arrogant. And, even then, the voice or perspective of the Commission was rarely a single, homogeneous one. The Chairperson's Foreword to the Report stresses the inescapable perspective of those involved in the Commission, while calling on others to challenge, critique and correct its limitations. Vigorous debate on the Report is required and welcomed. Indeed, a comprehensive review of its work is needed to determine whether it has fulfilled its mandate: 'Others [the Foreword reads] will inevitably critique this perspective – as indeed they must. We hope that many South Africans and friends of South Africa will become engaged in the process of helping our nation to come to terms with its past and, in so doing, reach out to a new future.'[3]

Many academics, journalists and others have boldly appropriated this good advice. Deborah Posel points to what she sees as hints of academic epistemological and methodological prowess in the Report. (She reminds us that it even drops the odd reference to Max Weber and others!) She then quickly adds that those who drafted the Report failed to develop these insights in a structurally sound manner.[4] Anthea Jeffery of the South African Institute of Race Relations, fêted by John Kane Berman, published a book entitled *The Truth about the Truth Commission*. She suggests that the TRC Report displays 'Orwellian shades', without discerning the hand of George Orwell in both the title and contents of her own book. Her concern is that the Commission sacrificed 'factual and objective truth' on the altar of a methodology that is fundamentally flawed in that it fails to do justice to the submissions of the masters of the old regime.[5] Barney Pityana takes a different approach. He argues that the Report is over-defensive and went too far in justifying itself against its 'cultural despisers'.[6] What he is saying is that it ought to have been softer on the liberation movements. He goes further, advocating a stay on all prosecutions that might stem from the TRC process. (Anthony Holiday, conceding that theologians (like Pityana) have access to the mind of God on all things, suggests that he was in this instance perhaps inspired not by his Father in Heaven, but by his Master on Earth, President Thabo Mbeki.[7] Holiday's needling does not make for a comfortable pew!) And finally there is Stephen Ellis, who states that the Report of the Commission 'represents probably the most far-reaching attempt by an official body to come to terms with the human rights abuses committed by a previous government anywhere in the world since the Nuremberg trials of the late 1940s'.[8]

At the heart of the debate on the Commission is, of course, the question of the complex relationship between truth and fiction. Albert Camus defined truth as being 'as mysterious as it is inaccessible' and yet, he insisted, worth 'being fought for eternally'.[9] Its discovery involves a long and slow process, to which the Commission could make no more than a preliminary contribution.

Testifying at a Cape Town hearing of the TRC into the killing of the Guguletu Seven in April 1996, Cynthia Ngewu, the mother of Christopher Piet, one of those killed, wrestled with what had in fact happened. 'Now nobody knows the real-real story,' she noted.[10] Memory is at best a tricky thing. It is fraught with trauma and often with incomprehension. Pamela Reynolds reminds us that it is 'raw memory' which emerges in testimony.[11] Memory gives expression to the inability of language to articulate what needs to be said. It is incomplete. Its very incompleteness is what cries out to be heard. There is also the testimony of silence. There is body language. There is fear, anger and confusion. There is a struggle between telling what happened and explaining it away. It takes time to unpack, understand and do justice to testimony. The Commission could not do so adequately in the time available to it. Historians need to engage in this process over time. Indeed, the question needs to be asked whether the 'real-real story' can ever be fully grasped.

This is a piece of reality that is frequently exploited by those seeking to discredit others who have suffered and are struggling to find words to articulate their deepest experience of what happened. Thus, Anthea Jeffery attacks the Commission because (according to her) it paid insufficient attention to the importance of factual or objective truth, by recognising the importance of what it called personal or narrative (dialogue) truth, as well as social truth and healing or restorative truth. The Commission deliberately chose to wrestle with these notions of truth in relation to factual or forensic truth.[12] It was not a court of law and (for good reason) it did not subject victim and survivor testimony to cross-examination. It did, however, through corroboration assess such testimony on the basis of a balance of probability.

Graeme Simpson is correct: '[M]ost of the legal and jurisprudential dilemmas presented by the TRC process are actually rooted in its own almost bi-polar roles as both a "fact-finding" and a quasi-judicial enterprise on the one hand, and as a psychologically sensitive mechanism for story telling and healing on the other.'[13]

The Commission resolved at its inception to provide maximum space for victims and survivors to speak. At the same time (prodded and forced by legal action initiated by perpetrators), it committed itself to due process of law, giving alleged perpetrators an opportunity to offer rebuttal. The outcome was a set of findings that, given the restraints identified by Simpson, sought to 'present as complete a picture as possible' of gross violations of human rights committed during the period stipulated by the mandate (1 March 1960 to 10 May 1994). There remains, of course, a huge amount of incomplete transitionary work yet to be undertaken – both by the courts with regard to 'fact-finding' and by government and civil society at the level of facilitating more story telling and healing.

The Commission never perceived itself as taking on the kind of academic or historical brief which many of its critics have ascribed to it. The Report is precisely what it states itself to be – a report of a state commission – although it is indeed a slightly more interesting one, I would suggest, than the common or garden variety. It is the work of a Commission located, perhaps, somewhere between the 'office holder' and the 'mirror-holder' in the academic sense referred to by Garton Ash. It sought to act as an independent agent and holder of a mirror in which the nation could see itself – and yet it was a mirror shaped and angled by an Act of Parliament and a legal brief.

Against this background, I offer five points of tensions or dialectics that shaped the Report: process and product; popular image-making and the Report; the mandate and the sins of the past; even-handedness and moral judgement; understanding past perpetration while preventing future violations of human rights.[14]

Process and Product

Aryeh Neier, in his careful review of the Report of the Commission, suggests that it is the open, transparent, public nature of the South African Commission that distinguishes it from other truth commissions around the world.[15] This presented the Commission with a primary methodological challenge in drafting its Report. The question was how (and how much) to report, when so much of the Commission's work had already been reported in the media. The Commission was confronted with a tension resulting from a transparent and publicly enacted drama on the one hand and the need to produce a report that was by definition less than final in two important senses on the other. Firstly, the amnesty process was still incomplete. This meant that a report needed to be filed without all the evidence being heard. And secondly, the open-ended nature of the truth-seeking, of memory recall and of dealing with the past was equally important.

Perhaps the most important contribution that the Commission has made to this process, to national and individual memory and to historians and others in search of 'the truth', is a well-stocked archive to be located in the National Archives. The Commission's Report is largely an annotated road map into the archive. It is in this next phase of inquiry that a rereading of the evidence that the Commission received still needs to take place. This academically challenging and morally imperative exercise of reading between the lines, hearing behind the words, looking behind the scenes and honouring the silence behind the words waits to be done.

Colin Bundy draws on Brent Harris's important Derridean critique of the archive. The challenge is important. The inherent limitations of any archive must be acknowledged. The destruction of records by the former regime means that a huge amount of documentation never made it into the archive at all.[16] This destruction constitutes perhaps the major violation of collective memory of this nation. Having said this, a significant amount of documentation was *not* destroyed. It needs to be archived and protected. Scholars, students and all interested persons ought to be given maximum access to these resources to ensure that the quest for truth continues. The Commission has recommended to the President that, while the protection of privacy and national security ought to be taken into account, these documents should be made available to the public. All parties involved need to ensure that this happens, especially considering the fact that there probably are some people within and outside government who would prefer these documents to be consigned to obscurity.

This places the onus to uncover the truth on academic historians and those of similar spirit. However, yet another question needs to asked: Can the historian ever capture the pain of testimony, the agony of someone else's memory or the trauma of translating 'raw experience' into the spoken or written word? This is perhaps where poetry, music, fiction and myth can contribute more to healing than any attempt to explain in some rigid, forensic way 'who did what to whom'. Antjie Krog's celebrated novel on the work of the Commission, *Country of My Skull*,[17] weaves fragments from different testimonies and interviews into a semi-fictional historical account of events. The Commission felt compelled to do both more and less than what Krog accomplished. Its Report was, above all, obliged to be more comprehensive and thus compelled to reduce or translate the richness of raw memory, or what has been called first-generation testimony, into the first stages of historical narrative. This narrative waits to be reviewed, rewritten and refined.

Image-making and the Report

John Thompson writes of the 'mediasation' of modern culture – of being subjected to sound bytes and instant image-making.[18] The press thus becomes a double-edged sword, communicating memory as well as dealing deeply with the past. Antjie Krog, journalist and poet, defines the 'unforgettable wail of Nomfundo Calata' at the first hearing of the Commission in East London in April 1996 as the 'definite starting point' of the Commission.[19] The images sent around the world were of people (mostly black, mainly women) weeping on stage. Other images can be added: Eugene de Kock[20] as 'Prime Evil'; Jeffrey Benzien[21] and his 'wet-bag' method of torture efficiency.

Once these images are imprinted on the public mind, it is difficult for society to see beyond them. And yet, image-making is not the responsibility of the media alone. The Report consists of five large volumes and few critics read it in its entirety from the first cover to the last. As I listen to people suggesting that something has been left out or ought to have been included, I find myself wanting to assist them in their search, while not wanting to sound too defensive. There are errors and many inadequacies in the Report. Sometimes there are interesting stories as to why these occurred. In some instances there is simply no excuse for these to have occurred. They should have been identified. It is at times tempting to explain why something is reported in a certain way, and what the political dynamics behind some aspects of the Report were. Sometimes I am even persuaded to suggest that it would be a good idea for a critic to read the entire report before being too vociferous in his or her critique.

The Report of the Commission, with the exception of a few of the earlier chapters, was written over a period of approximately six months, with different authors contributing different sections that needed to be welded into a coherent document. During the last three months these were adopted by the Commission, edited and sent to the printer before the writing of other sections was completed. Time, a limited mandate and (dare I admit it?) a fair amount of inevitable internal political squabbling and external political pressure often delayed the processing of the Report and it certainly ruled out anything that resembled a leisurely editorial period, which would have afforded time to write, rewrite, integrate and fine-tune the text. The level of pressure in the Commission was quite phenomenal. But then, what is written is written. The printed text takes on an independence of its own, both to engage and be engaged in by others.

Communication is a difficult process. First impressions, dominant images and master texts, as well as a range of different academic, political and personal agendas sometimes make it difficult to read or hear someone else's argument for what it is. Given the public and political profile of the Commission, this is particularly true of the debate surrounding its Report. It is important for the sake of the nation as a whole that the polemical debate about the past be kept to a minimum to ensure that the nation is given a chance to confront the truth about the past, in all its complexity. This will, of course, lead to a measure of conflict, not least because the different stories about the past often contradict one another. Conflict can, however, be part of the healing process. The words of Donald Shriver are compelling in this regard: 'One does not argue long with people whom one deems of no real importance. Democracy is at its best when people of clashing points of view argue far into the night, because they know that the next day they are going to encounter each other as residents of the [same] neighbourhood.'[22]

The difficulties of creating democracy out of a culture of gross violations of human rights are immense. It can be facilitated through what the Chileans call *reconvivencia* – a period of getting used to living with each other again. Above all, it involves being exposed to the worst fears of one's adversaries. It requires getting to know one another, gaining a new insight into what happened, as well as an empathetic understanding of how a particular event is viewed by one's adversaries.

The Mandate and the Sins of the Past

The statute of limitations captured in the mandate of the Commission raised the ire of as many inside the Commission as outside of its structures. Yet ultimately the Commission accepted the mandate, realising that there were other structures of state and civil society to deal with the many other consequences of the long years of apartheid. For the Commission to have dealt adequately with the impact of race classification laws, group areas, Bantu Education and the like was neither feasible nor provided for in the legislation directing its affairs. Clearly the gross violations of human rights identified in the TRC Act occurred within the context of these wider structures of evil. This is captured in the contribution on the historical context of the Commission's work.[23] The Bundy–Posel suggestion that the Report 'sheds remarkably little light on apartheid' is at best an over-statement. It was not the designated task of the Commission to provide a detailed unfolding of apartheid ideology. It was to show some consequences of this system, consequences that its mandate limited to killings, torture, abduction and severe ill-treatment.

Among the more significant criticisms of the Commission's mandate are those of Mahmood Mamdani. The burden of his critique is that 'the TRC's version of truth was established through narrow lenses, crafted to reflect the experience of a tiny minority; on the one hand, perpetrators, being state agents and, on the other, victims, being political activists'. He goes on to suggest that 'the violence of apartheid was aimed less at individuals than at entire communities.'[24] His concern is that the 'beneficiaries' of apartheid are let off the hook, not being required to contribute to the material restoration of those who have suffered.

The Commission did not focus on this matter, nor did it ignore the problem. It recommended that a wealth tax be considered as one option for reducing the gap between the rich and the poor. The TRC was part of a larger process, designed to give the nation time and space to deal with those events that brought it to the brink of collapse in 1990. If the underlying structures that gave rise to these events are not dealt with in this post-TRC period, the major confrontation facing this country may still be ahead. Sadly, the recommendations of the TRC have scarcely been addressed by the state, while the findings and recommendations in the Report on the business hearing have been ignored by business. Laying the past to rest may ultimately have as much, if not more, to do with material transformation, as with disclosure and truth telling. The one, however, cannot be separated from the other.

President Thabo Mbeki identifies two interrelated elements of national reconciliation in what he calls 'two nations in one country'. The first element of Mbeki's analysis of the challenge facing South Africa is the creation of a material base for assisting the grossly underdeveloped black nation to elevate itself from the vastly inferior material living conditions imposed on it by apartheid. The second challenge is the promotion of a subjective factor that sustains 'the hope and conviction among people that the project of reconciliation and nation-building will succeed'. The President recognises that reconciliation depends not only on an extended reconstruction and development process, but also on the public processes of facilitating co-operation and trust between people for whom these benefits are intended. Former President Mandela spoke of the 'RDP [Reconstruction and Development Programme] of the soul'. This is what the TRC was mandated to address.

Even-handedness and Moral Judgement

A commitment to impartiality in the hearings, investigations and findings processes did not imply moral indifference. Indeed, the Commission saw it as its responsibility to hold up a mirror to the past, enabling the nation to pass judgement on what had happened, with a view to creating a society within which past violations were not repeated in the future. It realised that perpetrators could both deny the past and expect the emergence of a new order in which the past is indeed seen to be a thing of the past. In addressing this matter, the Commission affirmed international human rights standards as a basis for judging the past. In so doing, it joined the world in stating that apartheid is a crime against humanity. This thrust the Commission into the 'just war' debate. It stated clearly that there was 'just cause' on the side of those fighting against apartheid, while identifying and naming individuals and organisations on all sides of the political divide who were guilty of violating the norms of 'just means' in pursuit of their goals. Its findings in this regard are less than *ex cathedra*. They do, however, affirm the importance of international human rights law and the place of the Geneva Protocols.

There are many South Africans who would argue that, given the nature of the struggle against apartheid, gross violations of human rights that were committed in the heat of battle should be tolerated, if not justified. Albie Sachs tells us that the ANC National Executive was divided on how to deal with such violations. He reports Pallo Jordan, former Minister of Environment, as saying: 'Comrades, I've learnt something very interesting today. There is such a thing as regime torture, and there is ANC torture, and the regime torture is bad and the ANC torture is good; thank you for enlightening me.'[25] But what of the murder, mutilation and torture that had been committed by the apartheid regime over decades? In this context the notion of a Truth Commission was born, with Kader Asmal suggesting that the violations of human rights on all sides of the conflict be investigated and acknowledged.

Against this background one needs to ask whether the ANC did not do itself an injustice in its rejection of the Commission's findings regarding gross violations of human rights committed by its followers. ANC criticism came quite literally before anyone could have read the entire Report. It had, quite simply, not yet been released. Some suggested that a meeting (which the ANC requested) could have helped. One hopes that the conflict lay no deeper than this, namely, at the level of inadequate communication and serious misunderstanding. If, on the contrary, this conflict extends to a refusal by the ANC to accept any comparative investigation of both sides of the conflict by the TRC, the situation is disturbing.[26] This, suggests André du Toit, constitutes 'the primacy of a particular moral perspective' that smacks of what Carlos Nino has termed 'epistemic moral elitism'.[27] The fact that the ANC itself initiated the idea of a commission, that it endorsed its mandate and conceded that gross violations of human rights had occurred in its camps and elsewhere in its submission to the Commission, means, I hope, that Du Toit is wrong.

To acknowledge gross human rights violations in the heat of battle, recognising the ever-present threat of spies having infiltrated one's structures, is not an easy thing. However, it must be done to create a culture of human rights for both the present and the unknown tomorrow. This should surely not be seen as an exercise in delegitimising the liberation struggle. No fair reading of the Report can come to that conclusion. It is a call for acknowledgement as a basis for creating a better tomorrow. Let us remember that the Skweyiya Report, in acknowledging such atrocities, recommended that those guilty of such acts should be prevented from holding government office.[28] The TRC deliberately chose not to go that far.

Understanding Past Perpetration while Preventing Future Violations of Human Rights

The mandate of the Commission was not only to determine who did what to whom, but also to address the vexing questions of why and how perpetration took place. It was to identify the 'motives and perspectives' of perpetrators. If we as a nation do not begin to understand why and how past atrocities occurred, we are likely to repeat such violations in one form or another.

Leon Jaworski, Chief Prosecutor in the earliest European war crimes trials after the Second World War, asks himself how it is that decent people murdered others so systematically. The question haunted him all his life and in 1960 he published a book entitled *After Fifteen Years*, in which he effectively says: 'Watch out. It can happen to you.'[29] Josef Garlinski, a member of the Polish resistance army and an Auschwitz survivor, reflects on the brutality he was required to endure from his Nazi captors and reminds us of this in his book *Fighting Auschwitz*. Having told his story with devastating human impact, he goes on to remind us that the young SS officers responsible for such deeds 'could have been your sons or mine'.[30] A black South African artisan, proud of his son's educational achievements and advancement in the South African Police, asked in disbelief how his son, a sensitive and deeply religious young man, could possibly have become a culpable member of the police riot squad sent into Mlungisi, the African township outside Queenstown, to quell an anti-apartheid uprising.[31]

The Commission made an initial attempt to address the question of motives and perspectives in the final volume of its Report.[32] However, a lot more work needs to be done. History suggests that evil and the capacity for evil is no respecter of tribe, nation or race. The identification of the social, material and psychological sources that provide the fertile ground for perpetration still needs to be addressed.

The academic historian has a great deal to contribute in this regard, and in so doing will need to deal not only with 'forensic truth', but also with those vexing notions of truth referred to earlier. I refer again to Garton Ash, who suggests that there are three ways of dealing with past atrocities: trials, purges and history lessons. Each requires a different kind of truth. 'I personally believe the third path, that of history lessons, is the most promising,' he writes.[33] And yet, as suggested earlier, it may take poets, artists and creative writers of fiction to complete the task.

Where Do Academics and Politicians Meet?

The furthest thing from the minds of those involved in writing the Report was the need to write an academic history. We realised that at best we could generate some material that others could forge into the kind of history for which Colin Bundy asks.

I conclude with two comments. Firstly, academics and politicians should indeed not get their roles confused. Both have a particular kind of work to do. An independent commission is neither a political caucus nor an academic workshop. And yet, academics do their jobs well in demanding that both commissions and politicians deliver more than they ever can. They hold up a vision that acts both as critique and lure. This is important. Secondly, with apologies to Immanuel Kant: The critique of pure reason is a wonderful thing. It is on this that Bundy and many others focus their critique. The critique of practical reason is equally important. Academics should be prepared to soil their shirts, both in order to understand political work as it happens in the rough and tumble of real life, and in order to be good citizens.

Chapter Three

The Politics of Memory in Divided Societies

Heribert Adam and Kanya Adam

The previous two essays evaluated the South African Truth and Reconciliation Commission's achievements in documenting the country's apartheid history, and in facilitating reconciliation in a divided society. Other societies have dealt with their iniquitous pasts in different ways, some more successfully than others. This contribution will examine the various ways in which countries have sought to come to terms with their histories, and the extent to which the means they employed were successful.

The Politics of Memory

Human memory is never a collection of fixed, stored data that can be downloaded or accumulated for later use. Social conditions determine what is remembered and how these events are recalled. Interests shape individual as well as collective memory, and memory, therefore, amounts to a contingent social construction.

Ian Buruma has rightly noted that '[m]emory is not the same as history and memorialising is different from writing history'.[1] If the two are equated, the distinction between falsehood and truth is lost. A history concerned with establishing factual events is to be distinguished from the interpretation of these events. Opinions about this interpretative and moral truth can legitimately differ, particularly in divided societies. Since individual morals, feelings and interests vary widely in a heterogeneous collectivity, it is problematic to assume a collective identity, without which there cannot be a collective memory. Only in a loose, metaphorical sense can we speak of a collective identity, a national character or a collective memory.

Collective memory constitutes the informal, widely accepted perceptions of past events in which the collective identity of a people is mirrored. This identity is strongly influenced by the official definitions, rituals and laws of the state. The memorials that a state erects, the national holidays selected, the museums subsidised, the speeches of politicians that celebrate or mourn the past and define a state's self-perception in laws and public institutions all contribute to collective memory that changes over time. Divided memories exist when sizeable groups within the same state simultaneously attribute different meanings to the same history.

There are no universally valid rules determining how an emerging democracy should deal with the crimes of a previous regime. It seems useful to explore empirically how different democracies have coped with the problem of state-sponsored crimes, how victims are recognised or compensated, how the new order attempts reconciliation between warring factions, and how the repetition of an unsavoury past is prevented.

Six forms of grappling with the past can be distinguished and compared in their historical context:

(1) Amnesia: post-war Germany, Japan, Spain, Russia.
(2) Trials and justice: Nuremberg, proposed International Criminal Court.
(3) Lustration: the disqualification of collaborators from public office; for example, the German Democratic Republic, Eastern Europe.
(4) Negotiated restitution and compensation: Germany's reparation to Israel and compensation for forced labour, Canada's and Australia's negotiations about the land rights of indigenous minorities.
(5) Political re-education.
(6) Truth commissions: Latin America and South Africa.

Several of these strategies are frequently employed simultaneously or with different emphases over time. Of all cases, two countries are of particular significance: Germany, because of its unique past with Auschwitz as the universal paradigm of barbarism, and South Africa. The South African Truth and Reconciliation Commission deserves critical scrutiny for three reasons. The TRC is regarded as a novel experiment of restorative justice and nation-building through reconciliation; it is often recommended as an international model for similar conflicts elsewhere; and its achievements are widely overrated outside South Africa, while largely dismissed inside.

We would argue, however, that the TRC's mandate was based on some flaws and problematic assumptions. One of these is the assumption that 'revealing is healing'. Legislated reconciliation also fails to recognise that only victims have the ability to forgive. Furthermore, the skewed composition of the TRC and its theological perspectives affected its credibility, and the quest for an official truth and common memory did not allow for pluralist interpretations of history. Above all, the focus on gross human rights violations freed the many beneficiaries of apartheid from responsibility and obliterated the reality of structural violence of racial laws for millions of victims who have not been recognised by the TRC process.

(1) Amnesia

In Germany, the post-war period up to the mid-sixties represented a typical example of official amnesia and private denial. Instead of dealing honestly with the shame of the past, the country was encouraged to forget the past, and to focus on the future and the rebuilding of the nation. The Nazi period was portrayed as an accident of German history: 'In the middle of the 1950s,' writes historian Norbert Frei, 'a collective consciousness had emerged that attributed solely to Hitler and his inner circle all responsibilities for the atrocities of the Third Reich.'[2] Germans as a whole were ascribed the role of a politically seduced people, of whom the war and its consequences had made victims.

In the communist German Democratic Republic (GDR), official anti-fascism denied all links with the Nazi past. Since the 'dark brown period' had resulted from a capitalist crisis, the heroic rise of socialism in the anti-fascist struggle had also taken care of all fascist remnants and preconditions.

In the West, the theory of totalitarianism reigned supreme in the ensuing Cold War. The free West proudly distinguished itself from both brown and red totalitarianism. Sociologist Helmut Dubiel asserts that 'the true scandal of German memorialising was not that the Nazi past was simply ignored, but immersed in the ideological competition between East and West'.[3] Both states accused each other of failing to draw the necessary conclusions from history. Each side blamed the other for perpetuating conditions in which freedom was denied.

There are two main explanations for post-war amnesia. The most widely accepted version holds that the economic and bureaucratic reconstruction required the inclusion of Nazi collaborators, given the scarcity of skills available. German rearmament in the 1950s, for example, would have been impossible without falling back on the expertise of previous officers. Large groups of colluders needed to be integrated into the new democracy, because they could not have been marginalised.

A second, psychologically based explanation focuses on the subconscious reaction to collective trauma. A fragile collective identity had to protect itself against an unbearable truth by repressing and rationalising it.

It was not until the late 1960s that the children of the war generation revived questions about the past, spurred on by the student revolt against authoritarian traditions and general politicisation. Yet another generation later, the meaning of the past is even more intensely debated. There is probably no other country that currently scrutinises and redefines its collective memory as thoroughly as Germany. An eleven-year debate about a central Berlin memorial for the victims of Nazism culminated in a parliamentary debate in June 1999, when it was decided that the Eisenmann memorial should be built as proposed.[4] The memorial would be dedicated exclusively to European Jews, and it would have an information and learning centre attached to it. Earnest arguments split all parties, and the overwhelming supporting vote surprised everyone. Public opinion surveys on support for the Eisenmann monument also revealed substantial agreement among the population. There was a definite split: 46 per cent were in favour of and 44 per cent were against the memorial, with 93 per cent of supporters in favour of its dedication to all Nazi victims. Parliament's decision to dedicate it exclusively to European Jews indicated that concern about negative foreign reactions outweighed local opinion.

Behind the German debate about whether the nation should define itself as a 'normal' polity stands the question whether the unified state should also shed the constraints on its 'moral sovereignty'. Full political sovereignty was restored with resocialisation into Western democratic habits. Later in 1989, national unification within European rules and values was the final crowning achievement. A growing number on the political right and centre now wishes to shed the moral inhibitions resulting from the Nazi legacy. Until the recent involvement of the German army in Bosnia and Kosovo, the country had shirked its responsibility to provide assistance to international human rights enforcement organisations with reference to its unique history of sixty years ago.

How should one evaluate this process of profoundly redefining collective memory? Is the decision for the Holocaust memorial the progressive acknowledgement of collective moral and political responsibility, although 'Germans collectively do not bear criminal and moral guilt'?[5] Or is the victory of the seemingly progressive remembrance of shame merely the monstrous tombstone in the final burial of an embarrassing past?

It would seem that the Berlin memorial, above all, fulfils the object of visibly exculpating the new 'Berlin Republic' from the suspicion of past nationalist ambitions. With narcissistic self-congratulation, the debate lays to rest the Nazi legacy by demonstrating that the self-confident unified state has successfully come to terms with its shame – just as the victims wished. Just as minorities around the world clamour for the 'vicarious virtue' of victimisation, as Ian Buruma has argued,[6] so the German political elite of all parties is now keen to demonstrate the opposite: that it has mastered the much more intricate task of coming to terms with being the worst collective perpetrator in history. This negative uniqueness, the ritual acknowledgement of the Nazi break with civilization (*Zivilisationsbruch*), is now almost paraded as a feature of a new national identity that is as interesting as the positive achievements of an economic miracle after total destruction in 1945. A shameful past as nationalist exhibitionism would be merely the other side of the dubious coin of denial and amnesia.

However, neither was post-war German amnesia a specific German characteristic, nor is the historical denial of collective infamy necessarily related to the development of a democratic culture. Britain, France and Holland had buried their colonial crimes until very recently, but are nonetheless considered model democracies. The United States of America still lacks a single national memorial to slavery or to the near genocide of the aboriginal people. Nations memorialise their own suffering, but not what they inflict on others. The Vietnam War Memorial in Washington lists the names of all the Americans who lost their lives, but not a single Vietnamese name.

In Japan, history textbooks do not mention the atrocities of the imperial army in Korea and China. *The Rape of Nanking*, Iris Chang's English bestseller about the murder of 30 000 inhabitants of the city, has not been published in a Japanese translation and is bogged down in arguments about its accuracy. The Tokyo government refuses a clear apology even to Chinese or Korean state visitors, despite the worldwide feminist concern about thousands of so-called 'comfort women'. Recently the official designation 'capitulation' was renamed the more neutral 'end of war'. National guilt is widely regarded as having been absolved by the first atomic bombs dropped on Hiroshima and Nagasaki.

Following political transformation, many nations rationalise their guilt with new myths. In Austria, collective memory redefined the popular enthusiasm for Hitler as 'forced unification', thereby portraying collusion as victimhood. In France, only the recent trials against collaborators of the Vichy regime have undermined the popular myth that half of the French population had joined the underground resistance against the German occupiers. Spain has totally avoided coming to terms with its forty years of Franco dictatorship because it would re-open the wounds of the civil war. Paradoxically, Germany has apologised for Guernica and paid compensation, but the Madrid parliament has not; Turkey still cultivates its cherished myth that the Armenian genocide never happened and is an invention of foreign propaganda.

The eighty to one hundred million victims of Stalinism still wait to be rehabilitated and properly recognised. Acknowledging that Marxism–Leninism had a rational, humanitarian goal, while Hitler's biological master narrative was by definition irrational, should not preclude comparisons between the racial genocide in Germany and the class genocide in the USSR.

This sketch of varied collective responses to past state crimes allows for some general conclusions. Grappling with the past is not a necessary precondition for a functioning democracy. As Michael Ignatieff has written: 'All nations depend on forgetting: on forging myths of unity and identity that allow a society to forget its founding crimes, its hidden injuries and divisions, its unhealed wounds. It must be true, for nations as it is for individuals, that we can stand only so much truth. But if too much truth is divisive, the question becomes, how much is enough?'[7]

It is commonly assumed that public interest in a shameful past fades away among later generations. They carry no personal guilt, unlike their parents who engaged in denial because they were psychologically incapable of admitting to the enormity of their own collusion with state atrocities. Paradoxically, public interest in and recognition of national crimes seem to increase over time. Subsequent generations feel free to accept collective responsibility for the sins of their ancestors although motivations differ in each context and divided memories prevail.

In their eagerness to prevent the gruesome past from haunting the future, well-meaning social engineers are intent on creating 'a common history' between hostile groups. In their most extreme form, they repress the airing of past hostilities, as Tito did with the enforced slogan 'Brotherhood and Unity'. Such totalitarian designs are the surest recipe for renewed conflict. 'By repressing the real history of the interethnic carnage between 1941 and 1945, the Titoist regime guaranteed that such carnage would return.'[8] Only a pluralist interpretation of history may at best achieve a shared truth, or at worst reinforce divided memories. History as an ongoing argument is still preferable to the myth-making of official collective memory.

(2) Trials and Justice

The prosecution of perpetrators of gross human rights violations requires clear winners and losers. Where there is a stalemate – as in South Africa, or in Chile between the democrats and the military – historical compromises and amnesties are negotiated. Prosecutions would most likely provoke new violence and even endanger the survival of the emerging democracy.

However, apart from the morality of pursuing justice for its own sake, there are good pragmatic reasons for trials of political criminals. Aryeh Neier, one of the most passionate advocates of punishment, has expressed the most convincing reason: 'When the community of nations shies away from responsibility for bringing to justice the authors of crimes against humanity, it subverts the rule of law.'[9] If the victimised see no one being held accountable, they may seek revenge on their own and continue the cycle of violence. Prosecution of individual perpetrators also counteracts the misleading notion of collective guilt. Individualising guilt does not smear the name of an entire group. Finally, indictments by the proposed International Criminal Court cannot be accused of constituting a 'victor's justice'.

However, there are also clear pitfalls to be avoided. If a sovereign state can head off ICC prosecution by bringing alleged war criminals before its own courts, a fair trial depends very much on the independence and quality of its judiciary. This spectrum can range from biased judges of the old order (as alleged in South Africa) to an internal 'victor's justice' where the judiciary has been purged and replaced with partisans of the new regime.

The ICC would become powerless if prosecutions could only be launched with the consent of the states involved in which the crime occurred or the alleged criminals live. A similar paralysis would ensue if vetoes by Security Council members could indefinitely block prosecution. NATO's unilateral military intervention in Kosovo without UN approval was a recent response to this predicament. NATO's 'military humanitarianism' postulated that gross violations of universal rights within a sovereign state necessitated outside intervention in the same way as aggression against a foreign territory would justify war in self-defence. Jürgen Habermas has argued that the NATO action anticipated a world citizenship that unfortunately does not yet exist as an enforceable order.[10]

If the ICC were to be the first practical indicator of a more effective world order for universal human rights, it would be even more imperative to prevent 'core' crimes rather than merely punish violators afterwards. It is doubtful whether the threat of indictment is sufficient to restrain a future Pinochet or Milošević. In fact, the opposite might happen. Faced with the prospect of being imprisoned in The Hague, future dictators may cling to power strenuously, resulting in more victims, rather than abdicate or remove themselves into unsafe exile.

A great step towards prevention of crimes against humanity could be the establishment of a similar international tribunal (or the inclusion of the task into ICC duties) to which aggrieved minorities could appeal for redress. The world lacks an impartial forum to which oppressed groups can formally turn for action against their government. With the realistic prospect of being brought to justice by an international body, armed resistance and civil war would be effectively discouraged. Should a sovereign state refuse to heed the verdict of the tribunal on the treatment of minorities, a variety of sanctions could be meted out against it. The state's chief representatives themselves could even be indicted for contempt of court. While the European Court in Strasbourg already hears complaints against unjust treatment by European governments and the International Court of Justice pronounces on inter-state disputes, aggrieved national minorities need to be offered a similar legal alternative to taking up arms.

(3) Lustration

The term 'lustration' is frequently used to describe all actions against former regime affiliates, from violent or lawless purges to formalised procedures, to a mere 'ceremonial cleansing' of the new order.[11] In this analysis, lustration is used in a narrower sense to define the regulated screening of collaborators for disqualification from public office. Victors establish categories of guilt and responsibility to which varying sanctions correspond. Typical examples would be de-nazification procedures in post-war Germany and 'destasification' after reunification.

Attitudes of the general public show remarkable similarities between the two cases, fifty-five years apart. Susanne Karstedt, in a perceptive comparative analysis of polling data, notes an initial strong approval of punishment of the top decision-makers and beneficiaries, but a readiness to exempt ordinary party members and recipients of orders in the lower echelons.[12] This reaction reflects and reinforces the notion of a 'betrayed people'. A small clique can be blamed, while the collusive silence of ordinary people transforms them into victims. With time, the call for indictment of the leadership fades and a general atmosphere of closure of the past takes hold.

Lustration is only possible in situations where extensive files of the previous regime reliably document collaborators. Disqualification from public office also presupposes the availability of sufficient skilled substitutes. This was the case in the reunification of East and West Germany, where the Eastern part was taken under the economic and bureaucratic tutelage of the West. In South Africa, the continued employment of apartheid administrators in the civil service for a while was not only part of the negotiated settlement but also a necessity in the absence of sufficiently trained personnel of the new order.

(4) Negotiated Restitution and Compensation

Even established democracies pay reparation to victims mainly under political pressure and rarely out of moral commitment or guilty conscience. The Canadian government finally paid a meagre average of $20 000 to the Japanese-Canadian survivors of Second World War internment camps more than thirty-five years later. Reparation amounted only to a symbolic restitution of their expropriated property.

Another dynamic is at work with regard to the long-standing grievances of native people. Canadian courts have found the main churches and the federal government 'jointly liable' for the horrific sexual abuse of thousands of aboriginal children. They were sent to religious boarding schools as part of a government effort to assimilate native youth. Hundreds of former students have filed individual and class-action lawsuits, seeking damages for their suffering, inflicted mostly by Roman Catholic and Anglican church officials. In the case of land claims and hunting and fishing rights by aboriginal groups in both Australia and Canada, powerful moral pressure is exerted. The scattered 3 per cent of the Canadian native population does not possess the voting strength, economic clout or physical power to force the national government to recognise its historical grievances. Yet despite strong opposition from influential oil, mining and forest companies, Canadian courts have recognised aboriginal land claims and forced the government to enter into good faith negotiations about transferring large tracts of crown land to native jurisdiction. Preferential fishing and hunting rights have long been granted, despite strong local voters' opposition and concern for conservation measures. Australia has even instituted a symbolic national 'Sorry Day' to create a collective memory of the country's illegitimate conquest by foreign settlers. Led by the Council of Aboriginal Reconciliation under the motto 'Walking together', Australia experienced its largest political demonstration for bridging the socio-political gap between black and white Australians in May 2000. A quarter of a million people walked across the Sydney Harbour Bridge in support of prioritising aboriginal reconciliation on the national agenda.

The moral politics of embarrassment are at work here. A state is forced by relatively powerless groups into a clear choice: either to forfeit its claims of a model democracy, based on the rule of law, or to live up to broken treaties and admit historical injustice. Since Canada proudly markets itself as an anti-colonial, multicultural model, it can hardly allow itself to be exposed as practising open internal colonialism. With the help of legal assistance by sympathetic lawyers, even powerless minorities can exercise power over indifferent governments. The Canadian state even bears the costs of the court challenges against itself and finances research into further claims in the name of historical injustice.

A political interest in acceptance by the international community motivated substantial German reparation to Israel and individual Jewish victims at the beginning of the 1950s, despite disapproval of the majority of the electorate. Foreign policy considerations also had a strong impact on the question of German compensation for an estimated one million out of eight to ten million survivors of forced labour in Nazi Germany. Paradoxically, it was globalisation, and the fusion of German and foreign conglomerates, that made the German side vulnerable to boycotts abroad and adverse court judgements in the United States.

Although the German government promises to treat all claimants equally, it can be expected that the strength of the claimants' lobby and the status of their government will play a decisive role. Sinti and Roma, unorganised homosexuals and Jehovah's Witnesses will surely be short-changed in the end. Claims of US citizens will be given greater weight than those originating from Eastern Europe. Constantin Goschler points out that only the end of the Cold War made these demands possible: 'Individual Nazi victims play a minor role in the calculation of East European states in light of their own interests in German support and therefore receive less endorsement from their own government than comparable claims originating from the US.'[13]

Even in a state with a government of liberation, the liberated victims cannot be sure of receiving material reparation. The South African government, Tutu admonishes, betrays the victims by ignoring the recommendation of the TRC to pay twenty thousand recognised victims a modest amount of R20 000 for six years. At the same time the TRC process illustrates the danger of establishing a hierarchy of victimhood.

Advocates of the TRC praise involvement of broad sectors of society in providing information. The communal experience of public hearings, of being heard and being officially recognised as victims, is said to be as important for the healing of trauma as the testimony itself. Unfortunately, this broad involvement also raises false expectations. In South Africa, many communities are disappointed that follow-up did not take place, and particularly that expected compensation for suffering has not materialised. 'We have stimulated hopes and then abandoned the people,' explains one Commissioner self-critically.[14] However, the TRC, with its limited resources and lifespan, was not empowered to fulfil the expectations it raised. It could merely make recommendations to Government, which was free to accept or to 'fudge' even the modest TRC suggestions. ANC leaders now argue that liberation should not be reduced to material benefits.

Speculations that 'the palpable insufficiency of reparation could stoke fires of revenge or further victimise the victimised as trivialising their harms or suggesting a payoff for silence' do not apply in South Africa.[15] Since a government of victims is responsible for non-payment, this would amount to a rejection of claims from its own ranks. Nor is anyone co-opted into silence. Those twenty thousand persons recognised by the TRC as theoretically eligible for compensation are envied by the millions of ordinary victims of apartheid laws who did not fall into the category of victims of 'gross violations of human rights'. Their suffering, caused by the expropriation of land in terms of the Group Areas Act, low wages under the discriminatory labour policy, and arrests under the pass laws, is trivialised by comparison; it is seen as not being worthy of restitution under TRC legislation. In short, by focusing solely on major transgressions against illegitimate laws, the TRC legislation ignores the structural, legal violence of a racist system. Mahmood Mamdani argues that the TRC concerned itself mainly with a select group of victims, instead of beneficiaries.[16]

(5) Political Re-education

Memory politics frequently include conscious measures for re-education, from the re-writing of history books to exchange programmes and the official re-definition of collective identity. It emphasises the importance of focusing on the suffering of one's adversary rather than on the pain of one's own group in order to achieve empathy and tolerance through a shared history.

Education for multicultural understanding always deserves support, but its impact should not be overrated. Strengthening the self-confidence of adolescents by developing a critical consciousness and knowledge of the rules of negotiated conflict resolution promises greater success as an educational method.

The lessons of Auschwitz do not lie in empty rituals of remembrance or in indoctrinating collective guilt. Political education in the next century needs to go beyond Auschwitz by keeping alive an awareness of and sensibility to future injustice. The lessons of Auschwitz are best preserved by exposing people's all-pervasive disposition for racism and discrimination.

The ashes and corpses of previous victims are best honoured by providing the living with insights about the causes of their fate. In Germany, this should include all victims of Nazism, not only Jews. Jews were certainly the most numerous victims, and in the paranoia of the Nazis their most dangerous enemy. Yet it seems wrong to dedicate the Berlin memorial exclusively to Jews, as the German parliament decided to do. A promise of similar memorials for the other victim groups elsewhere leads to rivalry and establishes a hierarchy of suffering. Above all, the false impression is created that Jews were murdered because of their particular behaviour, while in reality Jews were convenient scapegoats, and interchangeable.

Memorialisation in the form of an official monument always suggests that the Nazi past has been laid to rest once and for all. Some consider such finality an advantage. A truth commission, writes Martha Minow, 'fails to create potential closure afforded by criminal trials that end in punishment.'[17] However, continuing soul-searching should be welcomed rather than regretted. Political education is advanced by disputes over interpretations of past events that are easily consigned to oblivion with the closure of an authoritative judgement. The more controversial a memorial in the centre of Berlin, the better for raising consciousness. Rather than please, it ought to hurt national self-satisfaction like a thorn.

The central memorial need not even be confined to Nazi victims. Fascist mentalities, in the form of xenophobia and violence against foreigners, survive among an alienated minority, particularly in former East Germany, where few foreigners lived before. To highlight this continuity, the memorial could open itself to the future and engrave the names of all foreigners murdered for racist reasons in the post-fascist state.

The unique Nazi crimes could illuminate how and under what conditions universal individual predispositions emerge and are successfully mobilised in a mass genocidal movement. In this way the 'normal society' of the 'Berlin Republic', because of its abnormal past, could prove to itself and to the world that it has learnt to mourn all victims of discrimination.

(6) Truth Commissions

Truth commissions were first established when the successors of the military dictatorships in various Latin American countries came under pressure to reveal the fate of the thousands of alleged dissidents who had disappeared. The South African TRC differed from its Latin American counterparts in that it was established by an Act of Parliament rather than by presidential decree. It held open hearings instead of in camera investigations, and made amnesty dependent on full disclosure by perpetrators. The TRC saw itself in the tradition of 'restorative justice', forgoing punishment in favour of reconciliation. Assuming that 'revealing is healing', encounters between forgiving victims and remorseful perpetrators were meant to achieve this ambitious goal as the only alternative to continued strife.

Owing to TRC Chairperson Desmond Tutu's international stature, his hopes and predictions have entered the academic literature as empirical facts. In this vein, Gesine Schwan, in her celebrated Politik und Schuld, falsely credits the TRC with 'having engendered pity, empathy and remorse on the part of perpetrators by being confronted with the unspeakable suffering of victims.'[18] That was the intention of the TRC hearings, but in reality this only occurred in rare cases. Ironically, two of the worst killers, Eugene de Kock, dubbed 'Prime Evil' by the South African media as commander of the special Vlakplaas police unit, and his predecessor, Dirk Coetzee,[19] fall into this category of remorseful converts.[20] However, in most other cases, judging from participant observation and recorded confessions, apartheid's assassins tried to save their skins by applying for amnesty or turning state witness without recognising the moral turpitude of their actions.[21] The public shaming of confessing perpetrators presupposes a moral reference group that shares the shame. However, remorse is unlikely if exposed killers retreat into the ethnic enclaves for whom they committed their crimes and whose dominant attitudes range from understanding to open sympathy.

Typically, perpetrators acknowledged the suffering they caused, or even expressed coded regret, but rationalised their deeds in terms of the political climate of the time or their assigned role in the apartheid machinery. Like their political leaders in the National Party, they did not offer a genuine acknowledgement of guilt or acceptance of responsibility. None offered private compensation within their means.

Indifference towards the plight of victims was also displayed by black perpetrators on the other side, most prominently Winnie Madikizela-Mandela.[22] Despite an embarrassing beckoning for a sign of remorse by the TRC Chair, she finally complied only half-heartedly and reluctantly. The ANC leadership as a whole has yet to remove from office cadres within its ranks who have admitted to human rights abuses. The ANC only took collective responsibility for 'excesses' in the heat of the struggle. In fact, Mbeki criticised the TRC for its 'erroneous determination' that indiscriminate bombings or the taking of civilian hostages constitutes human rights violations. The TRC findings were seen by the ANC as an attempt to 'criminalise a significant part of the struggle of our people for liberation'. The TRC was accused of equating the ANC's unfortunate 'collateral damage' in pursuit of a just cause with the defence of an unjust one. To its lasting credit, the TRC has always insisted that no such moral levelling was intended or indeed possible, but even in the fight for a just cause, the Geneva Protocols have to be upheld.

The South African debate has confirmed the insight Michael Ignatieff has gained from the Yugoslav conflict – that it is relatively easy for both sides to acknowledge each other's pain: 'Much more difficult – indeed usually impossible – is shared acknowledgment about who bears the lion's share of responsibility. For if aggressors have their own defence against truth, so do victims. People who believe themselves to be victims of aggression have an understandable incapacity to believe that they too have committed atrocities.'[23]

While truth commissions can confirm the factual truth of an atrocity, they usually fail to establish a common interpretative truth. This moral truth of why something happened and who is responsible for it, is always heavily contested. Divided memories prevail because truth is tied to institutional and collective identity. Apportioning blame in a moral narrative affects the standing of a political party or the self-respect of a people. Even if something is an obvious truth to any 'objective' outsider, it might be far from acceptable to an insider. For a member of the 'in-group' the belief in the wickedness of the other or the goodness of itself is not just a myth that can be unmasked. It is part of an identity, a daily reality to be lived by, a lens through which the world is interpreted and a tool to give meaning to life. As Ignatieff has rightly stressed: 'It is unreasonable to expect those who believed they were putting down a terrorist or insurgent threat to disown the idea simply because a truth commission exposes the threat as having been without foundation. People, especially people in uniform, do not easily or readily surrender the premises upon which their lives are based.'[24]

Particularly if a truth is imposed from the outside, it is rejected. Foreigners should therefore refrain from interpreting history for locals, no matter how high their academic standing outside and how good their intentions. It is also wise to guard against the interpretations of internal exiles, of people of the same ethnicity but little ideological credibility among their own group: human rights activists or cosmopolitan minds who are viewed as sympathetic to the enemy. If collective identity is to be redefined successfully, it has to be communicated by credible ideologues from the inside.

The South African TRC neglected to enlist such figures from the Afrikaner intellectual or religious establishment. Unlike the Chilean Commission, with four members from the old and four from the new regime, none of the seventeen members of the South African TRC belonged to the formerly ruling National Party. (The two Afrikaners on the Commission were members of rival parties and were isolated among the rest of the ANC-orientated staff.) This skewed composition of the TRC, comprised of otherwise well-intentioned people with predominantly legal qualifications or theological training, nevertheless compromised the reception of its findings. Appointing reasonable hard-liners from both sides to argue about a shared historical truth in the calm of a committee room almost promises better results than to select presumable non-partisan, 'objective', politically low-profile representatives of various interest groups, as stipulated by South African legislation. If ethnic fundamentalists had achieved some minimal consensus, they could have communicated their controversial compromises far more effectively than any Nobel Prize-winning personalities. In fact, the more the outside world heaps praise on interlocutors to reinforce their difficult reconciliation, the more suspect they become among their followers. Honour should only be bestowed once results have been achieved.

The South African historic compromise initially benefited from having a range of credible leaders on both sides. With little internal democracy and authoritarian traditions in both the ANC and the NP, followers trusted their leaders blindly. Nelson Mandela and Joe Slovo could sell a controversial negotiated settlement to their sceptical constituency on the basis of their hallowed record of suffering and militancy. The conservative, cautious F.W. de Klerk was given an overwhelming mandate to negotiate, because nobody suspected his team would surrender all political power in exchange for preserving economic privileges.

However, more than sanctions and the rising costs of minority rule, it was the very nature of racial domination that distinguished South Africa from Yugoslavia. Mobilised ethnic identity in the Balkans prevented reconciliation while discredited racial identity in South Africa facilitated compromise. Long before negotiations about the abolition of apartheid started, the system had been delegitimised from the outside as well as from the inside. Most Afrikaner intellectuals had defected from the ruling group and were championing 'reform'.

Furthermore, the economic interdependence limited ruthlessness in apartheid South Africa. Terror was not applied indiscriminately against all members of an 'out-group', as under fascism or the ethno-nationalist strife of Yugoslavia, but mainly against political activists. The vast majority of 'non-whites', although suffering under heavy discrimination, could escape direct attacks on their life by being apolitical and complying with the law of the state. Unlike fascism, which placed its victims outside the law, denying them any personal rights, apartheid ruled through a supposedly equal legal system.

Racial discrimination in such a context does not lend itself to the same group cohesion and collective trauma as ethnic mobilisation. Unlike Nazi ideology, based on imaginary national blood bonds of common ancestry, apartheid needed to racialise culturally different whites in order to unify a weak demographic base, but ethnicise black people in order to divide and rule. This artificial and imposed social engineering had to fail because it lacked the freely embraced legitimacy of ethno-nationalism elsewhere. When the Cold War ended, Eastern European leaders turned successfully to previously suppressed nationalism to fill the ideological vacuum. In South Africa, costly segregation could finally be abandoned because the elites on both sides would benefit from reluctant co-operation. In short, the discredited racism lacked the appeal of a just cause because even apartheid advocates had come to see blacks as victims while the humiliated, the colonised, eschewed vengeance in the name of non-racialism and reconciliation.

A once powerful Afrikaner nationalism had fallen victim to its own economic success through state patronage. Once a mild African nationalism merely claimed political power and civil service positions without threatening the accumulated wealth and relative cultural autonomy of its historic adversary, Afrikaner nationalists unravelled into heterogeneous interest groups and different identity definitions without a common enemy. Graves of ancestors, territory acquired in ethnic cleansing or conflicts over holy sites, as in other nationalist conflicts, would be the last issues on the minds of black or white South Africans. Instead, a thoroughly Americanised society worries about access to the latest consumer goods and capitalist diversions. The white 'haves' are silently thankful that black 'would-be-haves' now keep a huge mass of black 'have-nots' reasonably pacified and, if necessary, under authoritarian control. It is this constellation, not a Christian ethic or democratic consensus, that enabled a truth commission to go through the ritual of grappling with the past in order to proclaim in vain a reconciled memory for the future.

Conclusion

Collective memory of human rights violations could be separated into two broad categories of cases to which appropriate responses differ: historical injustice and contemporary abuses.

Historical injustice comprises cases where blameless groups were the victims of state aggression a long time ago. Few direct survivors exist and the claims of their descendants relate to appropriate recognition of past injustices rather than to the restoration of the situation before the event. Victims of Nazi atrocities, Japanese imperial expansionism, Stalinism and colonial conquest and slavery fall into this category. Punishment of perpetrators is no longer possible. Repossession of expropriated property or forced resettlement of people after civil wars or ethnic cleansing would create new strife and injustices, or might no longer be feasible because of economic development that has taken place in the interim. In these cases collective responsibility consists more of symbolic restitution than material compensation. The best way of doing justice to the collective legacy is by keeping the memory of the injustice alive and mourning the victims through political education about the historical crime.

Contemporary abuses call for both justice through legal recourse, as well as the development of new institutions to facilitate reconciliation or, perhaps more realistically, peaceful co-existence. Particularly where sizeable historical antagonists share the same state (South Africa, Northern Ireland, Rwanda, Latin America), truth commissions together with trials of perpetrators can affirm victims, contribute towards common norms, and even create constitutional patriotism. Where ethno-nationalist groups do not support common nation-building (the Balkans, Israel/Palestine) and where mutual atrocities engender divided memories, separation in independent or semi-autonomous polities would seem the only feasible solution. In such cases, international trials in which state criminals are prosecuted for recent abuses could also act as a deterrent. An international forum to which aggrieved groups can turn for redress would constitute an alternative to renewed violence.

Part II:
Reflections

Chapter Four

The Right to Truth[1]

Patricia Valdez

Twenty-two years have passed since a *coup d'état* placed Argentina in the same position as Brazil, Chile and Uruguay. Whether under military or civilian governments, all of a clearly authoritarian nature, the people of the majority of the Latin American countries were suffering from the systematic violation of their human rights.

The new regime adopted a methodology intended to breed terror so as to erase all traces of those who were being kidnapped and to paralyse those who wished to maintain their struggle against repression. New words and phrases emerged during this period. 'Disappeared' was the word used to describe those whose fate was to be perpetually uncertain. 'Born in captivity' was the phrase used to describe the children of pregnant women who had been kept alive only until they gave birth. Once born, the kidnapped babies were placed in the homes of the military, the security forces, or even of outsiders somehow related to either group, who were unable to have children of their own. Destroying the identity of children in this manner meant denying them the right to know their own history, to know who their ancestors were, and to be part of their real family.

The breakdown of the rule of law led to many years of intense conflict in Latin America. With the restoration of democracy, significant pressure was placed on the state to assume its undeniable duty to take action against the perpetrators of crimes against humanity. The duties of states and the rights of victims, established by international law, were vigorously promoted by the action of non-governmental organisations and the victims' families, all working to bring injustice to an end. The legal debate that was generated in the national arena and in international forums also contributed to this cause. The rights of victims and of society as a whole to know the truth emerged as a new principle with significant force.

The duty of a state is defined by four essential elements of equal importance. Therefore, the achievement of one of these elements does not free a state from pursuing the other elements. These four elements are:

(1) Truth: investigating human rights abuses and making the facts known to the public.
(2) Justice: prosecuting perpetrators of human rights violations and punishing the guilty.
(3) Reparation: compensating the emotional and physical harms caused.
(4) Lustration: removing those known to have committed, ordered, or tolerated these abuses from the security forces in order to create an honourable force that acts according to the values of a democratic state.

In Latin America, following decisions made by the newly established democratic governments or as a consequence of the peace agreements reached by the states and the insurgent groups, special bodies were created to address the states' legal duties. These bodies have been generically named 'truth commissions'.

These commissions have conducted investigations, published reports, generated public debate, and in the case of Argentina the CONADEP – National Commission for Disappeared Persons – constituted the first step towards the development of penal processes. Still, this was not enough.

Therefore, twenty-two years later, Argentine society – doubtlessly the one society that has made the most effort to end impunity – is still trying to discover the fate of every victim and demanding that the perpetrators of crimes be brought to justice. These efforts are not limited to victims' families or human rights activists. Individual and social wounds run so deep that society as a whole continues to regard its quest for justice in relation to crimes committed during the dictatorship as fundamentally important. The persistence of this search is testimony to the value given to justice as the most appropriate channel for the resolution of conflict. This persistence is reflected in the various ways of remembering and paying homage to the victims: demonstrations against perpetrators in front of their homes, domestic and international court actions that make creative and intelligent use of the available laws, films, plays and art exhibitions, to name but a few.

South Africa attracted the attention of the entire world with its apparently irresolute apartheid regime and the manner in which this regime insulted the moral conscience of the international community. Today, all those concerned with justice, the international press, and the academic community devoted to the study of transitions have turned their attention to the Truth and Reconciliation Commission. This is because South Africa has embarked on a distinct path towards justice. This path combines, in an innovative manner, listening to accounts of the victims' suffering, instituting a broad methodology for recording these testimonies, proposing various options for reparation, while trying to find an effective way of obtaining information from the perpetrators in exchange for amnesty.

The attention South Africa is receiving for its process of transition is clearly sympathetic. This can partly be attributed to the almost mythical figure of Nelson Mandela, President during the first period of transition, who remains a symbol of personal integrity and service to his country. But the sympathy also results from a conscious awareness of the difficulties of the democratic transition process, which has to deal simultaneously with the severe crimes of the past and contemporary problems of a complex social and economic nature.

Without knowing what the long-term results of the TRC's work will be, it is possible to point to a series of achievements and challenges that have emerged so far. Clearly, the South African experience adds some unique procedures to the international tradition of 'truth commissions'.

Firstly, the TRC has developed an excellent *dissemination policy* that reflects an explicit commitment to an open and transparent process – clearly different from the Latin American experiences. The Commission's work went public in various ways. It obtained impressive coverage from radio, television and the print media. Findings were made available via the Internet too. Journalists followed and recorded the process in detail, and alternative dissemination channels were established by grass-roots organisations. This resulted in unquestionable benefits for South African society and ensured that no South African can legitimately state today that he or she has no knowledge of the levels of perversity the apartheid regime reached in South Africa.

Secondly, the work of the Commission is remarkably *transparent*. The Latin American commissions conducted their investigations with the kind of confidentiality and secrecy that reigned supreme during the dictatorship years. The fact that perpetrators seemed to be following the process closely made them feel that this was necessary; they only went public with their findings after the final reports were published.

This secrecy seemed to be justified by threats of new coups or retaliation against the heads of the commissions, and by the fact that state intelligence forces had not been dismantled,[2] paramilitary groups were still 'on duty',[3] and newly established democracies still remained under the influence of an autonomous military force based upon spurious laws.[4] Furthermore, defence ministers still holding office were proved to be the intellectual authors of various terrible crimes.[5]

In South Africa, the open procedures were a result of the manner in which perpetrators were dealt with: Amnesty was granted only after disclosure, and amnesty hearings were public events. In this way, the TRC was not faced with the legitimacy debate encountered in Latin America. In the latter, the processes the commissions engaged in were not accompanied by proper legal procedures and guarantees, and therefore revealing the names of perpetrators became problematic.[6]

Thirdly, the South African Commission made recommendations regarding a *reparation policy* that the state should adopt in order to compensate the victims for the injustices suffered. The existence of a detailed proposal, which intended to address the state's duty to compensate victims, is well-known. In Argentina, which has clearly taken the lead in this area, the design and implementation of the reparation policy was addressed after the Commission's work and all the trials were over. In Chile – where the situation perhaps resembles the South African experience most closely, owing to its emphasis on reconciliation and the responsibility of the state – the government regarded this issue as one of great importance, yet it obtained little response from society. Finally, in the case of El Salvador, the Commission made recommendations that were obligatory for both signatories to the Peace Agreement. Although the United Nations paid close attention to the implementation of these recommendations that were based on information provided by the Special Rapporteur, they were not fully executed. The fact that the Commission did not have the credibility or force that emanates from a governmental decision could be one of the reasons for this.

It is envisaged that South Africa will start implementing its reparation policy once the victims' names have been disseminated in the Commission's final report and Parliament passes the laws that will ensure its implementation. Still, it is clear that the severe lack of balance, resulting from the Commission's impossible task of providing, over a very short period, reparation for the different cases reviewed, constitutes a deep problem.

Those who have confessed to the crimes they committed and were absolved by the Amnesty Committee were able to find a swift solution to their problems. Yet the victimised families who had to face their pain anew – and whose hopes for justice were raised – will have to wait for one, maybe several parliamentary sessions to see a state policy on reparation passed. And then they will have to wait for the resources to be made available and for the means of its actual implementation to be found. Must it always be the same? Should the victims always the ones to do the 'waiting'?

This is the result – apparently unexpected – of having attached the Amnesty Committee to the TRC. The Amnesty Committee is a body of a diverse nature, ruled by a different dynamic. The amnesty process constitutes the greatest challenge faced by the Commission and is probably the one that will stand out at the moment of an overall evaluation of the work of the TRC.

The Amnesty Committee seems to have emerged from the study of other national experiences and its structure was designed to ensure a swift definition of its responsibilities. Its work is aimed at preventing the persistence, years from now, of a divided society resulting from a lack of justice. This seems to have happened in Chile, where the Commission[7] emphasised the detailed recording of each victim's statement and the public recognition of each one's dignity, while no perpetrators faced any trial or legal process – a consequence of a self-amnesty law passed by the military government before democratic elections took place. South Africa regarded reconciliation as the main issue in its initiative, looking for an intermediate legal instance that would force all those interested in benefiting from amnesty to provide substantial information to the TRC.

Some of the more evident limitations of the TRC have been noted. The Amnesty Committee has still not achieved its goals, and its work has progressed at a much slower pace than that of the rest of the Commission. The Commission offered a more swift and efficacious way out to the authors of crimes than to the victims or their families. This is proving counter-productive. Future studies will hopefully demonstrate the degree of efficacy of the amnesty process in obtaining information about what happened and in identifying the authors of the crimes. It is hoped that the names and positions of those who participated in the amnesty procedure will be established. Such studies will ideally also show whether members of the liberation movement or state agents were the ones to accord greater value to the process, and therefore to make the best use of it.

Truth commissions operate within a dual reality: Their investigations need to be deeply neutral, yet their results will be deeply political. The complexity of the transitional processes and the emphasis on reconciliation make the task of providing a balanced final report a challenging one.

Societies have long endured the deep-seated pain of torture, the loss of those who 'disappeared' or died, and faced abuse and humiliation on a daily basis. Victims do not want the truth commissions simply to record their stories and tell them what they already know. Society hopes that these commissions will go further by solving the puzzle of what happened, by assigning responsibility, and by making use of the state's credibility and power to establish a clear difference between the new and the previous political systems.

A truth commission, as its name implies, plays a specific role in establishing the 'truth' in relation to crimes that were committed in the past. But they can only be efficacious if, in the long term, they see themselves as merely a step in or a component of a much broader process. Such a process must involve the re-establishment of the rule of law, wherein the role of justice is fundamental.

There is still much debate about the extent of a commission's contribution in terms of justice and reconciliation. Studies and analyses of more than ten different cases that show some similarities still do not agree upon a set of key measures or elements that ensure a commission's success. Although no one doubts the value of its contribution during periods of transition, there is no unanimous opinion about the way in which it should be combined with the legal processes that derive from the state's duty to punish those who have violated human rights. However, it would be somehow misleading to place this debate exclusively in the sphere of the nature of truth commissions. The real challenge is overcoming injustice in a permanent and lasting way.

Today, these dilemmas and the means to resolve them have become part of a specific area of study in which different disciplines participate: transitional justice. Academics, lawyers, human rights organisations, political leaders, government officials, and the victims or their families have all become part of this debate. It is, essentially, a political debate with a strong ethical content, which is looking for an answer to the following question: Do democracies risk their stability when they punish or when they forgive those who have violated human rights?

Even when the threats of repeating the past have diminished or disappeared, or when the perpetrators of severe human rights violations have lost their fundamental powers, it is still important to seek an answer to this question. The answer is directly related to two important issues: demonstrating that all citizens are equal in the eyes of law and overcoming the injustice that otherwise remains at all levels of the public sphere.

The main deficiency of contemporary societies manifests itself in the inadequate functioning of their public institutions.[8] The absence of a culture of accountability both in public officers and public institutions, combined with the weakness of control agencies reflects a deep-seated injustice, which affects the quality of democracy.

The exercise of searching for and disclosing the truth is the first step in a larger process that needs to address the state's responsibility regarding the enforcement of justice and compensation of victims of severe abuses. This is the healthiest way of engaging in this process, which starts with the transition from an illegitimate regime, but has to continue towards the establishment of a public policy that aims to defend the rights of all citizens at all levels.[9] However, the implementation of a process based on the concept of 'the reality of what is possible' when addressing the best manner of breaking with the past, will probably bring about tidier and more predictable procedures.

However, these procedures tend to ignore the fact that historical and social history is built with uneven bricks that are not placed at the same time and will not last forever. Elements of social memory, combined with a widening of the citizenship base as people begin to exercise their rights, are what bring about democracy in our societies and strengthen a democracy's level of institutionalisation. This is why countries such as Argentina are still fighting important legal battles to implement the right to truth. This is also why Spain's initiative to prosecute Augusto Pinochet destabilised coalitions and consensus throughout Chilean society, forcing its leaders to rethink the way of correcting what was left undone at the time of a military-based transition.

The right to truth is an undeniable obligation of states towards their citizens and towards the international community.[10] Separating this right from the right to justice may have results that are less difficult to implement in certain moments in history. Yet this means that future public policies, which are essential to facing old problems that re-emerge immediately after transitions, will inevitably be more limited. These problems include citizens experiencing difficulty in accessing justice; security forces having to rethink their composition and duties; impunity as social behaviour; and widespread corruption.

Encouraging public debate on what has happened (and here the South African Truth and Reconciliation Commission seems to have taken the lead) without regarding these facts as having been dealt with when the Commission's work has finished, will promote respect for the rule of law. It will also pave the way to building a social memory of the past. Permitting the dynamics of the conflict to evolve, and the actors of civil society and democratic institutions to express themselves freely, is one of the best ways of preventing all types of authoritarianism, thereby building a truly democratic political culture. This culture will make it possible to face issues arising directly from past abuses.

A look at the last few decades proves that reconciliation is not brought about by governmental decrees, that free elections do not instantaneously establish democratic institutions or ensure that they function efficiently. It is important to place human rights in a privileged position. Fighting for a permanent culture of human rights has resulted in legal, institutional and political efficiency extending beyond the period of transition.

Chapter Five

A Diminished Truth[1]

Mahmood Mamdani

Amnesty for crimes with a political motive was part of the compromise that ushered in a post-apartheid South Africa. It was written into the Interim Constitution and embodied in the very structure of the Truth and Reconciliation Commission (TRC), which was divided into two halves: the Amnesty Committee and the rest of the Commission. The two halves differed both in their manner of appointment and in the weight given to their decisions. The main Commission was appointed through a transparent process. A selection panel composed of members of civil society and government was appointed to consider 299 nominations from different stakeholders. After interviews, the panel submitted a short list of twenty-five to the then President Nelson Mandela, who appointed seventeen Commissioners on 29 November 1995.

The Amnesty Committee was established after the main Commission, independently of it and without a transparent process. Mr Mandela appointed three Commissioners and two judges to the Committee on 24 January 1996.

The Amnesty Committee focused on perpetrators, the main Commission on victims. The Amnesty Committee's decisions are binding on both the TRC as a whole and on the government. By contrast, the main Commission's decisions are confined to the status of recommendations.

The TRC could have been called the Amnesty Commission, but it was not. It has been known popularly as the Truth Commission rather than the Reconciliation Commission – rightly so, I now think. For I think the real power of the Commission was exercised through the work of its main body. That was the power to define the terms of a social debate and, in so doing, define the parameters of truth seeking.

To recognise the enormity of this power, one needs to make a clear distinction between a social debate and an intellectual debate. The TRC's version of truth was reported as news in the media. It was discussed on talk shows and television programmes. It framed the outlines of a social debate. My question is: What kind of truth did the TRC produce and will its version of truth hold?

Is there a single truth of apartheid or are there several truths, each fashioned by a different vantage point? If the latter, which truth comes closest to capturing the experience of the most?

The TRC's version of truth was established through narrow lenses, crafted to reflect the experience of a tiny minority: on the one hand, perpetrators, being state-agents; and, on the other, victims, being political activists.

The TRC has received some 21 400 statements from people claiming to be victims, and has so far found that 80 per cent qualify as such.

This diminished truth was established through an analogy with Latin American dictatorships. It was an analogy embraced enthusiastically in two conferences that preceded the establishment of the TRC.

Everyone agreed that the two situations presented numerous similarities: gross human rights abuses in the course of a protracted confrontation between power and resistance, an ongoing struggle without an outright victory in sight for either side, a global situation underlining the need for compromise while also facilitating it and, most of all, the question of how perpetrators and their victims might live together in a new society.

These similarities were true but they did not exhaust the whole truth. The Latin American analogy obscured what was distinctive about apartheid. For the violence of apartheid was aimed less at individuals than at entire communities. And this violence was not simply political. It was not just about defending power but also about dispossessing people of the means of livelihood.

In other words, the Latin American analogy obscured the colonial nature of the South African context: the link between conquest and dispossession, between racialised power and racialised privilege, between perpetrator and beneficiary. Moreover, the Latin Americans did not face the question confronting South Africa: How will those who continue to be the beneficiaries of apartheid, a substantial minority, and those who continue to be its victims, the majority, live together?

A different commission would be needed to answer this question. For it would have to produce a truth that would capture both the distinctive violence of apartheid and the distinctive relation between beneficiaries and victims.

Imagine that a truth commission had been appointed in the Soviet Union after Stalin, and this commission had said nothing about the Gulag. What credibility would it have had? The South African equivalent of the Gulag was called forced removals. Between 1960 and 1982 an estimated 3.5 million people were forcibly removed, their communities shattered, their families dispossessed and their livelihoods destroyed. These were not inert outcomes of socio-economic processes, but outcomes of active violence by state agents.

These 3.5 million victims comprise faceless communities, not individual activists. They constitute a social catastrophe, not merely a political dilemma. Were these removals not gross violations within the terms of reference set by the law? Why, then, did the TRC not include these people among 'victims'?

The answer, it seems, is relatively simple. Like the pass laws, the Group Areas Act and other hallmarks in the legal umbrella of the TRC, forced removals were not illegal under apartheid. It seems the TRC considered as a gross violation only that which was a gross violation under the laws of apartheid!

One needs to recall the question Hannah Arendt posed in relation to another crime against humanity, the Holocaust: What happens when crime is legal, when criminals can enthusiastically enforce the law? Perhaps the greatest moral compromise the TRC made was to embrace the legal fetishism of apartheid. In doing so, it made little distinction between what is legal and what is legitimate, between law and right.

This is not to say that the TRC ignored the issue of beneficiaries. It did hold institutional hearings. But it understood as beneficiaries only those who gained from corrupting the system, who were able to turn links to public power into private advantage. Benefit, too, was defined as a corruption outside the law. So the TRC focused on torture, murder and rape, all outside the law, ignoring everything that was distinctive about apartheid and its machinery of violence.

Why did the TRC define the boundaries of truth seeking so narrowly? Was it to reinforce the political compromise of 1994 that the Commission turned the political boundaries of the compromise into the analytical boundaries of truth seeking? By reinforcing a political compromise with a compromised truth, did it not turn the political compromise into a moral compromise, thereby obscuring the truth?

In its attempt to define the truth pragmatically, did the TRC not suffocate a much-needed social debate on how to go beyond the political compromise of 1994, how to go beyond the political reconciliation between state agents (perpetrators) and political activists (victims as a minority) to a social reconciliation between beneficiaries and victims? The TRC invited beneficiaries to join victims in a public outrage against perpetrators. If only we had known, it seemed to invite beneficiaries to say, we would have acted differently; our trust has been violated, betrayed, abused. So, beneficiaries too were presented as victims. But, in spite of the best intentions, their intended salvation has a paradoxical and unintended outcome.

On the one hand, the more beneficiaries were outraged at gross violations, the less they felt responsible for them. Not only did they see no need to be forgiven, they actually experienced forgiveness as humiliation. Thus the growing opposition to the TRC process in the white community in general, and the Afrikaner community in particular.

On the other hand, the more beneficiaries appear complacent, indifferent, callous and lacking in empathy, the more victims are outraged. They feel forgiveness to be undeserved. The more they feel so, the more they demand justice. So, the TRC ends up fuelling the very demand it set out to displace: justice!

The TRC's great achievement has been to discredit the apartheid regime in the eyes of its beneficiaries. This is no small achievement. History tells us that to drive a wedge between perpetrators and beneficiaries has been the political requisite for every successful revolution.

In its eagerness to reinforce the new order, however, the TRC created a diminished truth that wrote the vast majority of apartheid's victims out of its version of history. The unintended outcome has been to drive a wedge between the beneficiaries and victims of apartheid. In doing so, the TRC has failed to open a social debate on possible futures for a post-apartheid South Africa.

Chapter Six

Truth without Reconciliation, Reconciliation without Truth[1]

Frederik Van Zyl Slabbert

It is 10 May 1994, a sunny autumn morning at the amphitheatre of the Union Buildings in Pretoria. Along with thousands of other people I wait for the inauguration of Nelson Mandela as the first democratically elected president of South Africa. I am still light-headed with disbelief at the pace with which national reconciliation has taken place since F.W. de Klerk delivered his epoch-making speech on 2 February 1990 in the Parliament of the old South Africa.

Immediately thereafter De Klerk called together all the traditional Afrikaner organisations – the churches, the cultural organisations, the Broederbond – and for three days they deliberated upon the best way forward and how to create a climate which could reduce the tension and uncertainty. Their declaration showed the necessity to work together for a common future and to try systematically to get to know the ANC and all other struggle organisations better. The right-wing groups made it clear that they wanted nothing to do with these changes, and some of the more militant struggle groups agitated for an intensification of the armed struggle.

When Mandela came out of jail he went straight to the Cape Town Parade. In his impromptu speech he emphasised that it was a very dangerous time for the country. The fears and mistrust of the past were still with us. He took the hand De Klerk held out to him and said they, and all of us, had to begin working on national reconciliation.

Shortly afterwards, they jointly formed a reconciliation committee comprising political, church and business leaders, and produced a plan of action. The idea was to establish similar committees at local government level, in schools and universities and non-governmental organisations. The aim of all these reconciliation committees was for people to speak directly and frankly about the past so that as many people as possible would be informed about what had happened, with the aim of ensuring that these mistakes would never be made again.

The thorny issue of accountability for serious crimes against human rights had to be settled. Mandela and De Klerk called an amnesty congress at which the senior officers of security forces on all sides, selected lawyers, church leaders and representatives of Spain, Chile, Argentina, Uruguay and Germany were present. These are all countries that had to make peace with a divisive, traumatic past. For three days there were serious and frank discussions about who did what and who took which decisions. The whole debate happened in public, with national and international television coverage. The final session was held *in camera*, and it produced an amnesty declaration. There would be collective amnesty for all, but where there was *prima facie* evidence of individual responsibility for misdeeds, justice had to take its course. After sentencing, a personal amnesty could be considered. This was not an ideal state of affairs, but everyone agreed that it was more important to work towards a common future than to continually dwell upon a fractured past. At the press conference Mandela took De Klerk's hand and said, 'We must forgive but never forget.'

Mandela worked tirelessly with right-wing groups to draw them into the process of reconciliation. Eventually first Carel Boshoff,[2] then Constand Viljoen[3] committed to the process. Doing so isolated fanatics such as Eugene Terre'Blanche[4] and his followers, and considerably reduced the possibility of violence. Both De Klerk and Mandela worked to stabilise the situation between Inkatha and the ANC and to stop the violence in Natal. Eventually Mangosuthu Buthelezi[5] could see that there was also space for him in the new South Africa. In the meantime the negotiating process for an Interim Constitution progressed relatively smoothly and it was decided to set up a Government of National Unity for five years, to hold a democratic general election, and that the top structures of the civil service, except in extreme cases of irresponsibility, would remain unchanged for the five-year term, with the instruction that they share their knowledge with their potential successors during that period. As far as possible, affirmative action would be reconciled with knowledge and competence. The civil service and the private sector committed themselves to making as much knowledge and training as possible available to the new democratic government during this transitional process.

The elections went by peacefully and effectively, and here we all are now sitting at the Union Buildings, waiting for the inauguration ceremony to begin. There is an underlying optimism and excitement in all of us. The reconciliation process has exceeded everybody's wildest hopes. It could have been a hundred times worse. Who will ever forget how Mandela and De Klerk hugged each other at the ceremony where each received the Nobel Prize for peace? There was not a dry eye here or in the rest of the world.

Mandela is sworn in and starts speaking. He talks about the time before and after his liberation; about the process of reconciliation to date. It is stirring, raw and sincere. There is a deathly silence. He ends, 'I now say in front of all of you and the whole world: The greater part of my productive life was destroyed by an inhuman system that was maintained by our fellow citizens. It caused immeasurable pain and suffering. But if I look at where we are now and the promises that the future holds for all of us, then I have no hesitation in saying to F.W. de Klerk and his people: What I and my people suffered under your party's rule we will never forget, but we forgive you, and I invite you, and them, to build a new country with us.'

Mandela holds out his hand to De Klerk. De Klerk gets up, takes the hand offered to him and they look each other in the eye while there is tumultuous applause all round. Eventually De Klerk gets the chance to say something: 'Mister President, you have pre-empted me. Before you can forgive me, I must confess so that you and the world will know what I am asking forgiveness for. I entered the politics of our country with verve and enthusiasm because I, and so many of my fellow party members, believed in the rightness of what we were trying to do. Gradually I began to realise that what we wanted to do could not be implemented and had no justifiable moral foundation. When I became state president this realisation became even stronger. That is why I made the speech of 2 February [1990], which marked the beginning of the process that has brought us here today. But, Mister President, never in my wildest dreams did I imagine the extent of the harm and pain our policies had caused. My colleagues and I dismissed those who tried to make us aware of this as propagandists with hidden agendas. It was the reconciliation process, which you and I initiated, that opened my eyes. Together we travelled across the country and I heard first-hand how people had suffered under our policies and security laws. I did not want to believe what I heard coming out of the Eugene de Kock hearings. But I say to you now and to the whole world: De Kock was right. He and so many like him could not have acted in isolation. We who governed made it possible. It is no use to claim that we did not know. We did not want to know, and if we knew, we did nothing about it. There can be no reconciliation without forgiveness. But there can also be no forgiveness without confession.

'I want to confess today on behalf of my people and myself, before you and the world, that we were fundamentally and completely wrong. That we almost wreaked irreversible damage on our country and its people. For that I ask your forgiveness and that of your people. I also beg forgiveness for your personal suffering. But, Mister President, my people and I do not just need the forgiveness of you and your people. I also ask forgiveness from the young people who died unnecessarily for an indefensible cause, and especially from their parents. I also ask forgiveness from the thousands of officials we pumped full of a false patriotic duty to implement an impossible policy. Especially, I ask forgiveness of the security staff in the police and army who had to stand at the forefront of oppression. We misled them horribly. Yes, I even ask forgiveness of De Kock, that we made it possible for him to become what he became.

'Mister President, if the forgiveness you offer me also allows for my confession, then I again take the hand you have held out to me and I say to you: Let us begin rebuilding this torn country of ours together.'

Mandela and De Klerk embrace each other once again in front of the whole world. Again there is not a dry eye here or anywhere else in the world.

As Jannie Gagiano would say, 'I dreamt I was awake when it all happened.' But of course I am awake and it was all just a dream. To bring truth and reconciliation together in our country would at the very least require a process of this magnitude. Reconciliation on such a collective and social scale has to work by means of an awe-inspiring power of example, a cleansing ritual loaded with the symbolism of atonement–forgiveness–reconciliation. The truth referred to here is not the truth of the law and science, but the truth that comes from confiding and acknowledging, a sort of confessional truth. There is no guarantee that if it happens, there will inevitably be reconciliation. But at least at a leadership level the example of personal reconciliation needs to be made. If there is mistrust, estrangement and a lack of confession and forgiveness here, how on God's earth can a general climate of reconciliation be fostered? In both De Klerk and Mandela's autobiographies it becomes clear that their relationship systematically deteriorated. After reading De Klerk's autobiography I was filled with revulsion. There is not the faintest trace of personal accountability for what happened in this country under his party's rule. Instead there are excuses and self-glorification. He is the born reformer who knew from the beginning what had to happen. At the Nobel Prize ceremony De Klerk and Mandela could barely hide their contempt for each other. Mandela's willingness to forgive was never reciprocated by De Klerk's confession. On the contrary, De Klerk behaved as if forgiveness was his due.

That is why the Truth and Reconciliation Commission was doomed from the start to fight an uphill battle as an instrument of national reconciliation. In fact, if anything made it clear that my dream was totally unrealistic, it was the reality exposed by the TRC process. The indescribable cruelty, torture, pain, confusion and senseless suffering experienced by the victims was never, other than in highly exceptional instances, answered with confession and accountability. One got the impression that the few who did come to confess had no other choice because the evidence that had emerged from the De Kock hearings was so damning against them. And even when some of them came to testify, the grey safari suit and shoes tucked away for the occasion, they still tried to evade, conveniently forgot, and transferred responsibility. The general impression they created was that they genuinely could not understand why they were the ones who had to come forward. They had just done their duty; they had only been the foot soldiers of the policy-makers.

And the policy-makers were beyond revolting. The senile arrogance of P.W. Botha who told the whole TRC process to get stuffed; De Klerk, legalistic, small-minded and trying to be clever: of course there were gross violations and he did not feel happy about them, but he knew nothing about them personally and never took such decisions. Do the people who sat in the B.J. Vorster,[6] P.W. Botha and De Klerk cabinets really expect us and the world to believe they took no decisions responsible for the misery? Or, that they knew absolutely nothing about it? This after decades of anti-apartheid struggle, murders, court cases, petitions, and so on? Even if they did not accept the TRC as a valid or useful instrument for reconciliation, was there any indication from them that there was a relationship between confession and reconciliation, that reconciliation without confession was not possible?

The response is usually that they were involved in an anti-communist struggle, and that it was not a game for the faint-hearted. But the Total Onslaught Strategy only reached maturity later, under Botha. By then the policies of apartheid had been mercilessly implemented for over thirty years. In fact, it was the implementation of this policy that required a Total Strategy against a Total Onslaught. The pass laws, the Group Areas Act, the homeland policies, the law on separate amenities. The consequences of these policies were repeatedly spelt out in South Africa and abroad through research, conferences, seminars, protests, and so forth. This is the policy that shaped the interdependent process of liberation and oppression. A process in which success was defined as the destruction of the other.

So the climate was created in which all sides were guilty of cruelty. A necklace murder cannot be separated from the murder of an MK soldier. Winnie Mandela who glared at Desmond Tutu with fixed, bitter eyes while he begged her to say that she felt just a little bit sorry. Her entire attitude said, 'Stompie was a traitor, he betrayed the struggle. The struggle was the fight against apartheid. It was a holy fight. Can't the meddlesome priest understand this?'

When De Klerk delivered his speech on 2 February, my very first reaction was: Do he and the NP really understand what they have unleashed here? Coincidentally I had, from Oxford, spoken to him on the phone the week before. A business associate, Dick Enthoven, had seen him in Johannesburg. They had started talking and from the discussion Dick had got the impression that De Klerk wanted to talk to me. I asked Dick why. He was vague and uncertain but said

De Klerk had given him a contact number. Because I was due back in South Africa for a short break from Oxford, I phoned De Klerk. He was quite friendly and amiable but I could not figure out what he wanted to talk about. When I told him I was coming to South Africa, he said I should visit him if I had the chance, but not before 2 February. According to him there was going to be a 'little acceleration' in policy.

Imagine that: The end of apartheid and the start of negotiations for a completely democratic alternative was 'an acceleration' of policy! When I met De Klerk in his office after 2 February and asked him why he had made the speech, his answer was that he had, on the one hand, experienced a 'spiritual leap' away from apartheid and, on the other hand, that he would have been crazy not to take the gap presented by the fall of communism in Eastern Europe. I left the meeting with the distinct impression that he did not really understand the implications of what he had done, and especially that he was convinced that he could control the process throughout. He was completely unaware of the problems that lay ahead, particularly at a security level. When I took my leave of him I commented that he had inherited a difficult security situation. He was somewhat surprised. 'Do you really think so?' he asked.

The one thing the TRC demonstrated clearly was that De Klerk, the NP and the security forces were totally unprepared for the moral and ethical implications of the dismantling of apartheid, and that, if it were to lead to national reconciliation, it would require creative political actions from them all. De Klerk had no remorse and seemed to be offended, as if South Africa and the world could not appreciate the greatness of his deed (and it was indeed great); the NP was totally confused and unprepared; and the security forces were furious about the betrayal and deceit practised upon them. They were especially upset because the politicians pretended they had been totally unaware of the work the security forces had had to do at the coal-face of oppression to keep the system alive. It was this work, exposed by the TRC, that filled good, loyal supporters of the NP with shame, and persuaded many of them to confess their unknowing accountability. But not De Klerk and his buddies.

I do not for one moment want to suggest that the ANC or other struggle organisations were all a bunch of innocent, naïve victims. Testimony was also given of gruesome deeds and cruelty on their part. Variations of the 'just war' philosophy were also produced, which sometimes sounded strange, and examples of sanctimonious struggle piety were plentiful. But the example set by Mandela, whatever his personal feelings, was one of unqualified reconciliation. From his visit to Betsie Verwoerd,[7] his actions regarding the 1995 Rugby World Cup Final, and his negotiations with Constand Viljoen, up to his many speeches immediately after liberation and his inauguration on 10 May 1994, it was clear that he wanted reconciliation. He repeatedly stated his willingness to forgive. This example influenced his followers and I do not doubt for a moment that it played a crucial role in the smooth unfolding of the first five years. But the example of a willingness to forgive on the one hand, without confession on the other, makes national reconciliation almost impossible.

Against this background it is valid to ask whether the TRC was the most suitable instrument to achieve the goal. Before answering this question I wish to state that Alex Boraine is a very good friend of mine. He is not the first friend with whom I have differed fundamentally on an issue, but who nevertheless remains a friend. Boraine was primarily responsible for the legislation that eventually resulted in the establishment of the TRC and he later became Deputy Chairperson of the TRC. Now that the most important tasks of the TRC have been completed, both he and Tutu, who was the Chairperson, are at present lecturing in the United States. The world, especially the United States, is much more fascinated and impressed by the TRC than people in South Africa are – a case of the prophet not being honoured in his own country. Alex is currently a visiting professor of transitional justice at New York University. I tease him, and tell him it is time he came round to permanent justice. In any case, long before, during and after the TRC hearings I argued with him and with people close to the TRC. The following points I regard as the most important: The TRC is based on suppositions and assumptions that, even if they are not demonstrably invalid, are nevertheless misleading and ambiguous. What is the notion of truth assumed here? It must be universal and transferable, otherwise the entire process is senseless. By definition it cannot be a relativistic truth because, as someone once said, 'If someone tells you there is no such thing as truth, he is asking you not to believe him. Don't.' That is why you cannot have your truth and I mine if we want the same reconciliation. We must at least agree that we are referring to the same truth for which confession, forgiveness and reconciliation are being asked, otherwise it could become quite a mess. So how do we get to this truth? Here, it is not about verifiable scientific truth in the pure sense of the word. In a traditional society, truth is determined by the priests, a king, a captain or group leaders. In modern industrial societies, the truth of accountability is determined by the country's prevailing justice system. The fact that we speak of an international tribunal of justice assumes that on an international level there exists such a generally acceptable process of cross-examination, defence and delivery of testimony, and that the judgement of the court is accepted as valid and true. If there are reasonable grounds for doubt, the right to appeal is granted. In other words, the truth of accountability is determined through law. This is the closest that we sorry sinners can get to the truth.

Now the TRC comes along and says that it will determine truth without legal process. How will it do this? By giving people the opportunity to recount the terrible things that happened to them, and giving others the chance to tell how they did those terrible things, and then to ensure that there is reconciliation between them? Let me concede immediately that something rings very true in a confession. When someone says, 'I am sorry, I did it,' we are prepared to believe such a person ninety-nine per cent of the time. (Even then they are sometimes lying.) But what do you do when people do not want to confess? If you have reasonable grounds for believing that the person is guilty, you take him or her to court. The TRC expressly states that it is not a court, however. It has the right to summons people to appear before it, but it cannot, through ordinary legal process, cross-examine people in order to determine accountable truth. If it wished to be this type of court, it would have had to become a special court for specific purposes of the prevailing justice system. But then the TRC would never have fulfilled its mandate within the given time-frame and court cases would have continued for several years.

Because the TRC cannot force accountable truth by means of confession, it becomes a sort of quasi-court where those summonsed or volunteering to appear are confronted with a mass of circumstantial evidence and an implication of guilt, which cannot, however, be proved by means of legal process. This causes everyone listening or watching to think: 'The bastard is guilty.' Whether it be Winnie Mandela, De Klerk, P.W. Botha or the leader of a defence unit, their instinctive reaction is: 'Go to hell.' The victims become embittered, the suspects become embittered, and both question the validity and usefulness of the TRC. The only exceptions are those individuals who were almost forced to make a confession because they were revealed through normal legal process as people with an obvious burden of guilt. For example, Steve Biko's murderers as a result of the De Kock hearings. There they were, pathetic in their evasive admissions. Jeffrey Benzien was an exception. In front of the TRC, crying, he sat on someone's back to demonstrate how he had tried to smother Tony Yengeni. Yengeni sat there, listening to him. Nobody doubted for a moment that Benzien was telling the truth.

But what about reconciliation? The assumption is that truth leads to reconciliation. But this is demonstrably nonsense. The divorce courts prove this every day. Biko's widow made it crystal-clear in front of the TRC, and I have great understanding for her point of view. There stood the murderers of her husband, shameless in their lack of remorse, trying to obtain amnesty on technical grounds. Why should she forgive them, even if they were telling the truth? But, it can be argued, the truth is at least a precondition for reconciliation. Again, evidence for this is of doubtful value. There are plenty of examples showing that legally, technically accountable truth has led to revenge, hatred and retribution. But what about confessed truth? The chances are better, but there is no guarantee that this is either necessary or sufficient. The assumption that truth leads to reconciliation or that it is a necessary prerequisite is based on sentimental theological assumptions that very often bear no relation to reality.

Can there be reconciliation without truth? Of course there can. Often truth is the first victim of reconciliation. Many married couples are reconciled precisely because the parties do not want to know or hear about the past. Is this real reconciliation? What, in fact, is real reconciliation? It is a relationship that is restored to the extent that the parties can move on in peace while accepting each other's integrity. If this had happened collectively in South Africa, we would be winning now. In Spain, a formal decision was taken not to speak about the past. To what extent is Spain a non-reconciled country? In Chile it was decided to grant a general amnesty without accountability. What evidence exists that if Chile, like South Africa, had tried to establish accountable amnesty outside the process of law, it would be a better-reconciled country today? The only available evidence is South Africa itself. Is it a reconciled country? Read Antjie Krog's *Country of My Skull*, Jacques Pauw's *Prime Evil*, and think back to Max du Preez's television programme about the TRC.[8] The answer is self-evident. But simply the way the TRC Report was received is indication enough. F.W. de Klerk and Constand Viljoen saw the whole process as retribution by the ANC and, in the case of De Klerk, also as a personal vendetta on the part of Alex Boraine. Thabo Mbeki sought a court order against the release of the Report because it placed apartheid and the struggle on the same moral level. After the Report had been tabled, Tutu and Boraine left the country. There are no follow-ups to consolidate the reconciliation facilitated by the TRC. In fact, what reconciliation? The impression is rather that everyone would like to forget the whole affair as quickly as possible.

But what about guilt? How far should it stretch? Is guilt possible without accountability? If I did not know, should I have known? If I knew but did nothing, am I accountable for the murders that took place, for the suffering under apartheid? What about the fact that I was an unknowing beneficiary of apartheid? To whom should I confess? From whom should I ask forgiveness for what I did not know, but from which I nevertheless benefited? And if I was aware but was too scared to do anything about it, how can I now rectify something I did not do? There are an infinite number of possible answers to these questions. One could start with the 'original sin' entrepreneurs: the theologians and priests who know what is going on in God's head. We were all born and received in sin. That may well be, but it will not help us get to Biko's murderers. Then one could start with the social philosophers, who will say that the real guilt should be at the door of colonialism, capitalism, nationalism, communism, socialism, and so forth. Once again that may be true, but it will not help us get to Biko's murderers either. Mahmood Mamdani, the political scientist, becomes very agitated because the TRC process allowed the great majority of those privileged under apartheid to get away scot-free. He has a point, but what mechanism does he suggest to address collective guilt? Expropriation of property? A once-off tax? But this has everything to do with retribution and nothing at all to do with reconciliation. Can one build a better future through retribution than through successful reconciliation without truth? I do not know.

What I do know is that there are only two means of arriving at the truth in a social context: one is through the legal process and the other through personal confession. And I can lie even when I confess. Whether both are needed or just one is sufficient for reconciliation is an empirical question that cannot be predetermined by means of simplistic assumptions of a romanticised, sentimental morality.

Does this mean that we should not be interested in the truth about our past? Of course not. That truth will be exposed to us through research, drama, literature, journalism and film. This is the great value of the work of Antjie Krog, Jacques Pauw, Max du Preez and so many others. And, also of the TRC process. Nobody can remain unmoved by the terrible deeds exposed by that process. Hopefully, through it we will learn to avoid similar horrific deeds in future. Probably we will find that the truth about the past holds infinitely more lessons for us than were exposed by the TRC.

And what about reconciliation? It is absolutely necessary if we want this country to turn the corner. But it will probably take many years, if not decades, before it becomes meaningful to all of us in our daily lives. If the political leadership does not want to set the example, the TRC and the courts will not be able to do it. The 1999 election campaign was also not too encouraging in this regard. Perhaps we will have to privatise the reconciliation process.

I know the TRC was established with the best intentions. I debated the issue at length with Alex Boraine. Cultural philosopher Isaiah Berlin used an Immanuel Kant phrase for the title of one of his works: 'Out of the crooked timber of humanity, nothing straight was ever born.' He made the point that the cult of sincerity is one of the curses of the twentieth century. It is quite simply not good enough. You can be sincere and stupid, sincere and uninformed, sincere and ignorant, sincere and incompetent. All we can hope for is that we are sincere enough to admit our mistakes and to avoid them in future. Nothing is more dangerous than a dogmatic and sincere ideologue.

Was the entire TRC process a failure? Yes, if one wanted to bring truth and reconciliation together. No, if it made us all aware of where we come from and the direction in which we must move. What is its usefulness to today's politics? I think all the parties concerned want to get away from the TRC as quickly as possible. My information, which comes from the former President's office, is that from the outset the new government was never very keen on the TRC. The ANC was always in favour of a general amnesty and a fresh start. It was the NP that prevented this. My nose tells me that, to sustain peace in KwaZulu-Natal and accommodate the former generals, Mbeki's government will sooner rather than later find a means of circumventing the amnesty terms of the TRC. Then, with or without the TRC, we will have to start working on reconciliation. In any event, it is going to be an uphill battle.

Chapter Seven

The Language of Potential

Alex Boraine

My colleagues and I have travelled extensively and have been in debate with numerous people from many countries, including Guatemala, Argentina, Northern Ireland, Ethiopia, Rwanda, Bosnia, Serbia and Kosovo. These people have watched the South African model with enormous interest, fascination and almost overwhelming approval, so much so that sometimes we, rather than they, have had to raise what we think are problems within the Truth and Reconciliation Commission.

It has been argued that the TRC's major problem is that it was over-ambitious, that it attempted to do too much, and therefore lost some of its focus. This may well be true. The fact that our hearings were open, in distinction to the hearings of any other commission that I know of, has been criticised. I would have to disagree with this. Concern has been expressed about some lack of due process in our proceedings, and I would agree that at times the TRC was inefficient and disorganised, particularly in the very beginning of its work, for example, if one looks at the first public hearings in East London. I think we made many grave mistakes and simply did not take them seriously enough.

The composition of the Commission has also been criticised, perhaps with good reason. In Chile, for example, it was decided to have four commissioners from the right and four from the left, so that there would be a better spread. However, the Chilean commissioners were nominated, while our process of appointment was much more arduous. Our poor approach to reparation has also been criticised, and I would agree with this criticism. It was a result of some internal dissension, a lack of responsibility in some regards, and the fact that the Act stated that we could not implement reparation, but simply had to submit a proposed policy of reparation. Many victims rightly feel that they have been ignored and abandoned.

A fundamental criticism of the Commission is that there has been no reconciliation. R.W. Johnson, in an article that appeared in the *New York Times* a couple of weeks after our Report was handed in, wrote the following: 'The final report of the Truth and Reconciliation Commission, a 3 000-page verdict on the entire apartheid era that was released on Friday, appeared to have done something for truth but very little for reconciliation.'[1] I wrote a response to the *New York Times*, and said this:

> History will judge whether or not Johnson's criticism is accurate. It is nevertheless worth making two points in this regard. The first is that while truth may not always lead to reconciliation, there can be no genuine, lasting reconciliation without truth. Certainly a litany of lies, half-truths and denial are not a desirable foundation on which to build the new South Africa. Second, it is readily conceded that it was not possible for one commission with a limited time-span and resources on its own, to achieve reconciliation against a background of decades of oppression, conflict and deep division.[2]

So, from the beginning, there was an acceptance that the task of reconciliation is too vast, too all-pervasive, too daunting for a single commission to make a reality. The following statement was made in a *New York Times* editorial after the Report was handed in: 'No commission can transform a society as twisted as South Africa's was, but the Truth Commission is the best effort the world has seen and South Africa is better for it.'[3] This statement was made by Tina Rosenberg, which gives it far greater power and strength than if it had come from one of the TRC Commissioners.

I want to proceed to the argument that the Truth Commission was not actually established to bring about any kind of reconciliation. The ANC called for a truth commission at a meeting of its national executive. When some of us discussed this at the request of then President Mandela, the point was made that if you have a truth commission, it has a kind of Orwellian overtone, which almost suggests that 'we are now going to discover the final truth'. But what we were supposed to do was to ensure that truth would serve the process of reconciliation, and this was our recommendation in the first draft of the Act that appeared before the Parliamentary Standing Committee on Justice. With hindsight, it may not have been a good decision, because I think it raised expectations, and people rightly ask what became of reconciliation.

Jakes Gerwel has made two important points about reconciliation and the TRC.[4] He noted that the Commission was never expected to reconcile the nation; it was there to promote reconciliation. Further he stated that the process of reconciliation has already begun, and that the Commission was intended to encourage the further development and promotion of that reconciliation within every area of society. He reminds us of what South Africa was like in 1989, when there was literally blood on the streets, when there was a threat of enormous bloodletting, when people were nervous and terrified. But the common sense of both parties to the conflict resulted in a commitment to negotiation politics, which probably resolved the fundamental conflict at that time. So reconciliation, if it is understood in this sense, had already begun. Therefore we should not imagine that there has been no reconciliation in this country whatsoever, and that the Truth Commission has failed in its work. Reconciliation began long before the Truth Commission became a reality; it continued during the TRC process; and it will need to be worked on for a very long time to come. Jakes Gerwel's appeal is that '[w]e do not pathologise a nation in relatively good health by demanding a perpetual quest for the holy grail of reconciliation'.[5]

Then Deputy President Thabo Mbeki delivered his now famous speech in Parliament entitled 'Two Nations' in May 1998, when Parliament was discussing reconciliation and unity. In it he argued that reconciliation had not really started and that it needed to go considerably further. In his view, we had not actually realised a reconciled society: 'A major component part of the issue of reconciliation and nation-building is defined by and derived from the material conditions in our society which have divided our country into two nations, the one black and the other white. We therefore make bold to say that South Africa is a country of two nations.'[6]

I believe that he is over-simplifying the matter. We have many groups within South Africa, implying that enormous reconciliation is needed, not simply between blacks and whites. I think that his is a convenient way of stating it, but circumstances are a lot more complicated and complex than he suggests. In conclusion, he stressed that the overwhelming majority of people in South Africa have not abandoned the goal of unity, peace and reconciliation, and still hope that their dream will come true one day. He cautions that we may not become complacent in the face of widespread deprivation, which could lead to 'a mounting rage to which we must respond seriously'.[7] He quoted the African-American poet Langston Hughes in support of his concern. The question the poet raises is: 'What happens to a dream deferred?', and the poet's conclusion is: 'A dream deferred explodes.'[8]

That is how serious the situation is. It is and must be the concern of the entire nation, not merely of a single commission. President Mbeki continued the same theme at his inauguration:

Because we are one another's keepers, we surely must be haunted by the humiliating suffering which continues to afflict millions of our people. Our nights cannot but be the nights of nightmare when millions of our people live in conditions of degrading poverty. Sleep cannot come easily when children get permanently disabled physically and mentally because of lack of food. No night can be restful when millions have no jobs and some are forced to beg, rob and murder to ensure that their own do not perish from hunger.[9]

The will of the government is clear, but is the management, the translation and the implementation of that will present?

The TRC, to some extent, did achieve remarkable reconciliation amongst many of the approximately twenty thousand people who came to it, and the nearly eight thousand perpetrators. But it didn't end there – I shall provide two examples. First, all of us who served on the Commission have been contacted by various groups, institutions, schools, universities and clubs, who have told us how they formed their own 'mini-commissions'. They have tried to take the process that they witnessed day after day and night after night in the media into their own communities; they have tried to make it work where they are, through story telling and truth telling. I think that this is probably much more powerful than whatever the TRC may have achieved.

The second example relates to the killing of American exchange student Amy Biehl. All of us know about this tragic incident. Many of us have marvelled at the remarkable generosity of spirit of her parents. But there's an even greater miracle. About six weeks ago, a new youth club was opened in Guguletu. The Biehl parents attended the opening of the club, which was started by two young men – two of the men who received amnesty for killing Amy Biehl. It surely points to the need for a wider definition of justice, which includes some aspect of restorative justice. This is exactly the kind of multiplier effect that is taking place almost unknown to ourselves, because we only hear about it almost by hearsay.

Let me stress that although there were many who publicly forgave those who had hurt them so grievously, there were many who were not ready to forgive. During the early stages of the Commission's work we made the mistake of almost demanding that people forgive. We soon realised that we had no right to demand of those who came to us that they should forgive. Our job was to create a climate and the circumstances in which this could become a real possibility.

It is important that our Report be made widely available if the work of reconciliation is to develop and spread. One of the greatest disappointments for me is that we struggled against all odds to meet the deadline of handing in a five-volume Report to President Mandela at the end of October; yet, to this day, we have no idea what Government will do with the forty pages of recommendations contained in the Report.

One of these recommendations is that the Report should be disseminated in such a way that it will reach as many people as possible – through radio, through tapes, through video, through articles and posters, so that youth clubs, churches and organisations can debate its issues. It is such debate that will lead to a deeper sense of reconciliation.

I am particularly disturbed by the lack of response to our recommendations regarding reparation to victims. We still have no idea whether Government accepts the recommendations partially or as a whole, or what it will do about the matter. I am very sympathetic towards the many demands that are made upon the state, but in my view the silence is deafening. We need to hear Government's response, so that we can achieve some closure as far as the victims are concerned. Perhaps it is also the role of civil society to read these recommendations, and to bring pressure upon both the public and private sector to do something about them.

I want to suggest a qualification to the wide use of the notion of reconciliation. First of all, to speak of reconciliation as though we can live in total harmony is absurd. The very essence of politics is based on different points of view – different values, different cultures, different arguments. So reconciliation ought to be viewed as an exchange of ideas in a climate of mutual respect and peaceful co-existence. Then we can start debating and discussing with a view to building a nation and reconciling peoples that have been divided for a long time and remain divided in many ways. The question of individual reconciliation is obviously an important one. To see two people who are enemies actually reconciled is a miracle, and we must work for that. But it will not happen throughout society.

Even if we imagine reconciliation at its very best and its highest, the questions are: Can it ever transcend the individual to reach the community or even a nation as a whole? Can a nation confess, repent, make restitution, seek forgiveness, be healed? José Zalaquett has said that the same philosophy that underpins Judeo-Christian beliefs about atonement, penance, forgiveness and reconciliation was the basis for the work of the Chilean Truth and Reconciliation Commission.[10] Hannah Arendt, a Jewish philosopher who certainly was not a devotee of the Judeo-Christian faith, nevertheless argues that there are two major components in any attempt to bring about reconciliation.[11] The first is dealing with those circumstances that are irreversible. How do we deal with them? This remarkable woman points to the possibility of forgiveness. And then she speaks of the problem of rebuilding, and raises the possibility of a covenant, of making promises and holding people to those promises, so that we may not only deal with the past, but actually go forward into the future on the basis of a new covenant. Karl Jaspers discusses the question of German guilt, and distinguishes between criminal guilt, political guilt, moral guilt and metaphysical guilt.[12] His understanding enabled Martin Niemöller to say the following: 'We have let all these things happen without protest against these crimes and without supporting the victims. We should not blame the Nazis only. They will find their prosecutors and judges. We should blame ourselves and draw logical conclusions.'[13] If anyone took a stand and suffered as a result of it, it was Niemöller. But he identified himself with his nation and with its actions.

Willy Brandt is another quite brilliant example of a leader who sought to reach out to communist Poland in the interest of reconciliation. In 1970, he signed a treaty that resulted in forty thousand square miles of German territory being returned to Poland. Both symbolically and practically, Brandt, as leader of the German nation, apologised to the Polish people who had suffered grievously as a result of Nazi policies. Many will recall his kneeling silently at the Warsaw War Memorial as an act of confession and repentance for offences against the Polish people. During the Second World War, Willy Brandt had fled Germany because of his opposition to Nazism and had lived in exile in Norway. And yet it was he who knelt and asked for forgiveness.

While it may not be possible for an entire nation to be reconciled, perhaps there is a huge and awesome onus on leaders of nations to apologise symbolically, and then to move forward. I believe that it was with this in mind that Desmond Tutu asked certain leaders in South Africa to make similar gestures. He asked Nelson Mandela to show public atonement in Church Street, Pretoria, where ANC cadres had planted a bomb on 20 May 1983. Similarly, he asked Mangosuthu Buthelezi to show atonement at Kwa-Mashu in KwaZulu-Natal, where women and children had been massacred in the 1980s, allegedly by IFP supporters. He asked the leader of the Pan-Africanist Congress, Stanley Mogoba, to hold a special service to symbolise atonement at St. James Church in Cape Town, where PAC members had massacred churchgoers on 25 July 1993. He asked F.W. de Klerk to go to the scene of the Boipatong killings which occurred in June 1992. Tutu appealed to all of them and concluded his appeal with these words: 'Would it not be wonderful if the leaders of these political parties could go to the site of a notorious atrocity committed by their side and say, sorry, forgive us? No qualifications, no buts or ifs.'[14]

Leaders in this country and other countries have often missed remarkable opportunities to lead a nation towards a deeper sense of reconciliation. Antjie Krog was a speaker at a conference that was held prior to the formation of the Commission.[15] She referred to the Anglo–Boer War that took place in South Africa between 1899 and 1902. In introducing this subject in relation to reconciliation, she quoted a remarkable poem by Eugéne Marais. She reminded her audience that twenty-six thousand women and children died in British concentration camps and elsewhere during the Anglo–Boer War. After the war, a royal commission on war was appointed, but it did not investigate crimes against the local population. The intriguing question that Krog posed was this: 'Wasn't the mere fact that the abusers of the war were never exposed perhaps not a key factor in the character that formulated apartheid laws?' She asked a further penetrating question: 'What would have happened if a British Truth Commission had recorded reports of injustices during the war, and what would have happened if acknowledgement had been made by the British about the wrongs, and if forgiveness had been asked for?' She speculated whether, had there been some public recognition of intrinsic humanity, the course of our history would have taken the turn that it did. We shall never know, of course. But I believe that any public confession by those involved in these kinds of violations, whether it was then or now, would drastically alter the history of South Africa, particularly in relation to race and power. There can be little doubt that the deep resentment felt by many Afrikaners helped to shape their own determination to survive at any cost.

In trying to assess the contribution that the Commission made towards unity, reconciliation and reconstruction, it is helpful to remind ourselves of the fundamental philosophy contained in the Postamble of the Interim Constitution: 'This Constitution provides a historic bridge between the past of a deeply divided society characterised by strife, conflict, untold suffering and injustice and a future founded on a recognition of human rights, democracy and peaceful co-existence and development opportunities for all South Africans.'[16]

It was with this in mind that the TRC was called into being. The question which Justice Mohamed raised when he handed down his verdict in a case that was brought against the Commission was: 'Consider if the TRC had never existed. Think about what would have happened if the silence had not been broken, if the right to be heard had been turned away. Because of this opportunity for both perpetrator and victim, there are enormous new possibilities in South Africa.'[17]

Surely a reliable test for reconciliation is whether it is accompanied by or at least leads to the achievement of economic justice. Wilmot James has put it this way: 'The TRC did valuable groundwork, now the nation's task is to underwrite emotional healing with material redress.'[18] As has been stressed from the beginning, unacceptable anachronisms exist in South Africa. Only when the mass of people who have been both emotionally and economically prejudiced by apartheid begin to believe that there is a new horizon to aspire to, will they be able to embrace a commitment to reconciliation.

In Argentina, the use of the word 'reconciliation' was deliberately avoided. Firstly, because the word was used by the Roman Catholic Church, which underwrote the military dictators and was complicit in many of the acts of terror that took place. Secondly, it is a word that is used very easily by perpetrators;

victims take a little longer to come close to it. And that is perhaps how we should approach it.

Can we be reconciled? What do we mean by reconciliation? Let's face the facts. Most whites don't trust blacks. I'll take it further: Most whites don't like blacks. Most blacks are deeply suspicious of whites, with some cause. We should not feel guilty about this. We are a product of divisions imposed upon this society and it will take a very long time before we begin to like each other, and more importantly, before we begin to trust and respect one another.

We must rid ourselves of these feelings of constant guilt and resentment. We should begin to move away from the stereotypes of race and prejudice, and proceed to something new. I shall conclude by quoting Adam Michnik, a man who spent much time in prison, where he was treated very badly. When the conflict had been resolved and the restoration of Poland had to begin, he said:

> The image of the enemy is a moral and political burden because you are negotiating with someone who only yesterday you called an oppressor, a murderer or a terrorist. You promised your followers this person would be severely punished as a reward for the oppression they had lived through. Your followers meanwhile are telling you, 'Justice requires punishment.' They ask, 'how can you negotiate and talk to a person who is responsible for all the disasters of our people?' I am negotiating because I've chosen the logic of peace and abandoned the logic of war. This means that my enemy of yesterday must become my partner and we will both live in a common state. He may still be my opponent, but he is an opponent within peace, not within war.[19]

It seems to me that this is the situation we face in South Africa and we have to break free from the servitude of past ideas and views. Every time somebody does something that creates trust, or does something that breaks down a wall, that person provides new opportunities for others to do the same. We have to distinguish between individual and national reconciliation, both of which have taken place in many instances. When we speak of the Rainbow Nation, I think we misunderstand what Desmond Tutu was saying. Perhaps he was saying that speaking of a nation being healed after the long-term existence of deep wounds means speaking a language not of fact, but of faith. This does not make the call for a Rainbow Nation illegitimate; rather, it challenges society to become what it is called to be. The image embodies a promise of what is possible in the future. It is the language of poetry. But let us not ever make the mistake of speaking as though we are the Rainbow Nation. When Tutu speaks of the Rainbow Nation as the people of God, he understands that he is speaking the language of potential.

Sometimes his words are misinterpreted, as a claim of who we are. We know that it is not true and dismiss it as cheap rhetoric. Michael Ignatieff put it well: 'Societies and nations are not like individuals, but the individuals who have political authority – and I would add moral authority, and some institutions within societies – can have an enormous impact on the means by which individuals come to terms with the painfulness of their society's past.'[20] I believe that this is where the Commission was, and this is where we need to be.

Chapter Eight

Reconciliation in Africa?

Jan van Eck

Since I first started working in Burundi in June 1995, I have discovered that countries like Burundi and Rwanda have problems that make South Africa's problems pale into insignificance. These daunting problems include a horrendous dimension of violence that one can hardly believe. At the time that the people who are involved in this violence commit such atrocities, they actually believe that they are completely in the right. They believe that they have no alternative. The violence is so all-encompassing that one feels the need to identify a group that is inherently 'evil'; otherwise it is beyond comprehension.

Over a period of three months in 1994, eight hundred thousand to one million people were murdered in Rwanda. The figures vary, as nobody has been able to count the victims. Those who lost their lives belonged mainly to the Tutsi minority, which forms 14 per cent of Rwanda's population. Today, only two hundred to three hundred thousand Tutsis remain.

The Rwandan situation is particularly complicated because killers and victims have to share the same country, very unlike post–World War Two Europe. This raises the following question: If the Jews who survived the Holocaust in Germany had not all left Germany, would it have been possible for Germans and Jews to be reconciled? We would definitely conclude that the Nuremberg trials would not have been possible. We have to ask this, because the consequences of the Holocaust, the most horrendous genocide in living memory, could nevertheless be managed in a situation where the victims were absent.

However, in Rwanda every Hutu is considered guilty either of crimes of commission or omission, because the Hutu government executed the genocide in this country. Therefore the Hutu population is subject to massive collective guilt. The Tutsis are all considered victims, even those who did not suffer, and therefore a feeling of entitlement is present. This culture of victimisation on the one side and collective guilt on the other side is setting the scene for a repeat of the genocide of 1994.

This is the main point I want to make: 'Justice' sought through revenge and retribution will sow the seeds for further atrocities.

From 1960 to the early 1990s, Rwanda was governed by Hutu majoritarian power government that eventually embarked on a policy of exterminating the entire Tutsi population. The Hutu government of Rwanda treated the Tutsis abominably, while the international community paid little attention. Many thousands of Tutsis were killed in the 1960s. Those who survived fled to Uganda, Tanzania and elsewhere, and lived in exile for thirty years.

In 1990 the Tutsi Rwandan Patriotic Front (RPF) invaded Rwanda from bases in Uganda, and violent conflict continued throughout 1991 and 1992. Although a series of peace accords were negotiated between the Hutu government and the RPF in late 1992 and 1993, the death of Hutu President Habyarimana in a plane crash in April 1994 initiated an explosion of violence and brutality.

The RPF were accused of assassinating Habyarimana, and Hutu soldiers, the presidential guard and the militia began to murder Tutsi civilians and moderate Hutus. Evidence has shown that the massacres that ensued were part of a well-orchestrated campaign of genocide. In July 1994, the Hutu government fled Rwanda, and the RPF declared victory and established a new government. Between eight hundred thousand and one million Tutsis had been killed from April to July 1994. Approximately two million refugees, mainly Hutu, were estimated to have fled Rwanda for Zaire and Tanzania.

In Rwanda there is little, if any, desire for reconciliation with those guilty of genocide. This is to some extent a generalisation, but at present the Tutsis show no sign of wanting to share power with them. The Tutsi government will not even consider amnesty. When speaking at a Genocide Conference in Rwanda in 1996, I referred to the amnesty clause of the TRC Act. The audience was completely unreceptive to the notion of amnesty and was firmly of the opinion that the prosecution of those who had committed atrocities was the only option.

There is no inclusiveness in government. The Hutu population has no real political representation, and those who believe in majoritarian (Hutu) rule – not violent rule, but a Western-style democracy – are not allowed to participate in the body politic of Rwanda. Therefore many Hutus join the violent rebel movements. Negotiations are not being considered. When people voted in the local elections, they had to line up behind the candidate of their choice to show their support – transparency taken a bit too far!

I must emphasise that my criticism arises from a perspective of deep sympathy and a deep understanding of the psychological damage that has been inflicted on the entire population of Rwanda. I understand why people are not doing what we believe they should do. They need to be encouraged and assisted to move slowly and with determination towards a process that will lead to a healing of the nation.

Reconciliation was the first issue I discussed in Rwanda and Burundi. In Burundi, the issue is equally controversial, although the number of people murdered in the most recent genocide is not as high. In Burundi, there have been multiple massacres over the last thirty years. Between 1965 and 1993, more than one million people were exterminated.

However, the biggest problem for both Rwanda and Burundi is that the extermination of Tutsis continues: In the Congo, Laurent Kabila delivered an anti-Tutsi speech which led to the killing of Tutsis; Robert Mugabe has made a similar speech in Zimbabwe. The Congo conflict has made anti-Tutsi sentiment even stronger. The Tutsi communities therefore suspect, not without cause, that there is a widespread regional policy of genocide against them as a minority group. This is the hard reality of the conflict in eastern Congo, and if this conflict is not resolved, there will never be peace in Congo or Central Africa.

While we should not promote notions of ethnicity, the most fatal mistake we make when trying to resolve conflicts in Africa is not to acknowledge its existence. Not accepting ethnicity as a reality is the ultimate mistake. We have to work with this reality and shape it into something positive, instead of entrenching it and allowing it to be manipulated.

The ultimate consequence of massacre upon massacre, and of torture of an unimaginable magnitude, has been the total dehumanisation of the entire population in Rwanda and Burundi. In South Africa, the aim of apartheid was to dehumanise a majority in the eyes of a minority. In Rwanda and Burundi, dehumanisation has taken on an extreme dimension: On the one hand, every Hutu is committed from birth to exterminating Tutsis, simply because they are regarded as foreigners. (They are assumed to be descendants of the Nilotic people of former Abyssinia, or, according to legend, cattle farmers who came from the sky with their cattle.) On the other hand, the Tutsis believe that the Hutus can never be trusted: they are genocidal and want to exterminate all Tutsis. So if we attempt to reconcile, to suggest power-sharing or co-operation, the Tutsis will claim that the Hutus will kill them if given the chance.

To complicate the matter further, the Hutus regard the Tutsis as oppressors. When the Belgian colonists arrived, they decided that the Tutsis with their Caucasian-type features were more attractive than the Hutus, who had Bantu features. They also considered the Tutsis more intelligent, because they were good warriors. The Belgians decided that the Tutsis would govern the Hutus on their behalf, and during the colonial years the Belgians used the Tutsis to oppress the Hutus. This changed when Rwanda became independent, when the Hutus came to power in Rwanda. Burundi remained a monarchy for a few more years, and then it became a Tutsi-dominated dictatorship.

The dehumanisation of the people in this region is standing in the way of reconciliation, impeding any progress towards nation-building and negotiating an acceptable agreement. The question asked of South Africans is what we have done to make our miracle happen. The Central African Great Lakes Region regards South Africa's transition, and the Truth and Reconciliation Commission, as the models from which to learn. It is looking for, and always has looked for, a success story in Africa. There have been few. So South Africa's story is the one they look at. But South Africa also needs to find out from other African countries what they think about our achievements, and we have a responsibility to share our experiences and our achievements with countries that are being destroyed by the trauma they are experiencing.

The first step in Rwanda and Burundi would be to negotiate a political solution, a social contract. This is what South Africa did: We negotiated a compromise, a mutually acceptable political settlement with which we could live. The Truth Commission had to operate in the spirit of this agreement, because there were no clear winners and losers. Therefore, before Rwanda and Burundi can start speaking about justice, there needs to be a political settlement. South Africa could not have prosecuted members of the South African Defence Force or South African Police in 1994, as it would have meant the end of peaceful transition.

In Burundi, the present Tutsi government has unsuccessfully tried to prosecute those who killed the first democratically elected president in 1993. The real perpetrators are hiding and cannot be prosecuted, because such a step could result in their sabotaging the negotiation process in Burundi. Neither can people from the majority Hutu community, who are accused of having committed acts of genocide, be prosecuted, because the government now needs to negotiate with them.

As the desire amongst Burundians to negotiate with one another and to try to find a solution has become stronger, prosecutions have actually been discontinued. For example, the Speaker of Parliament is an important political partner in the reconciliation and negotiation process. He had previously been charged with acts of genocide (although these charges were later proved to have been fabricated). Once there is a desire to achieve a political settlement, it becomes clear a country needs to determine the measure of justice to be implemented that will not destroy the spirit of reconciliation.

In Africa there are two other relevant examples of compromises made in the quest for peace – Mozambique and Sierra Leone.

Although Mozambique is seldom discussed, unbelievable atrocities were committed in this country during the war between Renamo and Frelimo. No formal amnesty was declared in Mozambique, but there were no prosecutions.

Mozambique regarded this not as a matter of choice, but as the only way of bringing war to an end. And thus it was done. Should we regard Mozambicans as unprincipled?

Sierra Leone was over many years destabilised by foreign powers and manipulated by regional powers. The result was continuous war and incessant killings. Ecomog forces were sent in, but did not assist in the peace-making efforts. Eventually, the rebels formed a government of national unity with President Kaba, the original democratically elected president. This was seen as an unwelcome development: Rebels accused of the most horrendous human rights violations were suddenly part of governing the country. Human rights organisations continue to campaign against this deal. However, it is seen as creating peace in Sierra Leone. Should human rights organisations sitting in London be evaluating what is appropriate for Sierra Leone?

On the other hand, Uganda is regarded as a model state by many people, but not by many of its own citizens. No opposition is allowed, and virtually all members of the government that was ousted by President Yoweri Museveni have left Uganda to form rebel movements. A referendum will be held in Uganda in 2000 to decide whether Uganda should become a multi-party democracy. President Museveni opposes multi-party democracy, and there is no doubt that the result of the referendum will be that Uganda will not become a multi-party democracy. A new rebel movement called the Citizens' Army for Multi-Party Politics (CAMP) has already been formed, and Ugandans are taking up arms to fight for a multi-party democracy. Yet the world community is not exerting any pressure on President Museveni to cancel this referendum, in spite of knowing that it is likely to lead to internal conflict of a magnitude that Uganda will not be able to survive. Already the whole north and west of the country are being destabilised. Although amnesty has been offered to the northern resistance army, which operates from Sudan, no negotiations are taking place with rebel movements.

Africa is suffering from the total destruction of its economy. On a global level, it is being marginalised. Investors are leaving Africa in tremendous haste. The people of Africa want an end to war, and if we do not adopt a more pragmatic approach to the conflicts of Africa, this will never happen. Without conflict resolution there will be no development, and a country that is not developed lacks resources. In countries where resources are scarce, such as Burundi and Rwanda, different ethnic groups start manipulating resources. Thus ethnic competition is partly a result of the scarcity of resources.

Having produced a model of reconciliation, South Africa has established a set of principles for achieving political transition and a certain level of justice. I believe that these principles could be of great use to the rest of the continent, and that South Africa has a duty to share its experiences. Because Africa does not believe in solutions that are not African, it has an enormous interest in the South African experience. I believe that the Truth Commission and all its members, having been involved in one of the most exciting and valuable tasks of the South African transition, are in a position to take its message to a much wider audience that needs to be reconciled.

The situation in Burundi and Rwanda must be resolved, because it lies at the root of the Congolese conflict. I strongly believe that South Africa can use its good offices in these countries, and share its experience of how to reform and transform, so as to prevent a repetition of the horrendous acts of violence that have been committed in the past and threaten to continue unabated.

Neither Dull nor Tiresome

Kaizer Nyatsumba

An assessment of the Truth and Reconciliation Commission's possible legacy in the no-longer-so-new South Africa is no easy task in a country such as ours, where the TRC represents different things to different people. It is perhaps no exaggeration to say that there are many important institutions in the country, the TRC being one of them, which have won greater acclaim abroad than they have here at home. Sadly, there appears to be a tendency in certain quarters not to assess things in a disinterested, dispassionate manner, but rather to criticise everything that does not accord with people's own prejudices.

In South Africa today, there are as many views on the TRC as there are people with strong political views. Indeed, many people's reactions to the TRC, from its inception through to the much-publicised submission of its Report to former President Nelson Mandela, have depended largely on at least two very important things. Firstly, how those people felt the past had to be dealt with in the new South Africa, and secondly, how they themselves related to that past.

For example, there were at least three divergent schools of thought when it came to how our country's ugly past was to be dealt with. There were those, especially within the ranks of the National Party and the Inkatha Freedom Party, who were of the opinion that we as a country had to let bygones be bygones, that the past should simply be erased from our collective memories. That way, it was argued, we would stand a better chance of achieving reconciliation without allowing the past to stand between us.

Then there were others, chiefly the now ruling African National Congress, who held the opposite view. It was important, they argued, that the wounds of the past should be opened to allow for a lasting, more cathartic healing to take place. It was vital, therefore, that a truth commission–type structure be established before which perpetrators could open their hearts and seek amnesty from prosecution.

Anybody who could show that he or she had violated others' human rights in pursuance of a political goal would then be granted amnesty. Remorse was not part of the equation.

The third school of thought, which included the Pan-Africanist Congress and the Azanian People's Organisation, argued strongly for the unconditional release from prison of those who were there because they had dared to fight against apartheid. It also argued for the wholesale prosecution of those who had destroyed numerous families, maimed and murdered in order to prop up apartheid, an abominable system which had been widely denounced as a crime against humanity. Although some of their comrades and cadres were later to benefit from the TRC process, AZAPO and the PAC were not interested in being reconciled with their former oppressors.

I think it is important to consider the origin of the TRC before turning our attention to how the Commission has been regarded and how its final Report was received. Upon its return from exile, the ANC was dogged by allegations that the organisation was guilty of gross human rights violations in its camps. Just as had happened to President Sam Nujoma's SWAPO a few years earlier, organisations like Amnesty International and the IFP and its conservative (and sometimes outright right-wing) backers in Germany and the United States repeatedly hounded the ANC about this matter. Various press conferences were called to highlight the ANC's alleged lack of tolerance for dissension, and a book by one Mwezi Twala, entitled *Mbokodo: Inside MK*,[1] was sponsored by one of these organisations and given maximum publicity to embarrass the ANC.

The strategy was simple enough: Harass and discredit the ANC as much as possible, and use every opportunity to portray it and its leadership as blood-thirsty terrorists who could not be trusted at all, let alone with power. Three commissions were therefore appointed to investigate the ANC between 1991 and 1993: the pro-IFP Douglas Commission, the Amnesty International Commission, and the Mandela-appointed Motsuenyane Commission.

Although by and large they differed in the emphases they placed on human rights violations and the context within which these occurred, without exception the three commissions were very critical of the ANC, and, understandably, the wide publicity that followed was very embarrassing and damaging to the organisation.

If I remember correctly, the Douglas and Amnesty International commissions went as far as recommending a blanket ban from public office for those who were implicated in human rights violations that had taken place in ANC camps. The Motsuenyane Commission recommended a strong censure of those who were involved. Needless to say, some of those who were implicated by these commissions are today in high positions both in government and in the public service.

In its reaction after a meeting of its National Executive Committee, the ANC accepted 'collective responsibility' for those violations and called for the setting up of a truth commission to investigate past human rights violations across the board. Predictably, some of those who had been calling for the prosecution of those ANC leaders implicated in human rights violations, immediately changed their minds. They did not support an across-the-board truth commission before which they would have to bare their souls, but neither were they in favour of prosecutions.

This debate raged on during the multi-party talks at the World Trade Centre, primarily between the ANC and the NP. As the country approached the 1994 elections, there was a lot of panic within the South African Defence Force and the South African Police and, consequently, much pressure was placed upon the NP and its negotiators. Finally, an understanding was reached that amnesty would be granted to all those who told the truth about their actions provided that they were politically motivated. These conditions were included in the Postamble to the Interim Constitution and eventually led to the TRC as we know it.

Now the TRC has come and gone, except for the Amnesty Committee, which still has a few months to go. Left in its wake is a raging controversy about its legacy: Did it manage to reconcile us as a nation, and do we now know much more about that terrible part of our history than we did before the TRC's inception? The one thing that cannot be said about the TRC is that it was dull and tiresome: It remained controversial and very much in the news to the end.

It is my contention that domestic responses to the TRC should be viewed against the way in which the Commission was received by different interest groups. It makes little sense to expect, for instance, that parties like the NP and the IFP, which were opposed to the creation of the TRC from the very beginning, would have been impressed by the Commission and its work, let alone by its final Report to the President. The same would apply to parties like AZAPO and the PAC, although some of their members have been beneficiaries of a process to which these organisations were opposed.

However, no matter how one looks at the TRC and from what vantage point one does so, the one inescapable conclusion is that by and large its mandate has been a misnomer. Certainly, the Commission has been able to shed some light on events for members of families who did not know how their loved ones met their ends, by whom they were murdered or where they were buried. We can say confidently that there are certainly individuals and families whom the Commission helped to discover the truth about their loved ones.

Unfortunately, it is my contention that we cannot say the same about reconciliation. The sad truth is that, for a host of reasons, South Africans are not any more reconciled now, especially across the racial divides of old, than they were before the inception of the Commission. We have had wonderful and very moving examples of reconciliation taking place between victim and perpetrator or a victim's family and a perpetrator after the truth had been told. However, such reconciliation as has taken place has not found resonance across the country.

The IFP and the NP believe that the TRC was part of an attempt to discredit them, and are still of the opinion that the best way of dealing with our past would have been through granting blanket amnesty to all those who participated in the conflict. They also believe, wrongly in my view, that the Commission was largely biased in favour of the ruling party, both in terms of its composition and in the manner it conducted itself. After all, there was that unfortunate decision two years ago by the TRC's Amnesty Committee to grant blanket amnesty to thirty-seven ANC and ANC-aligned individuals, among them TRC Chairperson Desmond Tutu's son, Trevor Tutu.

The PAC and AZAPO would have preferred the heroes of the liberation struggle who were involved in a 'just war' to have been released unconditionally and those who had fought on the side of apartheid prosecuted. After all, no less a body than the United Nations had declared apartheid a 'crime against humanity'.

Interestingly, the ANC itself was not very happy with the Commission, as could be seen from its ill-advised decision to seek an interdict against the TRC to force it to excise from its final Report any unflattering references to the organisation. Quite clearly, the ANC had followed the TRC route without fully considering the implications of its decision. This much became clear early in the life of the Commission to those of us in the media who received telephone calls from the ANC and were lobbied with regard to the Commission. It was suggested that we might want to make the point in our columns that the two parties to the conflict of the past, those who had fought to maintain so evil a system as apartheid and those who had fought to end it, could not morally be equated with each other.

The argument, of course, was sound, and it was one to which I was then and am now very sympathetic. Indeed, morally there was no way that apartheid's assassins could be compared with ANC–PAC–AZAPO guerillas. Those who fought to ensure the continuation of oppression had no moral defence, for the system they sought to perpetuate was so vile that it had been rightly condemned as a 'crime against humanity'. Those who had fought against apartheid, however, were liberators, and morality was on their side.

The problem that some of us had with the calls we received was two-fold. Firstly, the distinction was something the ANC should have sought to have adopted either during the multi-party talks at the World Trade Centre or when the relevant TRC legislation was passed. Secondly, if we went ahead and raised the very legitimate concern the ANC was expressing, we could in future legitimately be seen as people who merely parroted the views of others.

I will turn now to an assessment of the domestic responses to the TRC.

Apart from the political discontent in certain political quarters, to which I have already referred, the TRC had by far its best public reception in its own country early in its existence. Many South Africans, especially white South Africans in whose names these terrible atrocities were committed by successive NP governments and their security apparatuses, were shocked at the barbarity and brutality described graphically before the TRC. Those of us who followed events closely in the media can remember an avalanche of letters to various newspapers by white readers who were delighted that the ugly past was being dissected publicly. They were grateful to be made aware of the full extent of what had been done in their name and, together with many black South Africans, found the process to be immensely cathartic. Stories about the TRC were read religiously and Max du Preez's programme entitled *TRC Special Report* watched avidly on television every week.[2]

This did not last long. The early relief soon gave way to deep-seated resentment among some of our white compatriots, who began to feel that people who had committed similarly ghastly deeds on the side of the liberation movements were not subjected to the same kind of rigorous cross-examination.

Perhaps because the Commission went on much longer than it should ideally have done, the public gradually became inured to the sensational stories told at the TRC, unless the people making an appearance before the Commission were high-profile individuals like ANC Women's League President Winnie Madikizela-Mandela. In the process, the TRC became discredited and, in some instances such as when it granted a blanket amnesty to the thirty-seven ANC-aligned individuals, managed to discredit itself. Another example: In terms of the law the Commission was correct in its insistence on a personal appearance before it by former State President P. W. Botha. But in some quarters that stand-off also contributed to the erosion of the Commission's integrity because it was seen, wrongly in my view, to be vindictive in its dealings with a frail old man.

As I have already argued, the greatest failure of the TRC was in respect of reconciliation. In fact, with the benefit of hindsight we can now say that it was extremely ambitious of the government to have hoped that the TRC would assist with the reconciliation process. Although I myself claim no authority on the Chilean model, it is not my impression that in addition to unearthing the truth about the past, part of the brief of its commission was explicitly stated to be reconciliation. Whatever reconciliation occurred would appear to have been a by-product of that process, a result of the healing power of the truth.

In conclusion, I wish to make two points. The TRC has been perceived abroad as having been a large part of the so-called miracle of our relatively peaceful political transition, yet it is my firm view that the country cannot be said to be much more reconciled at the moment as a result of the Commission. Indeed, it is my contention that fault lines are developing daily in our society, and that unless the new tensions are handled carefully, the once much-talked-about Rainbow Nation will prove to have been a very useful marketing tool, which was actually a charade.

The two individuals who could have helped to rehabilitate the TRC in the eyes of the general public, and for posterity, were President Thabo Mbeki, in his capacity as the leader of the ANC, and former President F.W. de Klerk, in their response to the final Report of the Commission. Unfortunately, they were the very people who tarnished its image further by challenging the Commission's findings – Mbeki because he did not like what it said about the ANC and De Klerk because he did not like what it said about him. In the end the ANC failed in its court challenge, but to date the country does not know what the Commission had to report about De Klerk.

His Name was Henry

Albie Sachs

At a lecture I gave in New Delhi in December 1998, which was in effect a report on the Truth and Reconciliation Commission's Report, I told the following story: I was in chambers at the Constitutional Court in Johannesburg just over a year ago, and in a state of some excitement because I was told that somebody called Henry had arrived at reception. I took out my security pass, went to the security door, opened it, and saw him there. He had telephoned me some days before to say that he had been part of the group that had organised the placing of the bomb in my car in 1988. He was going to speak to me at the TRC and he wanted to see me before he did so. He came through the door, he was shorter than myself, slim, younger, he walked to my chambers; he with a military gait, I with my judge's ambulatory style, looking at each other without looking. Both of us were curious. He was thinking, 'Who is this person I helped to try to kill?' I was wondering, 'Who is this person who wanted to blot me out?'

His name was Henry. He told me that he had been to Potchefstroom University, had been a bright student. He had good parents, especially his mother, who was a very moral person. He was selected to go into the army – he said he was a good soldier. He rose quite rapidly through the ranks and was selected for special operations. Then he described how he had been part of the team that had organised taking photographs of my car. He told me about other commando attacks that were being organised at that time to kill other people in Mozambique. And then, he began to look at me rather quizzically. He began to speak in an almost petulant tone, as he looked around my chambers, the pictures on the wall, the comfort, the pot plant. He told me that he had been one of those dismissed from the army as a result of the Goldstone Commission findings.[1] He had received about R150 000 and invested it in a company with a certain Eugene de Kock, and had subsequently lost the money. He was quite aggrieved, and told me that he too had been injured, he had received a bullet wound in his leg. The implication was that the generals were now either still in the security forces or they had received large 'golden handshakes'. They had been treated well, while he was one of the foot soldiers who had been abandoned. And here was I, the person he had tried to kill, sitting in my office as a judge, part of the new elite, receiving a good salary, successful.

Usually when somebody comes to visit me, I show the ordinary civility and shake hands when I receive them, and I shake hands when I say goodbye. But with Henry I experienced a very cheap emotion, I wanted to say to him: 'Henry, I'm sorry, I can't shake your hand, you know why.' But I resisted it. I said to him that normally I shake the hand of someone who visits me, but I couldn't shake his. I told him to speak to the TRC, to tell them what he knew, to contribute to the store of knowledge that our country has about its past, to be as honest as he could. I said that maybe he and I would meet afterwards, then we could see. I forgot about him after that.

What was this body called the Truth and Reconciliation Commission, which was somehow going to humanise the relationship between my would-be assassin and myself? It has been subjected to two major critiques. The radical critique, alluded to by Colin Bundy, more or less says that by identifying gross violations of human rights, which affected a certain number of individuals at the forefront of the struggle, attention is taken away from the deep, systematic, pervasive dispossession and humiliation of the majority of people. It actually serves a negative purpose. And from that point of view, it undermines any possibility, contradictory as this may seem, of reconciliation. It is an important perspective, and one of the many perspectives that have emerged from this deeply engaging, profoundly affecting, brilliant, difficult, dark, intense process that we all participated in and watched and argued about. While I acknowledge the importance of this critique, I think it is basically wrong, although it should be a part of the overall assessment. It has to be one of the many voices that make up the total symphony of the process.

Why focus on these individual cases of torture, assassination and violence, when apartheid itself was a denial of humanity that involved dispossession of land, suppression of language, culture, and personality? I think there were very good reasons for doing this.

First of all, these cases were hidden, secret and denied. The Group Areas Act was known, the Land Act was known, the wars of dispossession were known. But these were covert activities conducted in a clandestine way. Secondly, they were criminal even in terms of the laws of apartheid. Torture, assassination and fraud were crimes even in terms of South African law. That is one reason why they were secret. Something had to be done in relation to those crimes.

Thirdly, they had an intensely cruel, savage and affecting character. They were the epitome of domination and dehumanisation, and of organised, institutionalised control of one section of the population. Attacking these cases was doing much more than revealing the agony of certain individuals. It was exposing a system that gave rise to those actions, which covered up and condoned them, which rewarded the persons who committed them. It was a powerful counter-attack against extreme forms of immorality that were rooted in systematic, organised injustice. I believe that personalising these accounts, far from having been the weakness of the process, was its strength. The objective of the whole TRC process was to help humanise South Africa and to move away from abstract characterisations and categories. The oppressed are people, and there were contradictions amongst the oppressed. We had to make people realise that human beings were doing things to other human beings. Perhaps the most difficult part of the whole process was to acknowledge that the perpetrators themselves were human beings. They come from the same genetic stock, the same nation, the same race, in a broad sense, as we do. And for our own humanity, for our own strength, for our own glory, for our own confidence in the future, for our own reconciliation with our fellow South Africans, we must find a spark of humanity – *ubuntu* – in even the least of us, in even the worst of us.

The question was asked whether it would be right to try to develop some kind of psychological profile of Eugene de Kock. I heard Phumla Gobodo-Madikizela describing her five visits to the maximum security prison in Pretoria, to speak to and try to understand Eugene de Kock. I was filled with admiration for her, this slight African woman, going to meet the man, the killer, the representative of all the violence and terror of the centuries. And she went to meet him with courage and with psychological understanding, to try to find out who he was, and the reasons for his actions – through a form of dialogue, not forgiveness. I am proud to be a South African belonging to a nation that has the capacity and spirit to conduct these kinds of enquiries. They are not dehumanising to the person who has dehumanised so many others.

I think that even in terms of the transformation of our country, the process has created such a powerful and intense moral climate that it wipes out any possibility of denial. Even the most right-wing newspapers always start their editorials by saying that we have to acknowledge that terrible things were done in our name. Once that is done, it creates a climate which puts intense moral pressure on those who supported the system of apartheid to change, and to contribute towards change.

If the radical critique raises the question of what is meant by reconciliation, I would like to give my views on its meaning. Reconciliation doesn't need each victim to forgive each perpetrator, and for the perpetrator to apologise, and for the parties to embrace. That is asking too much, and it is inappropriate. There have been a few wonderful examples of exactly that, but what reconciliation really means is some kind of basically shared understanding of the terrible things that were done, and of who did them. Reconciliation also involves an understanding of how it happened and what the context was. Only when that understanding is there, can the nation move forward. We now take the work of the TRC, which has been so successful, for granted as though its achievements were given.

Reconciliation lies in converting knowledge into acknowledgement of the pain, in hearing the voices of the victims, speaking for themselves in their multiple voices, from all sides, from many different quarters, from all the sections of our society who have suffered pain in different ways. It lies in the perpetrators acknowledging, however haltingly, in whatever limited a way, at least something of what they did. Reconciliation means the nation, and the world, acknowledging that these terrible things happened.

The conservative critique takes two forms. The first concerns methodology, raising the question of what truth is. Anthea Jeffery's book entitled *The Truth about the Truth Commission* is a critique of what are called different concepts of truth.[2] The truth can be seen in very different ways. Prior to the establishing of the TRC I drew a distinction between what I call microscopic truth and dialogic truth. Microscopic truth is discerned when you observe a limited, prescribed field – you control the variables, you exclude everything else, and you make your observations in terms of the relationship between the variables. Microscopic truth can be found in positive science. It is what is examined in a legal case – one has to decide whether this person killed that person, with intent to kill on a specific date. That is all you really ask.

Dialogic truth is of a different order. It involves the multiple perspectives, experiences and interpretations of events of the different participants. It is a kind of a social truth. One of the difficulties about analysing the TRC lies in the fact that it was dealing with both kinds of truth at the same time.

I have since added two further categories of truth. There is logical truth, whereby you can deduce truth from a statement simply by a process of inference. There is experiential truth; Gandhi referred to 'my experiments with truth'. He did not commence with a systematic philosophy and then apply it to his life. He started off with his life, his experience, the phenomenon of being himself in a particular place in particular circumstances. And out of those lived experiences, he generalised. In South Africa, experiential truth is absolutely powerful and massive and vivid and varied for a great many people.

If the TRC did nothing else, it enabled this experiential truth to come out, wave upon wave. I think it is rather absurd to say that these statements are worthless because they were not given under oath. This is applying a kind of technical legalism that is appropriate when you are dealing with due process of law. You cannot convict without proper testimony, proper cross-examination, without narrow, microscopic examination. But when you try to find out what happened and what it meant to the people concerned, when you want to hear the voices, when dignity consists not only of the findings, but of the right to speak and be heard, of the right to be acknowledged, of personal pain becoming the pain of the nation, then the experiential side becomes predominant and very important.

I think the TRC Report is a brilliant document. I loved it because it was so uneven, it was rough, it had its seams, you could see the stitching, and it was authentic, it was real. It was not one of these boring, homogenised commission reports that are read only by a few experts. It contained the passion, the variety, and even the contradictions of the process itself. There are a number of findings that I did not feel all that comfortable with, but that was not important. The important thing was that in the process, the TRC put its findings down on the table, and was itself a protagonist, it was not simply recording history. It was a very active participant in the process. The TRC was 'a site of struggle', an ideological, conceptual, political, emotional, personal struggle.

The TRC's mode of operation was unique. I always mention something that was completely strange to me: that Archbishop Tutu cried. Judges do not cry. We do not have songs at the beginning of the process. We do not have a comforter sitting beside witnesses, patting their shoulders, giving them support. Court processes are not human in the way that the TRC processes were. There was something different, inventive and creative about the process. It was special indeed.

It was not the state setting out to prove anything. The state was not prosecuting, The process was not a denunciation. It was a platform, it was a vehicle, it was an arena, it was a site, it was a place, and the voices came out. The perpetrators spoke. How I wished that they had not come in their suits. They were tense and nervous. If only they had opened up, if only they had been human, if only they had cried, if only they had shown more emotion, the way Jeff Benzien did. How affecting that was – how contradictory it felt to see this man crying, this horrible person, who was yet somehow feeling ashamed of what he had done. As far as I know, it has never happened this way in any other country. It has not happened during show trials, nor as a result of torture.

The feature that also particularly strikes people is that all this happened across the board. If the success of the TRC is judged by the fact that it angered everyone on all sides, then it was hugely successful! There were no victors, and there were no losers. The TRC's approach was that it was going to look at everybody, nobody would escape its process. Again, this is unique in the world, as far as I know, and it gave the TRC an extraordinary credibility.

The second part of the conservative critique comes from those who find that amnesty is incompatible with justice. What does this word 'justice' mean? Does it simply mean sending people to prison, or repaying money? In terms of social processes, is that the beginning and end of justice? Is there no justice if you do not send someone to jail, or if you do not see a transfer of money?

This approach is too limited. From a practical point of view, the machinery for prosecution is dominated by the very people who were implicated in the crimes. From an idealistic point of view, the final objective is to enable us all to live together in one country. That was the great dream of Albert Luthuli and Oliver Tambo,[3] two people who made tremendous contributions: living together for future generations, stopping that cycle of domination and control.

The perpetrators paid a price. You saw them, tense, nervous, receiving counselling for post-traumatic stress. They have to look into the faces of their children, their wives, their neighbours, having confessed to the most grievous, horrible crimes. The victims received information, knowledge that they did not have before, where the alternative would have been nothing. Their pain was acknowledged, bodies were recovered and they were honoured. Their sacrifices were acknowledged as an integral part of the terrible trauma and travail that gave rise to the new South Africa.

There is still much to done in terms of reparation. I personally feel that the payment of money is not the primary response, as it can never be enough. You cannot put a price on a person's life. But to live in a democratic society, to feel that one is a free human being, that is worth everything, it is beyond rubies. I think symbolic reparation is important. Money alone cannot humanise and restore dignity.

The matter of reparation is not simply a question for the government. I think it is something for all of us to pay attention to. Someone said that she was willing to give 1 per cent of her salary to a public fund, to contribute towards the relief of those who suffered. I would like to support that by pledging a contribution. I am sure there will be thousands and thousands of South Africans who will respond in the same way. Not only the beneficiaries of apartheid, but those of us who survived, who delight and feel joy in the achievement of South Africa today. Perhaps you earn a generous salary and you can give a percentage of your salary for the next three years, to some kind of fund. I am sure there will be a huge response from ordinary people who are wondering what they can do.

Henry came back into my life. I was at a party when I heard someone saying, 'Hello, Albie'. I looked around, and there he was. He told me that he had given his information to the TRC. He mentioned Bobby, Farouk and Sue.[4] He was on first-name terms with people whom he had tried to kill. I felt so pleased that he had taken that step, and looked at him, and shook his hand.

A few days ago, Indres Naidoo came to see me about the re-publication of a book he and I wrote about Robben Island. He referred in the postscript that he has written to information given to him by Henry, suggesting that the bomb was meant for him (Indres) and not for me. Our book is true and at the same time out of date. And a strange kind of argument emerges between Indre and myself. I insist the bomb was meant for me, and he thinks the bomb was meant for him! It is curious that it is important for me, for my ego, my vanity, that I am the intended victim. I mention this simply to illustrate that the discovery of truth is a continuing, endless process. New information emerges continually, but what is important is that we are talking, as free citizens in a free country. The dignity of the South African nation has been restored. And for this unique contribution I thank the TRC.

Chapter Eleven

A Lot More to Live For

Dumisa Ntsebeza

Both the Preamble to the Promotion of National Unity and Reconciliation Act, No. 34 of 1995, and the Postamble of the Interim Constitution, Act No. 200 of 1993, recognise the need for reconciliation between the people of South Africa in order for peace and national unity to endure, and for the reconstruction of society to take place.

The Postamble recognises the granting of amnesty to applicants for acts, omissions and offences associated with political objectives and committed in the context of the conflicts of the past as central to the reconciliation process and the reconstruction of society.

The broader aim of the Truth and Reconciliation Commission, though this was not specifically spelt out, was to promote reconciliation and unity between not only perpetrators and victims, but also between beneficiaries and victims. This latter aspect I shall address later.

A number of assumptions were made when the two Acts of Parliament were debated and enacted. It was assumed that reconciliation would be a product of truth telling, and that the truth told would be the whole truth in its fullness. It was also assumed that once the victims learnt the truth about what had happened to themselves, to their loved ones, and to others close to them, they would find it possible, although not easy, to come to terms with the pain and suffering caused by evil acts. It was assumed that they would be able to forgive, even if they could not forget.

It was assumed that knowledge would compensate for the pain that, but for full disclosure, would remain for as long as the details of the atrocities remained hidden. Victims would find it possible to bring about closure to their suffering and pain. It was assumed that acknowledgement by the perpetrators, even if they did not show contrition and remorse, would assist both victim and perpetrator to revisit an act of the past that had caused so much pain to those affected by it. It was hoped that this exercise might cause all those involved to commit themselves to never allowing a recurrence of that ugly past.

This is the backdrop against which we should measure the successes and failures of the TRC as far as the process of reconciliation is concerned.

Testimony of Victims

We need to consider the testimonies of the victims and perpetrators as they emerged during the TRC process. I hasten to add that my own point of view is that this evidence does not 'prove' anything more than that people have reacted in different ways to the discovery of the details of the atrocities of the past. Some people confirmed that they were healed through the process of truth telling and official acknowledgement. Some were content to have the remains of their loved ones exhumed and reburied, and have shown no great enthusiasm for revenge through criminal and civil actions against offenders.[1]

Some victims have been healed through exoneration from blame, like those who were falsely accused of being enemy agents, whose true stories emerged during the TRC process. Some did not live to hear their names cleared. Maki Skosana was necklaced and killed because she was believed to have led a group of COSAS youths to their horrible death in the so-called zero-zero hour operation, when the grenades they were hurling at pre-determined targets were booby-trapped.[2] Her sister, Puleng Moloko, who had suffered the pain of her death and the humiliation of ostracism because Maki had been falsely accused, was happy that the truth had finally emerged. She did not insist on taking further court action against those who had murdered her sister.

There have been remarkable stories of people showing a willingness to forgive where one would not have expected such forgiveness. Beth Savage of East London was a victim of an APLA attack. She spent one month in intensive care, underwent open-heart surgery, and had to have her large intestine removed.[3] Yet she wanted to meet the man who threw the grenade, stating that she would meet him in the spirit of forgiveness, and that she hoped her attacker would forgive her too, for whatever reason! When she eventually met Xundu, now a major in the South African National Defence Force, she told the media that she no longer had nightmares about the attack.

Such instances of unbelievable testimony are legion – from victims who should be screaming for vengeful justice, but whose desire for giving perpetrators an opportunity to redeem themselves is motivated by their notion of reconciliation. Cynthia Ngewu, whose son was killed by the police in the 'Guguletu Seven' incident, said the following at the Forum on Reconstruction and Economic Justice in Cape Town on 19 March 1997:[4]

Cynthia Ngewu: What we are hoping for when we embrace the notion of reconciliation is that we restore the humanity to those who were perpetrators; we simply want to ensure that the perpetrators are returned to humanity.

Phumla Gobodo-Madikizela: Many people in this country would like to see perpetrators going to prison and serving long sentences. What is your view on this?

Cynthia Ngewu: In my opinion, I do not agree with this view. We do not want to see people suffer in the same way that we did suffer, and we did not want our families to have suffered. We do not want to return the suffering that was imposed upon us. So, I do not agree with that view at all. We would like to see peace in this country ... I think that all South Africans should be committed to the idea of re-accepting those people back into the community. We do not want to return the evil that perpetrators committed to the nation. We want to demonstrate humaneness towards them, so that they in turn may restore their own humanity.

It is true that there have been other victims who have rejected the notion of reconciliation, who insist on retributive justice, and who insist on the punishment of perpetrators for their apartheid-era crimes. We can count among these the Mxenges, the Seremanes, and some of the women of the Khulumani group.[5] Some have qualified their attitude by saying that they cannot find it in themselves to be reconciled with perpetrators whose identities they do not know, and the details of whose acts they have not had an opportunity to hear. Some have stated that they cannot be reconciled with the violators of human rights who have appeared before the TRC, but have peppered the hearings with lies, denials and obfuscations of the truth. Nkosinathi Biko, at the end of the amnesty hearing of the applicants who were responsible for his father's death, said that we are now no more knowledgeable about how and why Steve Biko was killed by the police than we were after the 1977 inquest, and therefore rejected any notion that he could ever be reconciled with his father's killers.[6] This is a qualified rejection of the process. It is a rejection that says that were circumstances different, had the applicants chosen to disclose fully all the facts, forgiving these miscreants may have been possible. For the Biko family, while appreciating the need for letting bygones be bygones, the basis for forgiveness would have been knowledge on the victims' side, and acknowledgement on the perpetrators' side.

There are other victims who seem to have been so shell-shocked by the extent of the depravity, brutality and heinousness of some crimes related in graphic detail at amnesty hearings, that they immediately denounced any notion of reconciliation.

In short, there are as many who have rejected the notion of reconciliation as there are those who have embraced it.[7]

Anthea Jeffery has criticised the TRC, accusing it, *inter alia*, of not evaluating evidence as a court of law would have done, and of relying on the testimonies of victims who were not subjected to cross-examination.[8] To this 'crime' we plead guilty. We never pretended to be a court of law, and we specifically said so. Our findings were based on a verification process conducted by the Investigative Unit and its researchers. The reliability of testimony was assessed on the basis of corroboration and balance of probabilities. We also ensured that persons who would be detrimentally affected by our findings had an opportunity to make representations in advance.

Another criticism is that we failed to contextualise the investigation into gross violations of human rights. For example, it has been argued that we should have examined and investigated the role of apartheid education and its lasting legacy that has wreaked havoc with and done irreparable harm to mainly black people.

This critique fails to take into account that the TRC Act emphasised a *specific* focus – the investigation of gross violations of human rights, namely, killings, abductions, torture and severe ill-treatment. We had only eighteen to twenty-four months within which to investigate thirty-four years of South African apartheid history. When we started our work in January 1996, we had nothing: no support staff, no systems, no office space (not even in Cape Town, let alone in other centres), no precedent, and Commissioners drawn from a range of political and cultural backgrounds. We literally hit the ground running, and once we started, we worked under tremendous pressure until we produced the Report.

That we were able to produce the Report is a miracle. We therefore ask our critics to look at our work in perspective. Months after the TRC commenced its work – following many internal debates – we decided that we would have to place the Report into some kind of context, hence the institutional hearings into the legal system (focusing also on the role of the judiciary), the media, business, the health sector, and so forth.

But we could never have done *everything*. We had neither the time nor the capacity to do so, and when our budget was cut by 25 per cent in 1997, the task simply became impossible. The reality is that we could not investigate everything.

Reconciliation

I would also like to examine the failures and successes of the TRC's reconciliation brief. I need to make two disclaimers. Firstly, it was never the duty of the TRC, contemplated or otherwise, to implement reconciliation. Our duty was to promote reconciliation, as the Act suggests. Secondly, if the view exists that it is still too early to establish whether the French revolution was successful (an assertion of E.P. Thomson's), then it is far too early to judge the failures and successes of the reconciliation process. Reconciliation is a process that, in my view, will span over many years to come, even generations.[9] It is a process that needs not only the TRC Commissioners, the committee members and the staff to see it through. Each and every member of society in South Africa – be they intellectuals or ordinary people, in organs of civil society or government, in big business or SMMEs, in NGOs or in the various state departments – needs to participate in this process, so that the whole nation can be reconciled.

Finally, there will be no reconciliation as long as the division between the 'haves' and the 'have-nots' exists. As long as the historical imbalance persists between the beneficiaries of South Africa's racial capitalism, who are mainly white, and the victims thereof, the black working class and the rural poor, there will always be a powder keg ready to explode at the tiniest spark.

An ANC member stated at a hearing in Grahamstown that it was all very well for Comrade Nelson Mandela to speak easily of reconciliation, because his circumstances had changed for the better since he was released from prison, whereas the speaker, also a victim of apartheid, and a former political prisoner, was in the same, if not a worse position than when he was released from prison.

This comment is not only fair, it goes to the heart of the matter. It is perhaps in this context that the TRC can arguably be regarded as having failed the victims. The TRC failed to speed up the process of interim reparatory measures to victims, which might have allowed victims to be reconciled with the fact that offenders were granted amnesty.

The victims of Brian Mitchell's murderous attack at Trust Feed came to the Commission to ask for moderate reparation, but payment was not forthcoming.[10] Quite some time after they had appeared before the TRC, they saw Brian Mitchell being released soon after his application for amnesty had been successful. It is therefore perfectly understandable that they rejected Mitchell's overtures when the TRC tried to arrange a meeting with them at his request, so that he could apologise and discuss with the community how he could repay his debt to them.

This rejection was a voice of protest against the TRC, which had released the perpetrator, while leaving the victims destitute, despite its earlier promise of reparation. Thus it could be argued that in respect of its reparation and rehabilitation policy the TRC has failed to promote reconciliation. This is an area in which a lot of work must still be done.

Those who think they have ready answers to the notion of reconciliation, I shall merely admonish that reconciliation is not an easy concept. It is confusing.

It is confused. It is complex. It makes a traumatic demand on those who are called on to forgive and forget. We need to manage the notion of reconciliation with care and responsibility. The concept should not become a political football. It deals with people's suffering. Let those of us who claim to know what ought to have been done or what ought to be done, err on the side of supporting the process critically. Like President Mandela, let us accept the Report of the TRC with all its imperfections as a fair reflection of people's real-life experiences – not as fiction, or as speculative conjectural rhetoric.

Conclusion

Finally, a record of a real-life experience that leaves one appreciative of the dynamics and complexities of reconciliation is the story of Beatrice Sethwale. She testified at a human rights violations hearing about the death of her son, a black police officer, who had been killed because he was a 'collaborator' in the apartheid system. She was asked how she felt about people who were saying that they would now like to work towards reconciliation, by first of all acknowledging that she herself had suffered. She replied as follows:

> I feel I am already dead and that this process will be a very long and time-consuming one. It will take a lot of effort to make me entirely normal again because I've actually become quite used to my pain and place where I find myself currently. I don't bear any grudges against anybody. But if you lose your confidence and your faith in other people, it is very hard to restore. My faith in my fellow human beings has been shattered but I don't bear anybody any grudges.

Indeed, to refer to Njabulo Ndebele's parable of the lion and the rabbit, for some or probably most victims of violence, it does not seem to matter that the rabbit has run away. The roof has not fallen. The pain that accompanied the hours of propping up the roof has since been forgotten. Besides, there is still food in the cave that is ready to be eaten – and that is always something to look forward to. It may well be that the lion has lost all faith in its fellow being, the rabbit. Its faith in the rabbit has possibly been shattered, but so what? It does not bear the rabbit any grudges. There is a lot more to live for. Perhaps after a long and time-consuming process, the rabbit will find it possible to return and be reconciled with the lion.

Part III:
Unfinished Business

Chapter Twelve

Reparation, Amnesty and
a National Archive

Mary Burton

The five-volume Report of the Truth and Reconciliation Commission was published and presented to the President of South Africa at the end of October 1998. It was immediately made available to Parliament and to the media, and received wide coverage in South Africa and internationally. Although there were challenges and criticisms within South Africa, the outside world has lavished praise on the Commission and on the perceived process of reconciliation in South Africa. Archbishop Desmond Tutu, Chairperson of the Commission, continues to be invited to speak on numerous platforms, and audiences respond warmly to his accounts of forgiveness, and to the changes that have taken place in South Africa. Here at home, however, the months have gone by and the Commission's Report and its recommendations seem to have faded from the minds of the decision-makers. The Commission itself is in suspension, except for a small team dealing with legal matters and with reparation, and for the Amnesty Committee, which must continue until all applications have been considered – a process that is likely to take several months more.

The Commission can take pride in many of its achievements, but in some areas it left important work still to be completed, or found that it could not meet some of its goals. Furthermore, there is unfinished business to be undertaken by other sectors of society if the tasks of the Commission are to be fulfilled, and if reconciliation is to be a possibility. The 'miracle' of reconciliation is seriously at risk of being damaged beyond repair if this work is not accomplished.

Let us consider the work still to be done by the Commission. The applications for amnesty have to be dealt with as soon as possible, and a report will then be produced by the Amnesty Committee. It is disappointing that the process is taking so long. The applicants, of course, have the right to have their matters considered, but it is awkward to have only one part of the Commission's work carrying on for so long. It is possible that the full Commission could be reconvened to consider the Amnesty Report, and then to prepare a codicil to the TRC Report. As time goes by, it seems less and less likely that the entire Commission could be available to do this work, but it is necessary to bring the entire body of work to a proper, formal conclusion.

The Role of the TRC

While the amnesty hearings and decisions continue to receive media attention, little is known about how the needs of the victims are being addressed. This is particularly painful for those who suffered and who now see the perpetrators being granted amnesty, while they themselves continue to feel abandoned. They have had to wait a long time for some kind of acknowledgement from the Commission, because it was necessary to undertake final reviews and confirmation of the findings for each of the over twenty thousand people who made statements to the Commission concerning the violations of their rights. Each person then had to be notified of the decision. This process has taken a very long time, but is now nearly complete, and the bulk of the notification letters have been sent out.

Those who were found to have been victims of gross violations of human rights (as defined in the legislation) are entitled to apply for reparation, the notification letter being accompanied by a Reparation Application Form. This is a fairly complicated document, and some people required assistance in completing it. Commission staff and a number of non-governmental organisations provided this assistance. When the Commission receives the completed form, the person's situation is assessed and the requisite information is then forwarded to the President's Fund, which pays 'urgent relief', which has been agreed to by Government. The process is under way, but not yet complete.

Another area in which the Commission still has a special responsibility lies in the sphere of information. When the Commission began its work, one of its expectations (and indeed an expectation of many people who had suffered violations) was that it would be able to give people more information about events that had been shrouded in secrecy. In a number of highly publicised cases this did occur, but in many thousands of cases it has not been possible to discover very much more than was already known. Furthermore, the TRC has not had the capacity to inform each deponent about the investigative work that was done, regardless of whether more information was gleaned or not. Many victims are understandably angry and disappointed about this. One of the possible remedies depends on the decisions still to be made concerning the TRC Archives. I shall deal with this issue in more detail later. The Commission itself is also preparing a sixth volume to its Report, which will contain a complete list of all those people who made statements to the TRC and were found to have suffered gross violations. It will also include all those people identified as victims through the amnesty process. With each name there will be a very brief summary of the violation that was suffered. The TRC hopes in this way to show a measure of its concern for those victims who were associated with its work, and to acknowledge their contribution to the process.

Finally, even though the Commission as a whole is in suspension until the completion of the amnesty process, it would be particularly appropriate for Commissioners to demonstrate their sense of accountability to the whole country by returning to the areas where it took statements and held hearings, in order to report back to each community. Many of the people who came forward to make statements and to give information feel that they have been ignored or forgotten. The Commission did not have the time or the capacity to undertake this task during its term of office, although there had been hopes that it would be possible. However, Commissioners could and should make themselves available for this work, possibly in co-operation with other organisations. This is happening to some extent through the participation of Commissioners in conferences and seminars, but it does not meet the needs of the more distant and less resourced rural communities.

The Role of Government

After the Report had been presented to former President Mandela and to Members of Parliament, there was a debate in Parliament that addressed major aspects of the Report, but did not consider the recommendations in any detail. Since then, the national elections held in April 1999 have brought in a new President, Cabinet and Parliament. It therefore seemed appropriate that the recommendations should be considered and responded to by the new government. The President's speech at the Opening of Parliament in February 2000 and the presentation of the national budget by the Minister of Finance were opportunities that could have been used to present Government's response. However, Government failed to take advantage of these opportunities. It is particularly urgent that a decision be made about the extent to which individual monetary reparation is to be made to each person found by the TRC to have been a victim. These people have been waiting anxiously, and expectations (which at first were generally modest) have grown.

The Commission's recommendations included a proposal for monetary reparation to be paid over a six-year period, to those victims identified through the TRC process. In addition, suggestions were made about memorials, community reparation and symbolic reparation. If the recommendation regarding individual financial reparation is *not* to be accepted, the government has a duty to inform the public about its intentions with regard to community reparation or symbolic reparation. These do have their place, but they need to be planned through a process of consultation and need to have wide acceptance, if they are to further the process of reconciliation.

When the question of reparation is discussed, it is imperative that the ongoing poverty and inequality in the country is addressed. Thousands of people suffered during the years of conflict and repression, and those who were formally identified as 'victims' are part of a much wider community in need. The Commission grappled with the question of whether it should forward a 'closed list' of victims to the government, or whether it should point to the fact that many more people suffered than it was able to access. It would be in the interest of peace and reconciliation if the government were to identify specific plans for development (particularly in the fields of education, work opportunities and health care) as part of a process of reparation and rehabilitation, and implement these with particular urgency.

The government should clarify precisely what its intentions are with regard to pursuing investigations and prosecutions in cases where amnesty was not sought or was refused. The Director of Public Prosecutions has been given the responsibility of taking this forward, and the Commission is making its assistance available.

Specific mechanisms should be sought for fostering reconciliation. President Thabo Mbeki has indicated that he is favourably disposed towards taking forward some of the ideas on a National Day of Reconciliation. This idea should not be allowed to drift away, but should receive attention before too much time elapses.

An urgent decision must be made about the TRC Archives: Where are they to be housed, under what conditions and with what resources? Who will have access to them, and how? The documents, as well as the films, tapes and other records, all form part of a national heritage, and need to be adequately cared for. If people had access to the stories of their particular family members, the archive would provide one way in which the families and descendants of those who suffered could find solace. A specific building could be made available. Provision for properly storing and cataloguing the material could be made. Mechanisms for facilitating access, while securing the confidentiality of certain records, would need to be put in place. Such a centre could provide one of the best possible memorial sites, and it is very likely that national and international funding would become available for it.

The Role of Society

The work of reconciliation, of dealing with painful memories and ongoing damage, needs to be tackled not only by the Commission and the government, but also by society as a whole. Non-governmental organisations, faith communities, educational institutions and individuals all have roles to play. Already artists are working their alchemy on the TRC material in drama, poetry, prose, painting and story telling (and probably other art forms too), recreating the experiences and enriching understanding.

If a TRC Archive is to be kept in a central place, copies of relevant documents and films could also be kept in 'Centres of Memory' located all over the country, perhaps in municipal libraries or schools. Churches and non-governmental organisations are expanding the process of working through trauma with 'Healing of Memories' courses. Groups of people and individuals have found ways of reaching out to express their regrets for the past and to contribute towards reconciliation. Many people have demonstrated that they yearn for ways of shedding patterns of division and conflict, but need help to cross these bridges.

A number of people have put forward the suggestion of a public 'Reparation Fund' to which they would willingly contribute. If reparation is not paid to individuals by the state, ways could be found to give particular assistance to those who need it most urgently, and whose need is a result of past violations; for example, educational opportunities for those orphaned by a politically motivated killing, or health care for someone physically or psychologically traumatised by torture, could be made available.

The concept of restorative justice, instead of a single focus on retribution and punishment, still needs discussion and thought. Not only legal experts, but also members of the public, should be encouraged to examine new ways of dealing with injustice and abuse.

International Responses

The TRC based many of its findings on the provisions laid down in existing international codes governing the conduct of people involved in war or in less formal conflict situations. There has been some public comment about whether persons acting on behalf of an oppressive government can be judged on the same basis as those acting on behalf of a liberation movement. The Commission made it clear that it held the apartheid system responsible for much of the suffering that was revealed. However, no party can be exonerated from human rights violations that were committed – international provisions identify specific violations of human rights that are not acceptable under any circumstances. Nevertheless, the experience of the TRC has revealed the need for more stringent international codes and more effective mechanisms for measurement. This area still needs more work, and South Africa has a significant contribution to make.

Conclusion

The South African Truth and Reconciliation Commission has attracted considerable international attention and admiration, and it raised great expectations in the hearts of many South Africans. Much remains to be done to complete the work, and it is very important that this opportunity is not lost.

Reconciliation will not come quickly, but in the meantime people need hope of a better life, and a belief that steps will be taken to deal with past injustice. We have to increase our efforts to improve matters, to do the best that we can – for the sake of South Africa, and for the sake of other troubled parts of the world, which look to us for guidance.

Chapter Thirteen

Burying and Memorialising the Body of Truth: The TRC and National Heritage[1]

Ciraj Rassool, Leslie Witz and Gary Minkley

On 15 April 1996, a large assembly gathered in the 'Municipal Castle' of East London's City Hall. They had filed past the 'equestrian memorial to the men of the Colonial Division who fell during the Anglo–Boer War'[2] and crossed the threshold to fill the six hundred seats in 'the wood panelled auditorium'. Clouding and clarifying their vision, the surrounding stained-glass windows of the hall depicted the 'four good qualities of municipal government: Plenty, Peace, Justice and Victory'.[3] Others ascended the 'beautiful marble staircase'[4] to bear witness to the first public hearing proceedings of South Africa's Truth and Reconciliation Commission. Before the media spectacle could begin, there was a long pause to give SABC TV 'time to cross to East London'.[5] Then, as the producer was alerted that the commercials had come to an end, the signal was given and Archbishop Desmond Tutu, Chairperson of the TRC, 'led his congregation in a Xhosa hymn'[6] and delivered a brief sermon to set the drama in motion: 'We are charged to unearth the truth about our dark past; to lay the ghosts of that past [to rest] so that they may not return to haunt us. That it may thereby contribute to the healing of a traumatised and wounded nation; for all of us in South Africa are wounded people.'[7]

Tutu, 'ritual performer', the man who 'minted our political discourse',[8] from the 'Rainbow Nation' to the 'new South Africa', now opened the gateway for a new history of reconciliation. The first witness then moved to her assigned seat in the Victorian hall to face the Commissioners on stage and to recover her 'small' story for the grand spectacle of the electronic monument to apartheid's past.

Beneath the arc of the television lighting, and in the glare of the camera, South Africa's 'real history', live and visual, and seeking to recover the past, was anchored into homes and public and private interior spaces in different corners of South Africa. In televised lessons of the past, broadcast to the nation, apartheid's hidden history was 'unearthed' and buried, and simultaneously revealed and revised as an essential 'building block' for the new nation.[9] This paradox, of the past being exposed and submerged, of history's simultaneous exhumation and burial (and reburial), lies at the heart of the workings and public representations of the TRC. Proposals to add symbolic images of the TRC's findings on to South Africa's heritage landscape – of Victorian halls, stained-glass windows, marbled staircases, and equestrian statues – are framed by this desire to memorialise and create a new national past, without disturbing the cemetery of history. This is particularly the case since all ideas on symbolic reparation and memorialisation, by necessity, have to encounter the dominant policy frameworks on heritage, which have been driven by the over-riding objective of national reconciliation.

Symbolic Reparation: The TRC Proposals

The TRC's Committee on Reparation and Rehabilitation was charged with the task of developing a cohesive policy on reparation and restitution. In terms of the Promotion of National Unity and Reconciliation Act, No. 34 of 1995, as amended, the TRC had to propose measures that would grant reparation to 'victims of violations of human rights'. It also had to aim to rehabilitate and restore 'the human and civil dignity' of such victims.[10] This legislative fiat posed difficult questions for the TRC. How was it to measure injury? And how was it to quantify suffering for the purposes of compensation?

Based on a programme of international research, national consultation and workshops with survivors, NGOs and academics, a number of recommendations were proposed to the President, the Cabinet and Parliament in 1998. The TRC argued that it was necessary to make sure that people who 'suffered gross human rights abuses [were] acknowledged by providing them with reparation'. This was necessary so that those 'severely affected by the conflicts of the past' could 'get over the past'. In making their recommendations, the Committee on Reparation and Rehabilitation had 'looked at individuals, communities and the nation as a whole', and noted that while reparation and rehabilitation could take the form of financial payment, this was not its only proposal.[11]

The Commission indeed proposed reparation and rehabilitation in five categories: urgent interim reparation, individual reparation grants, community rehabilitation, institutional reform and symbolic reparation.[12] A great deal of discussion has revolved around financial compensation, its magnitude, the timing of its delivery and the commitment of the government to honour the TRC's proposals. On the one hand, Archbishops Tutu and Ndungane have expressed their disappointment in what they perceive as the failure of the government to deliver on grants of reparation.[13] Within the governing party, the ANC, on the other hand, there has been a tendency to move the discussion away from an emphasis on money as compensation and to emphasise the possibilities of community restitution and symbolic reparation. Former Minister of Justice, Dullah Omar, under whose administration the TRC was brought into existence, has expressed the view that it would be impossible to compensate all the victims of apartheid. While recognising that there was some place for monetary compensation, Omar contended that 'our people did not conduct the struggle for individual reward'. There had to be a 'balance' between individual, community and general reparation in order to 'restore the dignity of apartheid victims', while the 'matters of reconstruction and nation-building' also had to be considered. This community reparation, he suggested, should take on symbolic forms such as the building of schools or monuments.[14]

The precise nature and form of such symbolic heritage displays have been the focus of some policy discussion within the TRC and in subsequent forums. The TRC, for instance, proposed the renaming of streets and public buildings 'to remember and honour individuals or significant events', the development of museums and the building of monuments through which events of the past could be commemorated. It also suggested that 'culturally appropriate ceremonies' be held and a 'National Day of Remembrance' be declared by the government 'to help bring about reconciliation'.[15]

The Department of Arts and Culture, Science and Technology (DACST), in its draft 'Portfolio of Legacy Projects', recommended that a 'national Wall of Remembrance' be constructed, along the lines of the Vietnam War Memorial in Washington in the United States, on which victims' names as well as the dates and places of their deaths would be inscribed. Drawing on the proceedings of a TRC workshop on symbolic reparation, DACST further proposed that alongside this wall, there should be an 'interpretation centre', perhaps in the form of an 'interactive museum', which would 'illuminate' the work of the TRC, 'its difficulties, its contradictions, its tales of heartbreak and inspiration'. This monument would 'contextualise the history of the era in which the sufferings and human rights abuses took place'.[16]

Some of these suggestions were echoed and expanded upon at a conference held eight months after the publication of the TRC Report to reflect on its achievements and failures. Calls were made by some for artistic productions in the form of dramatic performances and vivid paintings. Others, somewhat controversially, appealed for the death camps and sites of torture, such as Vlakplaas, to be declared national monuments, to pre-empt their disposal for commercial interests and their disappearance from the landscape of remembrance. But the idea that received most support was a proposal for an archive as a place 'where the records are available to people'.[17]

Museums and the Veil of Truth

While much has been noted in public debates about the failure of the state to provide financial compensation for victims, very little publicity has been given to the virtual lack of action in implementing proposals for symbolic reparation. Museums in South Africa have hardly begun to represent the process, evidence and findings of the TRC. The seeming official nature of the process and the sensitivity of the evidence may have inhibited curators, artists and cultural institutions from taking the initiative. Moreover, since the early 1990s, museums in South Africa have hardly taken up the challenge of reflecting upon apartheid's history. Instead, old collections and exhibitions sit uneasily alongside new displays – constructed as addenda – in which blacks have been merely added on to the existing pantheon of settler and white pioneering achievements, personalities, and local and national celebrities.

At the McGregor Museum in Kimberley, the add-on method has really come into its own. New displays place an emphasis on the pre-colonial past of communities categorised as 'indigenous'. Situated at the rear of the museum, this exhibition, called *Ancestors*, draws on both archaeology and what is seen as new history, to construct a racially inclusive past of the people of the Northern Cape. This enables the museum to insert itself into national debates about South Africa's public history and the 'heritage of all our citizens'.[18] At the same time many of the old displays, which contained even the most offensive of apartheid's self-depictions, were left untouched. And so, upon our last visit there in March 1999, in the large room on the first floor devoted to the Kimberley Regiment of the South African Defence Force, dioramas glorified the methods and tactics used by apartheid's army to counter the liberation movements of the 1970s and 1980s. These depictions of 'insurgents' and 'terrorists' repelled by heroic troops were the very type of histories that the TRC was trying to challenge.[19]

In contrast, the challenges of depicting the acts, deeds and mentalities of apartheid's death squads have been taken up in temporary displays, curated in the setting of art exhibition spaces. One of these art exhibitions which attempted to depict apartheid through an interaction with the process of the TRC was *Faultlines*, which opened on 16 June 1996, the twentieth anniversary of Soweto Day (now Youth Day). The setting for *Faultlines* was the Castle of Good Hope, a building that for centuries had been a symbol of insularity and colonial power. The exhibition presented itself as a visual inquiry by a group of artists into truth and reconciliation, and simultaneously attempted to initiate a process of 'liberating the castle'. Words from the archive of resistance at UWC's Mayibuye Centre, and those uttered and seen in the theatres of memory of the TRC, were re-imagined and re-inscribed into the space of the Castle.[20] Curated by Jane

Taylor, and including installations by, among others, Penny Siopis, Malcolm Payne, William Kentridge, Moshekwa Langa, Jane Alexander, Billy Mandindi, Randolph Hartzenberg and Clive van der Berg, its stated intention was to open up a 'proliferation of sites' where enquiries into the past could become 'everybody's terrain'.[21]

Many of the works challenged the sometimes very limited reading of the archive within a narrow apartheid/resistance narrative. Viewers were continually invited to visualise and imagine pasts that lay beyond the textual, archived record. Perhaps the most striking public display of the exhibition was a huge mural made of small black and white tiles, which appeared on the Leerdam wall of the Castle, below a set of flags indicating the various 'keepers of the Castle' over the past three centuries. Created by Vita Award–winning artist Kevin Brand, the mural replicated the photograph taken by Sam Nzima of two students carrying the body of Hector Petersen, the first person to be fatally wounded by police gunfire during the Soweto uprisings of 1976.

In spite of its intentions, *Faultlines* did not entirely provide the visual spectacle that would have opened up a proliferation of sites into apartheid pasts. Much of *Faultlines* remained within a narrowly documentary view of the past, with the artists offering their interpretation of an already 'uncovered' archive. This archive was by and large already classified into the very broad category of apartheid's resistance, with the apartheid archive continually being delineated and limited by the polar category of resistance. An examination of the visitors' book seemed to indicate that visitors hardly returned to *Faultlines* on completing their official Castle tour. Kevin Brand's mural, based on Sam Nzima's photograph, was not as distinct as one might imagine, the tiles often blending into the wall, making the image disappear.

In spite of its shortcomings, *Faultlines* possibly went further than any other exhibition in a museum to visualise the TRC in a public space. There have been other visual presentations, but these have either served as a backdrop for academic conferences, or have been individual works of art or installations by artists. One such exhibition was *Truth Veils*, which was held at the Gertrude Posel Gallery of the University of the Witwatersrand in June 1999 during the conference 'The TRC: Commissioning the Past'. Drawing on work by Kevin Brand, Bongi Dhlomo, William Kentridge, Zwelethu Mthethwa, Berni Searle and Penny Siopis, this exhibition brought together installations originally presented at other exhibitions, as well as specially commissioned work with an 'historical' component. Here, a selection of works of art addressed issues which emerged out of the TRC or on which the TRC was silent. Archival material was thus juxtaposed with commissioned work and pieces from the Wits Gallery's permanent collection.

The exhibition drew both praise and negative criticism. One critic claimed that 'the show forces viewers to examine the multiple and contradictory truths that haunt the physical and metaphorical landscapes of the TRC. The sheer volume and intensity of the material are overwhelming, as is the ragged journey between documentary footage of nauseating violence, and the more mediated conceptual surfaces of some of the works. I wanted all South Africans to see it.'[22]

Another review rebuked the curators for creating an exhibition that reduced art largely to 'an illustrative or, worse, decorative role', with its contents consigned to 'elements in a backdrop for the cheese-and-wine mingling of networking delegates'. While some pieces demonstrated the possibility of 'co-operation of aesthetic and intellectual capacities', the exhibition, for the most part, failed to 'bridge these functions ... in a more sustained manner'. The absence of a 'stronger motivating purpose' for the exhibition was adversely affected by an aestheticisation or, even worse, a sentimentalisation of 'testimonies and various tellings of apartheid's victims/survivors'. In criticising works by Sue Williamson, who 'aestheticised', and Jo Ractliffe, who 'sentimentalised', the reviewer suggested that the TRC had become 'something of an artistic and academic bandwagon, a shortcut to relevance and political importance. Overall, the exhibition's "greatest failing" was not to demonstrate a greater ethics of respect (and silence) in properly listening to what has been told'. For the 'greatest respect one can pay is the silence of attentive listening'.[23]

Sue Williamson is one artist who has consistently and with conviction tracked and engaged with the hearings of the TRC, attempting to represent its transcripts in aesthetic form. In *Truth Games*, a series of interactive pieces brought together images of accusers, defenders and events in question into works of art. Viewers were able to participate in considering processes of truth making by moving blocks of text around to reveal and obscure images of history.[24] In its successor exhibition, *Can't Remember, Can't Forget*, Sue Williamson added sound effects to visual constellations. Voice-over sound bytes of testimony and 'an ominous, swelling soundtrack composed by musician Arnold Erasmus' enabled viewers/listeners to interact with the intensity and the colour of the images. In this multi-sensory environment, exhibition goers were confronted with the question of truth as 'subject to manipulation, abuse and control'.[25]

Almost without exception, these works of art, which have drawn on and represented the processes of the TRC, occupy an ambiguous space between private artwork as aesthetic commodity and public rituals of memorialisation. They emerge out of a longer genealogy of 'resistance art', especially from the 1970s and 1980s, in which artists drew on, depicted and sold the South African liberation struggle. The occupation of this ambiguous space has been a source of professional admiration and heroic adulation. Yet there are sentiments that are deeply critical of the appropriative methods and self-inscription of artists and their works into the genres of struggle and recuperation. One critic went so far as to refer to apartheid being used as 'convenient subject matter' by the artist who 'expropriates the memory of what apartheid has already swiped or destroyed'.[26] While this might have been an extreme view, it does point to the question of what forms of art and aestheticisation are appropriate for the solemn processes and disturbing findings of the TRC. It also forces us to ask how artists are accorded recognition for their work, when they insert their art into the public domain as memorials to a traumatic past.

Truth Monuments and Commemorative Landmarks

One of the instant imaginings accompanying the end of apartheid was that many of the symbols and memorials that saturate the South African landscape would disappear. The central image of the conference 'Myths, Monuments, Museums', held at the University of the Witwatersrand in 1992, for instance, was the toppling of the Voortrekker Monument in Pretoria. Except for a few cases – most notably the removal of the statue of Hendrik Verwoerd from public display in Bloemfontein – these visual markers have remained in place under the auspices of a nation that regards racial reconciliation as foremost on the agenda. The most assertive demonstration against the historical depictions of past monuments has been to shroud them in black or to dress them in a very different cloth. General Louis Botha has been dressed up as a Xhosa initiate, and black cloths have been placed over a series of monuments in Johannesburg. In Adderley Street, Cape Town, Jan van Riebeeck was covered in black by an environmental awareness group, with a poster attached proclaiming 'No Shit on our Shore'. But these instances of the disturbance of monuments have been exceptions. On the whole, when the issue of removal or destruction of these monuments has come up for discussion, an all too familiar refrain has been repeated, that history would be destroyed – as if monumental structures encompass a neutral past.

The TRC has tended to approach these monuments in a similar reconciliatory fashion. This was most evident when the TRC hearings went to Bloemfontein. During a break in the hearings, the Chairperson of the Commission, Archbishop Desmond Tutu, took time off to visit the Anglo–Boer War Memorial in the city. Tutu made comparisons between the war and the subsequent antagonisms it had aroused, and the work of the TRC, which, he claimed, was trying to avoid a situation where the past would 'come back to poison the present'. He was particularly keen to point out that during the Anglo–Boer War in Bloemfontein, 'Afrikaners and black people had "stood together against [British] imperialism"'. This was presented as an example of racial reconciliation in the city, in particular, and the country, more broadly, even though there were very few 'white bums on the benches' at the TRC hearings.[27]

If the removal and reconfiguration of apartheid's monuments have proceeded at a snail's pace, the construction of new monuments has been haphazard and piecemeal. It was left to the government's Portfolio of Legacy Projects to present 'a coherent set of principles', which would enable different initiatives to be 'harmonised'. The Legacy Project had been set up 'to approve and facilitate the setting up of new monuments, museums … plaques, outdoor artworks, history trails and other symbolic representations'. These would ensure that 'visible reminders' of the 'many aspects of our formerly neglected heritage' would be created. While 'integrity' and 'broad participation' was emphasised, attention also needed to be given to the principles of 'inclusiveness' and 'balance'. With wide distribution envisaged throughout South Africa, new monuments would encourage a focus on national symbols with 'provincial and local participation'. The proposed Legacy Projects would thus 'communicate a stimulating message of rich cultural diversity' and 'acknowledge and celebrate South Africa's multicultural heritage'.[28] The result has been yet another instance of the add-on effect. The proposed Legacy Project on the Anglo–Boer War is set out precisely in these terms. In the words of the Minister of Arts and Culture, 'The broad impact of the war, not only on the Boers and the British, but also on black South Africans, will be captured.'[29] While many of the projects have been slow to get off the ground, the add-on effect has meant that they have had little impact on the urban and rural landscape of apartheid.

But a central discursive feature of the programme of monumentalisation was the life stories of leaders 'who have contributed to our legacy of democracy'. Commemoration sites and plaques would honour 'great patriots' who 'achieved honour against tremendous odds'. Their homes and 'other significant sites associated with them' should be declared national monuments and 'special, public ceremonies and exhibitions' should be held. A cenotaph 'for martyrs who fell in the armed struggle' and a cultural map of war graves were proposed.[30] Some leaders were singled out for special focus. Chief among them was Nelson Mandela. It was recommended that a project called 'The Long Walk to Freedom: The Mandela Trail' be introduced. This commemorative landscape of Mandela's well-established biography would offer 'a portrait of the society in which he lived and struggled' and give a 'context to his steadfast vision of a non-racial society'.[31] Other great men in the biographic pantheon envisaged by the Legacy Projects are Samora Machel, Albert Luthuli and Mohandas Gandhi. The latter, like Mandela, would have his own heritage trail, 'In the Footsteps of Gandhi', which would serve as a 'tribute' to his life and commemorate 'his bequest to the spiritual and political culture of South Africa'. It was particularly noted that Gandhi's philosophy 'resonated in the conduct of South Africa's "negotiated revolution", in the healing spirit expressed in our new constitution, and in the healing spirit of the Truth and Reconciliation Commission'.[32] The 'neglected heritage' that is being added on to the landscape of memorialisation is that of biographic monuments to leaders, who are being recast as the bearers of reconciliation.

Significantly, when the TRC promoted ideas of symbolic reparation in a popular publication to summarise its reparation and rehabilitation policy, it used a photograph of a street named 'Nelson Mandela Rylaan'.[33] Although the TRC consistently claimed that it was a vehicle of ordinary people, ordinary stories and ordinary lives, it was through naming and depicting the great men that the apartheid past uncovered by the TRC became memorialised. This may reflect a general discourse within the TRC process, in which testimonies provided by 'ordinary people' were continually inserted into a national narrative of great leaders and key events of resistance to apartheid.[34] As with the Legacy Projects, the populace is invited to view and narrate its history through the biography of great leaders.

While the Legacy Projects represent a carefully strategised and centralised programme on the part of the central state to add assertive and authoritative memorials and museums to the heritage landscape, local governments in different provinces have taken the initiative to establish community monuments. Some of these memorials have taken on the form of statues of great leaders of the struggle, such as the Mandela statue at Hammanskraal, and the Biko memorial in East London. Others have sought to depict resistance events through the medium of public art. In Cape Town, for example, the City Council has embarked upon a programme of memorialisation to 'honour heroes of the struggle'.[35] The first two of these monuments were unveiled on 21 March 2000, Human Rights Day, in civic ceremonies held at Guguletu and Athlone. A cement and stone memorial in NY1 Road, Guguletu, made by Lungile Maninjwa, honoured the Guguletu Seven, who were ambushed and killed by security police on 3 March 1986. In Thornton Road, Athlone, a sculpture made of similar materials by Tyrone Appollis commemorated the Trojan Horse incident of 1985, in which three children were killed by police who had hidden themselves on the back of a railway truck.[36]

At the unveiling in Athlone, the legacy of the TRC was presented in ambiguous terms. The TRC was explicitly praised for its role in uncovering truth. 'Without the TRC, the truth would not have come out [that] this thing was planned by the police,' suggested Minister of Transport and 'son of Athlone' Dullah Omar. Nevertheless, at Athlone the dominant image of reconciliation as the basis of nation-building almost receded from view. In a rhetorical flourish, the poet James Matthews listed the horrors of apartheid, and asked with irony, 'Do I offer bouquets of reconciliation?'; the choir and the assembled crowd deliberately omitted *Die Stem* as they sang the national anthem; and Dullah Omar, deviating from the dominant national task of reconciliation in his history lesson for the public gathering, referred to Human Rights Day as Sharpeville Day, thus evoking a memory of 'fallen heroes' who had sacrificed themselves in the face of 'apartheid violence'.[37]

Even though the Trojan Horse memorial was being presented as a monument to resistance, reconciliation was both the impetus and the underlying basis of its inauguration. The City Council had commissioned the memorial because 'many of the reconciliation processes' had revealed a lack of 'a proper memorial of the past'. Cape Town needed to 'honour the many who sacrificed their lives' and thus address the problem that many statues and sites depicted a racially exclusive history. It was the 'constitutional responsibility' of the council to build such memorials to redress the 'imbalances of the past'.[38] At the unveiling, however, the notions of reconciliation went further than a desire for a landscape of racial balance. In his speech, Omar drew parallels between the events of Athlone on 15 October and those in Guguletu the following day, when a 'second Trojan Horse incident' occurred, which resulted in more deaths occasioned by the same truck. This reference to the forgotten Trojan Horse served as a metaphor for re-reconciling communities on 'different sides of the line' on the basis of their common heritage of struggle. Continuing in this vein, Omar suggested that communities who had internalised the violence of apartheid, and who had turned on themselves through family violence, particularly against women, had to find ways to establish a society that respected human rights and was free of violence. It was in the principles and precedents of anti-apartheid struggle that the basis for such a reconciled society could be found.[39]

As in the case of installation art, these monuments, as forms of memorialisation, also raise questions about aesthetic integrity and artistic authority. The monuments at Athlone and Guguletu were specifically commissioned by a local authority. The artists who were commissioned, Tyrone Appollis and Lungile Maninjwa, were seen as rooted in their respective communities and as having the ability to express the sentiments and respond to the sensibilities of the community. This was not the case in East London on 12 September 1997, when Nelson Mandela unveiled a new monument to Steve Biko, erected alongside East London's City Hall, site of the first TRC hearing. The monument had been donated by 'admirers' of Biko, including Richard Branson, Peter Gabriel, Richard Attenborough, Kevin Kline and Denzel Washington. It was erected by the City Council of East London. At the time of its unveiling, the 'larger-than-life' brass statue of Biko was described as 'the first grand memorial to an anti-apartheid hero in a new South African city landscape still dominated by images of white men'.[40] However, the sculptor who had been commissioned to do the Biko memorial was none other than Naomi Jacobson, whose record as a sculptor of the African body had included a series of ethnological – even anthropometric – studies in bronze and cement fondu of 'tribal' heads and faces from colonial Namibia.[41] Through a remarkable twist of fate, the visual producer of racial representations had now become a memorial artist of post-apartheid heritage, commemorating a hero of the struggle. Naomi Jacobson's name, as inappropriate memorial sculptor, features prominently on the Biko statue in East London.

Installation artists, whose work depicts apartheid's traumas, such as Sue Williamson, continue to be celebrated in their own name. However, in Guguletu and Athlone in Cape Town, the names of Tyrone Appollis and Lungile Maninjwa, as functionaries of the 'community', have slid, almost naturally, into its nameless collective. The names of the artists neither appeared on the commemorative plaques, nor were they mentioned in the ceremonies on 21 March. Moreover, in a civic report on the unveiling of the 'simple monuments', published a month after its unveiling, Maninjwa and Appollis remained unacknowledged, while Mayor Nomaindia Mfeketo was depicted as 'a central figure throughout'.[42] As Lungile Maninjwa said immediately after the unveilings at Guguletu and Athlone: 'They talk about remembering, but they forgot about us.'[43]

The Body of Evidence

Benedict Anderson has suggested that 'it may be useful to begin a consideration of the cultural roots of nationalism with death, as the last of a whole gamut of fatalities'.[44] At the visual core of the TRC hearings were descriptions, representations and conflicts around bodies in various states of mutilation, dismemberment and interment within the terror of the past. Again and again, witnesses made claims in respect of body parts and human remains, making their visibility, recovery and repossession a metaphor for the settlement of the pasts of apartheid.

> Amanda Eunice Magwaca: I lost my husband, I want his remains, his bones, and I want to know what they did to him.[45]

> Ncediwe Mfeti: I have an interest in the commission making a thorough investigation ... even if it is his remains, if he was burnt to death, even if we can get his ashes, the bones belonging to his body, because no person can disappear without trace. If I could bury him, I am sure I could be reconciled.[46]

Within the TRC, exhumation, reburials and ceremonies of mourning emerged as a primary expression of symbolic reparation. Associated with death is the process of naming and marking in the form of the death certificate, the death declaration and, most visibly, in the headstone as the monument of remembrance. These are not merely private memorials. The rituals of death and the journeys and presentations of the body give the nation an inheritance that is recoverable, containable and ultimately buriable as the markings of history. Through the visuality of the body, presented in discrete and individualised cases, the past of apartheid becomes measurable, transparent, documentary and finite, allowing for the final fatality of apartheid and a rebirth at the threshold of a new nation out of 'exquisite cruelty'.[47]

The body of evidence presented to the TRC is also material. The physical markings of violence and trauma that were identified, held up and displayed provided tangible evidence of the individualised acts of history on each dismembered body: 'That hand, I want it back. That hand that is said to be in the bottle in Port Elizabeth, I would like it back.'[48] This kind of utterance, repeated again and again within the TRC process, identified body parts as sites of torture, physically recovering and re-membering the hidden past and uncovering and locating its source. Physical remains like those brought to a hearing by Joyce Mthimkulu and held up to be seen – 'scraps of her son's hair attached to parts of his scalp'[49] – envisioned these separate stories of remembrance with material life, truth's 'real' testimony. The physicality of mutilation was seen to embody the materiality of apartheid.

This metaphor of body parts was carried through even into representations of other dimensions of the TRC's operation and the TRC itself. With great regularity, the Commission was described as the 'truth body'. This body was seen to stand for 'our tortured past', 'our lost innocence', and seemed to demonstrate symptoms of 'paralysis', of 'hugs and restitution',[50] of 'pain that knows no political boundaries'[51] and of 'bringing grief'.[52] But the metaphor also extended to a more extensive grammar of history-making. So the demand for Dirk Coetzee's testimony to be heard was characterised as 'Dirk Coetzee's head sought' and the 'truth body' seen to be 'burying the past' and 'laying it to rest'.[53] Heads and burials, bodies and remains appear as metaphors for our attempt to resolve an unsettled past, functioning as powerful reminders of different histories that are being imprinted on the national memorial landscape.

While bodies of evidence litter the landscape of history, the call for an archive of truth seeks to institutionalise the empirical edifice of the body and its narratives into a world of letters.[54] Through the archive, the records of deaths and destruction, as well as the acts associated with them, will become both an account of a traumatic past and an appropriate memorial for the new nation. The archive, seen as a repository of empirical data, will also become a place of national recovery, providing healing and history. The body of truth, buried and protected in an archive, is invoked as the route to reconciliation.

Such calls may appear to open pathways to the past. Yet, they neglect the very way in which the archive and its fragments of evidence are constituted. Rather than opening 'windows on the past', the archive is 'itself an interpretation that influences future interpretations'.[55] Indeed the assembly of an archive can 'represent the fixing of knowledge, ending the instability of the meanings and the contestations over the truth of the past'.[56] In its process of silencing and forgetting, the archive frames what is delegated to it as a 'unified whole' and represses all that is left outside, 'denying its existence and consigning it to oblivion'. This consignation, ethical ordering and excision, Derrida suggests, is 'the violence of the archive', because it operates 'as an anticipation of the future'.[57]

Memorial Conclusions

In the landscape of memorialisation, the terrain of heritage has seen instances of recovery and repression. Artists have added their visual representations to the national quest for the truth of the past, while the state has embarked on a programme of commissioning the past. Scholars and cultural critics have debated the contours of memorialisation, as the state has displayed an ambivalence towards monetary reparation. All these initiatives claim the recovery and reconstitution – of history, the self and the nation. But in their efforts they are all subject to modes of repression. The authority of the artist, the appropriateness of state-directed projects, and the veneration of the archive pose uncomfortable questions for memorialisation. Heritage is never more repressive than when it claims to recover a national past. The discourse of reconciliation and the Rainbow Nation weighs heavily on the capacity of heritage to contest the past.

Chapter Fourteen

The Amnesty Process[1]

Linda van de Vijver

If these men be immune, then law has lost its meaning and man must live in fear.
Benjamin Ferencz, Chief US Prosecutor, Nuremberg

[T]here is a need for understanding but not for vengeance, a need for reparation
but not retaliation, a need for ubuntu but not for victimisation.
Postamble, South African Interim Constitution, 1993

The work of the Amnesty Committee of the Truth and Reconciliation Commission had not yet been completed at the time of writing this contribution.[2] A complete, global review of the amnesty process and the decisions of the Amnesty Committee was therefore not possible. This essay provides a broad overview of the amnesty provisions, why the process of amnesty was considered necessary, and whether it can be morally and legally justified. With regard to the latter, reference is made to both domestic and international law. Finally, two decisions of the Amnesty Committee are examined, with a view to considering the problems faced by the Committee in defining the nature of an act with a 'political objective'.

The Amnesty Provisions

The Amnesty Committee of the TRC was established in terms of Chapter 4 of the Promotion of National Unity and Reconciliation Act, No. 34 of 1995. Section 20 of this chapter authorises the Committee to grant amnesty to persons in respect of acts committed with a political objective if the following requirements are met by the applicant.

Firstly, the act, omission or offence to which the application relates must be an act associated with a political objective committed in the course of the conflicts of the past. An 'act with a political objective' is defined as any act or omission which constitutes an offence or delict associated with a political objective, and which was committed within or outside the Republic during a specified period by:

(1) any member or supporter of a publicly known political organisation or liberation movement on behalf of or in support of such organisation or movement, *bona fide* in furtherance of a political struggle waged by such organisation or movement against the state.

(2) any employee of the state in the course and scope of his or her duties and within the scope of his or her authority directed against a publicly known political organisation or liberation movement engaged in a political struggle against the state, and which was committed *bona fide* with the intention of countering the said struggle.

The following criteria must be taken into account in deciding whether an act is one associated with a political objective:

(1) The motive of the person who committed the act.
(2) The context in which the act took place.
(3) The legal and factual nature of the act, including the seriousness of the act.
(4) The objective of the act.
(5) Whether the act was committed on behalf of the organisation or institution of which the person who committed the act was a member.
(6) The relationship between the act and the political objective pursued, and the proportionality of the act to the objective pursued.

Secondly, in order to succeed with his or her application for amnesty, the applicant must have made a full disclosure of all relevant facts concerning the particular act.

A person who has been granted amnesty in respect of an act cannot be held criminally or civilly liable for that act, nor can any organisation or the state be held liable, and no person can be held vicariously liable.

Initially, applicants could apply for amnesty in respect of any act committed between 1 March 1960 and 6 December 1993. This latter date was later extended to 10 May 1994 by an amendment to the Interim Constitution. The final date for the submission of applications was 30 September 1997. The total number of applications received as at 30 June 1998 was 7 127. By this date, the Amnesty Committee had dealt with 4 443 applications and granted amnesty to 122 applicants, with a further 2 684 applications to be dealt with.[3]

The amnesty provisions were a necessary compromise reached during the negotiations which resulted in the Interim Constitution. The Postamble of the

Constitution called for the establishment of the 'mechanisms' required to address the issue of granting amnesty. The amnesty process placed the onus on perpetrators to apply for amnesty, and demanded the full disclosure of all relevant facts before it would consider granting amnesty to applicants. In this regard it is unique, and differs from the 'blanket amnesties' that were granted in, for example, Latin America. The amnesty process thus has the potential to meet the victims' need for truth and public acknowledgement, as the information provided is intended to assist in providing an accurate account of the nature and extent of human rights violations. In this way it was envisaged that we would learn from the past and strive to ensure that 'never again' would such transgressions of human rights occur.[4]

Nevertheless, of all the work of the TRC, it has been the one issue to cause the most debate, controversy, and criticism. In support of the work of the Amnesty Committee, Archbishop Desmond Tutu states the following in his Foreword to the TRC Report: 'Amnesty is not meant for nice people. It is intended for perpetrators. There are strict criteria to be met and we believe that the Committee has used those criteria to determine whether or not amnesty should be granted. Amnesty is a heavy price to pay. It is, however, the price the negotiators believed our country would have to pay to avoid an "alternative too ghastly to contemplate".'[5]

While most commentators would agree that the process is necessary as part of the promotion of 'national unity and reconciliation in a spirit of understanding which transcends the conflicts and divisions of the past',[6] words of caution, if not dissent, have been uttered. One commentator has put it thus:

> [T]he moral compromise entailed in suspending the rights to justice of the few who could succeed, is a bitter pill to swallow and has consequences which are borne by the entire society. This [Mxenge] family did have the evidence and information to succeed with criminal charges and civil claims. They not only suffered a dramatic and terrible loss, but they also had a killer who came forward and confessed – even before the TRC was established. In denying this family the right to a criminal prosecution and a potential civil claim…we have the kind of fundamental compromise of principle which lends itself to the perception of state sanctioned impunity for these gross violations of human rights.[7]

Challenges to the Amnesty Provisions

The applicants in the AZAPO case,[8] who were families of prominent anti-apartheid activists, applied for an order declaring the granting of amnesty by the

Amnesty Committee unconstitutional. Their contention was that the consequences of section 20(7) of the Promotion of National Unity and Reconciliation Act, which permits the Committee to grant amnesty, were not authorised by the Interim Constitution. The applicants also contended that the state was obliged by international law to prosecute those responsible for gross human rights violations, and that section 20(7) therefore breached international law.

The Court acknowledged that this section of the TRC Act limits the right of the applicants in terms of section 22 of the Interim Constitution to 'have justiciable disputes settled by a court of a law, or where appropriate, another independent or impartial forum'. However, in terms of section 33(2) of the Constitution, violations of the rights are permissible either if sanctioned by the Constitution or if justified in terms of section 33(1) of the Constitution (the limitations clause). The Court held that the Postamble to the Constitution sanctioned the limitation on the right of access to court.

The Court acknowledged that the granting of amnesty to perpetrators was difficult to accept, but justified the process as follows:

Every decent human being must feel grave discomfort in living with a consequence which might allow the perpetrators of evil acts to walk the streets of this land with impunity, protected in their freedom by an amnesty immune from constitutional attack, but the circumstances in support of this course require carefully to be appreciated ... Secrecy and authoritarianism have concealed the truth in little crevices of obscurity in our history. Records are not easily accessible, witnesses are often unknown, dead, unavailable or unwilling ... That truth, which the victims of repression seek so desperately to know is, in the circumstances, much more likely to be forthcoming if those responsible for such monstrous misdeeds are encouraged to disclose the whole truth with the incentive that they will not receive the punishment which they undoubtedly deserve if they do.[9]

The Court further noted that amnesty was a crucial component of the negotiated settlement itself, without which the Constitution would not have come into being. The Court also held that the amnesty process was not inconsistent with international norms, noting that:

Although the mechanisms adopted to facilitate that process [of a transition to democracy] have differed from country to country and from time to time, the principle that amnesty should, in appropriate circumstances, be accorded to violators of human rights in order to facilitate the consolidation of new democracies was accepted in all these countries [Chile, Argentina, El Salvador] and truth commissions were also established in such countries.[10]

The Court held further that international law was not relevant to determining whether section 20(7) was inconsistent with the Constitution. In support of this opinion, the Court noted that international conventions and treaties only become part of the municipal law of South Africa if they are incorporated into the municipal law by legislation.[11]

Furthermore, subsections 231(1) and (4) of the Constitution provide that an Act of Parliament 'can override any contrary rights or obligations under international agreements'.[12] Section 35(1) of the Constitution instructs courts engaged in constitutional interpretation only to 'have regard to public international law applicable to the protection of rights'.[13] The Court thus held that these principles of constitutional interpretation militated against finding a cause of action for domestic criminal prosecution in international law.

Amnesty and International Law

The insufficient attention paid by the Constitutional Court to international law in determining the constitutionality of the amnesty provisions in the AZAPO case has been the subject of some criticism. One commentator has stated:

> International law may not be binding, but it seems clear that the court should attempt as far as possible to interpret broad or ambiguous constitutional provisions in such a way that they conform to international law...Throughout the judgement international law is treated almost as an afterthought. After so much parochialism and outright hostility to international law by South African courts under apartheid, one would think that the new Constitutional Court would devote more time and intellectual rigour to considering the topic.[14]

It has also been noted that the Court did not refer to international human rights law which has had a significant influence on the South African Bill of Rights. Section 22 of the Constitution is similar to provisions in the American Convention on Human Rights and the American Declaration on the Rights and Duties of Man. These instruments of international law formed the basis of decisions of the Inter-American Commission on Human Rights in the 1990s, which stated that amnesties granted in a number of Latin American countries were not consistent with international human rights law.[15]

In 1973 the UN General Assembly had adopted the *International Convention on the Suppression and Punishment of the Crime of Apartheid*. Article 1 of the Convention defines apartheid as a crime against humanity, and declares that inhuman acts resulting from the practices of apartheid are crimes that violate the principles of international law and constitute a threat to international peace and security.[16] Article 3 provides that international criminal responsibility will apply to individuals and representatives of the state who commit the crime of apartheid.[17] How then can we reconcile the granting of amnesty to perpetrators of 'inhuman acts resulting from the practices of apartheid' with the principles of international law?

Diane Orentlicher argues that there exists a norm of international law to prosecute 'especially atrocious crimes' in domestic courts.[18] In her view, the principle that crimes against humanity must be punished is so important that it justifies an exception to the fundamental principle of international law that requires respect for national sovereignty. In support of her argument she cites one of the *Principles of International Co-operation in the Detection, Arrest, Extradition, and Punishment of Persons Guilty of War Crimes and Crimes Against Humanity*, which were adopted by the UN General Assembly in 1973. This principle states that 'crimes against humanity, wherever they are committed, shall be subject to investigation and the persons against whom there is evidence that they have committed such crimes shall be subject to tracing, arrest, trial and, if found guilty, to punishment'.[19]

According to Orentlicher, 'the law proscribing crimes against humanity has commanded a uniquely powerful commitment by the world community, which has resolved emphatically that it will not countenance impunity for massive atrocities against persecuted groups'.[20] In applying this rule to transitional societies Orentlicher adopts an uncompromising approach.

Firstly, she notes, it is a well-established principle of international law that a state's duties under international law are not affected by a change in government. Therefore, if an outgoing government did not fulfil its duty to punish atrocities, its successor is generally bound to fulfil the obligation. Furthermore, a state cannot evade its duty to punish crimes against humanity simply to satisfy antagonistic military forces or to promote national reconciliation. Ratification of an amnesty law through a form of democratic procedure would not alter this conclusion since nations cannot avoid their international obligations by enacting inconsistent domestic law.[21]

In a response to Orentlicher, Carlos Nino examines the case of Argentina.[22] An amnesty law had been passed by the military government in Argentina in 1983. Raul Alfonsin was elected President at the end of 1983, and created a commission to investigate human rights abuses. This was followed by the selective prosecution of military leaders, after Congress had declared the amnesty law null and void. Carlos Nino argues that the results of President Alfonsin's investigation and prosecution of human rights abuses in Argentina 'were nearly all that could be morally required under the circumstances':[23]

> The success, limited though it may be, was the product of a delicate equilibrium between many factors. I do not think that the equilibrium would have been fortified by the sort of international duty Orentlicher advocates. An international duty would perhaps have even further destabilised the process of promoting the trials. A legal duty selectively to prosecute human rights violations committed under a previous regime is too blunt an instrument to help successor governments who must struggle with the subtle complexities of re-establishing democracy.[24]

Antonio Cassese notes a number of important reasons why crimes against humanity should be recognised as being within the province of international criminal law.[25] Firstly, there is a need to establish a public record of atrocities committed – as an acknowledgment of peoples' suffering, and to offer them some sense of relief. The establishment of a judicial historical record also prevents a subsequent denial of events that occurred, and ensures that horrific events are not forgotten.

Secondly, justice is a preferable response to revenge, 'amnesia', or amnesty. The failure to prosecute atrocities leads to a desire for revenge, and it also allows future leaders to act with impunity. With regard to 'amnesia', or forgetting, we need only quote the words of Eli Wiesel, during the trial of Klaus Barbie: 'If we forget those people we murder them twice.'[26] Finally, the prosecution of perpetrators of war crimes and crimes against humanity establishes individual responsibility for the crimes, rather than the collective assignation of guilt.

Cassese accordingly argues that any law on amnesty in response to crimes against humanity is contrary to international law, but does concede that truth commissions, and the granting of amnesty, can be a better solution in certain circumstances, as in the case of the South African TRC.[27] A truth commission may be a suitable solution for a nation which is emerging from an oppressive regime and which is undergoing a transition to democracy. It may also be very difficult, if not impossible, to conduct prosecutions in certain countries, because of the secrecy and efficiency of the oppressive regime. Finally, truth commissions are to be preferred when the society is too fragile to survive the effects of politically charged trials. In other words, such a solution may be an acceptable compromise reached in the interests of peace.

Martha Minow[28] argues that an enquiry needs to be made into the particular historical and political circumstances of each case of atrocities before deciding how to proceed. Her contention is that if the goal of nation-building has real prospects for success, then efforts to reconcile, and probably the establishment of truth commissions, should be pursued. Furthermore, if the new government was a result of a political compromise rather than a total victory, then promises of amnesty should be considered. While amnesty will constrain responses to the atrocities committed, such constraints may be justifiable if the compromise produces a genuine democracy.

Paul van Zyl notes that prosecutions may simply not be possible in certain circumstances: where the prosecution of security forces that remain powerful may undermine the political transition, and where practical considerations prevent the prosecution of any more than a small minority of perpetrators.[29] In such circumstances, he argues, a state may derogate from its international obligations to prosecute and punish perpetrators of human rights abuses, if the following conditions are met:[30]

(1) There is persuasive evidence that the state is unable to prosecute those responsible for human rights abuses, or is only able to prosecute a small minority of perpetrators.

(2) The majority of citizens have accepted the transitional justice policy adopted by the state. For example, legislation may have been passed by a democratically elected parliament.

(3) The state is committed to complying with its other international obligations. For example, the state must attempt to discover the truth about victims, to identify perpetrators, and to provide reparations to victims.

(4) The failure to prosecute must not obstruct the state's commitment to fulfilling its broader international obligations. For example, blanket amnesties cannot be granted as this conceals the truth about the commission of human rights abuses.

Charles Villa-Vicencio has added two further conditions to Van Zyl's criteria:[31]

(1) The state must be committed to the reparation of victims and survivors.

(2) A decision not to prosecute must be transparent and victims must be consulted about the decision by means of an appropriate structure.

Villa-Vicencio argues that if these conditions are met, and if prosecutions are neither possible nor helpful, a state should pursue the truth commission route rather than attempting the prosecution of perpetrators:

The question is whether legal absolutism involving a 'duty to prosecute' is necessarily helpful or realistic in national and international disputes involving genocide, terror, and similar forms of lawlessness. Popular perceptions of law as the 'bulwark of freedom' and being 'of God not man' perhaps need to give way to more humble metaphors that capture the tension between political vicissitude and the codification of the law ... [L]awyers and judges need to adjust to what is required in a particular situation to meet a given goal. The necessity for this adjustment militates against the notion that a 'duty to prosecute' is a legal absolute.[32]

The Ideals of Restorative Justice

The advantages of the truth commission process will be appreciated if we examine the process within the context of 'restorative justice'. The TRC Report notes that the Postamble of the Interim Constitution constituted a 'commitment that included the strengthening of the restorative dimensions of justice'.[33] Restorative justice is defined in the TRC Report as a process that:

(1) aims to redefine crime: It shifts the primary focus of crime from the commission of offences against a faceless state to an understanding of crime as offences against human beings.
(2) is based on reparation: It aims to heal and to restore all concerned – firstly, victims, but also offenders, their families and the larger community.
(3) encourages victims, offenders and the community to be directly involved in resolving conflicts, with the state and the legal profession acting as facilitators.
(4) supports a criminal justice system that aims to hold offenders accountable, to ensure the full participation of both victims and offenders, and to overcome injustice.[34]

The TRC Report notes further that an 'individualised, accountable amnesty process' can make a 'contribution to the rehabilitation of perpetrators and their reintegration into the new society'.[35] In this regard, Judge Mahomed has stated that, without amnesty, 'both the victims and the culprits who walk on the "historic bridge" described by the epilogue will hobble more than walk to the future with heavy and dragged steps delaying and impeding a rapid and enthusiastic transition to the new society at the end of the bridge'.[36]

Accordingly, it is argued that the amnesty process is both a necessary and valuable step towards achieving restorative justice, which 'seeks to recover certain neglected dimensions [of the established justice system] that make for a more complete understanding of justice'.[37] The quest for restorative justice constitutes the means by which both victims and offenders, as well as their families and communities, and the nation as a whole, can learn to live together after decades of political conflict and violence.[38]

Defining 'Acts with a Political Objective'

Having established that, to some extent, consensus has been reached on the legal and moral aspects of the amnesty process, let us turn to a consideration of the more practical application of the amnesty provisions. It has been noted that 'the more interesting and controversial decisions'[39] of the Amnesty Committee were those concerned with determining whether the acts in question had a 'political objective'. Let us consider two decisions that were the subject of considerable public debate and criticism.

The one decision concerned the application of two members of a right-wing political party, Janusz Walus and Clive Derby-Lewis, who had murdered Chris Hani, a prominent ANC and SACP leader. The applicants contended that the murder was committed in order to 'create a situation where the followers of Mr Hani would cause widespread mayhem in the wake of the assassination'.[40] This would provide the right-wing with the opportunity to step in to restore order and take over the government of the country. The applicants also argued that the 'general position of resistance adopted by the Conservative Party as expressed in the speeches and utterances of its leaders amounted to implied authority for the assassination'. Their application was refused, as the applicants did not satisfy the requirement that the murder was committed 'on behalf of or in support of' the Conservative Party 'bona fide in furtherance of a political struggle waged by' the Conservative Party. In fact, the Conservative Party did not propagate violence at the time of the murder, and never approved or condoned the assassination. The application was also refused as the Committee was of the opinion that the applicants had not made a 'full disclosure of all relevant facts'.

Opposition parties and relatives of the two applicants were vociferous in their condemnation of the TRC after the refusal of amnesty, arguing that it was 'common sense' that Hani's assassination was politically motivated.[41] It was also suggested that the TRC was 'a mouthpiece of the African National Congress' and was applying the amnesty provisions inconsistently.[42]

In another case, four members of the Azanian People's Liberation Army (APLA) had murdered Amy Biehl, because she was white. The murder had not been ordered by the organisation, although it was consistent with the general ideology of the organisation. All the applicants 'submitted to the slogan "one settler, one bullet"',[43] which had been chanted at a meeting attended by the applicants immediately prior to the murder. The applicants stated that '[t]o them that meant that every white person was an enemy of the Black people. At that moment to them, Amy Biehl was a representative of the white community. They believed that by killing white civilians, APLA was sending a serious political message to the government of the day. By intensifying such activity the political pressure on the government would increase to such an extent that it would demoralise them and compel them to hand over political power to the majority of the people of South Africa'.[44]

The Committee accordingly decided that 'it must be accepted that their crime was related to a political objective', and granted amnesty to the applicants.

On the face of it, the planned murder of a prominent political leader is of a more 'political' nature than the random killing of a woman who simply happened to be in the wrong place at the wrong time. While these decisions are not intended to be presented as representative of the decisions of the Amnesty Committee, they raise some interesting questions. Is it possible to reconcile these decisions?

In the Walusz/Derby-Lewis decision, the Committee examined the legal requirements, and rightly concluded that the murder did not have a 'political objective' as defined by section 20 of the TRC Act. The decision on the application of the killers of Amy Biehl appears to be less carefully considered. Rather than examining the requirements of the Act, the committee simply concludes that 'it must be accepted that their crime was related to a political objective'. Yet it has been suggested that the murder was 'a mindless savage attack',[45] and an act of 'wanton brutality, like a pack of sharks smelling blood'.[46] The Committee also did not consider the question of whether there had been a full disclosure of facts. In fact, one opinion regarding the decision was that 'it became clear the truth would remain forever open to speculation and dismissal'.[47]

One commentator has suggested that the Committee was influenced by the fact that the amnesty application of Biehl's killers was not opposed by her family,[48] while the application by Hani's killers was opposed by the Hani family. It is further noted that 'section 20(3)(e) of the Act (acting in response to an order of a political party) was the pre-eminent and overriding criterion considered'.[49] Yet how the chanting of a slogan, a common feature of political rhetoric, can be regarded as an order, remains unclear.

Conclusion

While the amnesty process may have been necessary to the process of South Africa's peaceful transition from a repressive regime to a democracy, we need to be mindful of what such perceived condonation of violence means in the long term. Ronald Slye addresses the issue of 'privileging political violence' under the amnesty process, and notes that this 'sets a dangerous precedent for future political advocacy, and a dangerous signal to a society that is trying to establish popular legitimacy based on the rule of law'.[50]

Brendon Hamber has questioned 'whether knowing the truth actually translates into the prevention of future violence and more specifically into substantial institutional change':[51]

> In South Africa, the link between past and present calls for more draconian police action is not sufficiently explored. The impact of the granting of amnesty for political crimes, even with the truth recovery process, is also something that will only be seen in years to come. However, if the lessons of other countries are taken seriously, the threat of large-scale impunity and authoritarianism does loom. South Africa cannot recognise the roots of violence and criminality as residing in the historical dehumanisation of the apartheid system and simultaneously ignore the impact of politically motivated amnesties on the credibility of the criminal justice system.[52]

As we consider the impact of the amnesty process on reconciling and building a new nation, let us also not forget the question of whether the process contributed to the healing of individuals. In this regard, I will conclude with the words of the mother of Sicelo Dlomo, whose killers were recently granted amnesty: 'Myself, I disagree with amnesty. I am the sufferer. I'll never forgive these people who killed my son. This pain will never come out. We are unable to work because the pain is too much.'[53]

Part IV:
After the TRC

Chapter Fifteen

Of Lions and Rabbits: Thoughts on Democracy and Reconciliation

Njabulo Ndebele

You will all remember that famous tale of a lion that caught a rabbit in the act of stealing. Rabbit was helping himself to a meal he had found in a trap that Lion had laid in a cave. Lion was enraged and pounced on the thief. As Lion was about to devour the culprit, Rabbit screamed in terror that the cave was collapsing, and that both of them would be saved if Lion, who was stronger, propped up the ceiling with his powerful limbs, while Rabbit rushed to find help.

Lion, caught in the suddenness of a dangerous moment, and instantly grateful that he had not recklessly eaten a source of vital and timely wisdom, immediately sprung up on his hind legs, propping up the roof of the cave with his front paws. Rabbit sprinted away, and, of course, never returned. Lion remained there in the cave, a living rafter, holding his dear life in his own paws, and starting to realise with dread that he was becoming tired. Doom hung over him as he pondered why lions were also made to be vulnerable to fatigue. He prepared to be buried alive, as he finally let go of the roof. Nothing happened. His relief at being alive was momentary, as it dawned on him that he had been fooled.

Without doubt, many of us will admire this small animal, Rabbit, for getting out of a tight spot by means of superior intelligence. Our popular trickster did it again, reducing the brawny king of the jungle to a piteous fool. The narrative frame of the tale paints a story of escape in which the weak enjoy a moment of triumph over the powerful, and live to tell the story. The dramatic sequence of entrapment and escape attracts and captures our imagination, enabling us to recognise the most apparent point of the tale: that there is entertainment to be had at the expense of the powerful. By the same token, we appreciate the value of intelligence.

In the imbalance of forces at play, the rabbit was in danger of losing its life. In order to safeguard it, he deftly manipulated the lion into a position of trust, such that the instant violation of that very trust became a condition for restoring the balance, allowing him to escape with his life, and thus both of them continued to live. The moral considerations involved in breaking the trust become secondary to the higher goal of escaping with one's life.

We think further that, in the final analysis, no harm befell the lion. The cave did not fall in. He suffered only a slight loss of dignity, by being fooled. Furthermore, he remained behind to eat his catch.

But that would not necessarily be the end of our dialogue with this tale. Some would argue that the rabbit is not such a wonderful fellow after all; and that the lion does have redeeming qualities. When faced with the prospect of saving both his own and the rabbit's life, the lion was willing to suspend the act of meting out punishment, and to choose, rather, to co-operate with the rabbit, for the safety of both. What if, indeed, the cave had been collapsing? The rabbit's capacity to discover danger matched the lion's willingness and ability to keep danger at bay. There is thus a real basis for mutual trust, no matter how temporary.

All is well until we remember that the rabbit is, in fact, a petty thief. No matter how brilliant he is, anyone who dares enter into a pact with him in future is warned there is a good chance you may be betrayed. The very ease with which Rabbit got out of a tight situation should tell you to watch him closely in future. While you may admire his escape, he also leaves you with niggling anxieties. Surely there is something volatile and incendiary about this intelligence. The energy and brilliance of its inventiveness may not always wait for moments of self-defence to act themselves out. Rabbit may take advantage of anyone, and strike in unprovoked malice, wreaking havoc and causing chaos. Certainly, not only will Rabbit live to tell the story of his escape, he will live to steal again.

The tale presents us with at least two frames of interpretation. There is the larger frame, dependent on the most observable features of the drama: entrapment and escape. It yields an unproblematic hero against an obvious, powerful victim who deserved what he got. The lion, whose catch was being stolen, receives less sympathy in the light of his intention to punish, perhaps with death, a small but clever fellow. The second frame emerges from within the larger frame and subverts it. It is the frame of detail, which emerges as we ask further questions about the tale. It yields us a somewhat complex, vulnerable victim, and a brilliant hero with serious flaws. We discover, to our surprise, that we might sympathise with the lion, and have serious reservations about the rabbit.

There are many in this country who think that South Africa has been a cave facing inevitable collapse, and that its black citizens have been left holding the roof, while the whites have escaped to get on with their lives. But if the majority black population is the lion, it should be remembered that this lion was no longer king of the jungle, the colonial wars of conquest having taken his title away. And the rabbit had been stealing all along, albeit within an enabling code of legitimacy imposed by himself. The power of the black majority was rising steadily, leading to negotiations, which culminated in the elections of 1994. The contours of a lion were emerging once more, and the rabbit, fearing that he may be pounced upon, could see the value of the story of a collapsing cave.

Many have the definite impression that Rabbit is happily getting on with his life. Isn't this impression confirmed by a casual inspection of the divided landscape of our country? Who is still rushing to catch trains, buses and taxis, paying heavily to travel long distances to work and back? Whose children still attempt to get an education in overcrowded classrooms? Who is still dominating as boss in the workplace, and is still privileged to think and plan and issue instructions, albeit with decreasing confidence? Who continues to live in better houses and suburbs, playing cricket and rugby, while others live in neglected townships, playing soccer? Certainly, in this view, the negotiations leading to the elections of 1994 – and such instruments as the Truth and Reconciliation Commission – look like one big trick to keep the lion propping up the roof.

But the situation can get a little fuzzy, if not downright complicated. Let's consider this. According to the South African folklore of tribal politics, in which we, like all people, indulge from time to time, the Xhosas have become the rabbit running this country, while all the other tribes, black and white, are holding up the roof. But as if that were not enough, have you noticed all the new popular words – *Masakhane, Bambanani, Zama Zama*[1] – that prompt people to do something? There is no doubt about it: Rabbit language is taking over, while the other African languages are holding the roof. Of course, if the Xhosas are running this country and the Zulu language is running amok, it follows that the conspiring Ngunis are walking away, while everybody else is holding the roof.

Look at the Afrikaners, the big lions that dominated the army and the police, and probably still do, and who ruled with an iron fist for close to half a century. Look at them. They are holding the roof, while the English walk away with their second passports! This world is truly unjust. What about the coloured people in the Western Cape? Are they not holding the roof, while the alliance of the Democratic Party and the New National Party is walking away?

What about poor black workers? Are they not holding the roof, while the exploitative, manipulative, capitalist rabbits continue to prosper? Recently, new capitalists have arrived. They are as black as the workers. They may be rabbits themselves, but may feel that they are holding the roof, while the rest of their rabbit capitalists, who don't have to worry about being accused of greed and corruption, get on with their lives. And at some point the ANC must have felt that it was being made to hold the roof, while the Communist Party walked away with the Reconstruction and Development Programme. Or have black men left black women holding the roof? It's all very confusing.

Who, then, is the lion? And who is the rabbit? Identities seem to shift constantly, depending on the classification of participants in any particular situation. They can fall into any of the categories of race, ethnicity, class, political affiliation, geographical location, gender, generations, and numerous others. Depending on the function or location of a category in a particular drama, someone may be a lion today and a rabbit tomorrow. There is a constant ebb and flow of shifting identities in South African history, which constantly subvert any tendency towards simplification.

In fact, the greatest simplification, apartheid itself, constantly worked against the complicating forces of history, enforcing a tendency towards denial among its beneficiaries, often through willed ignorance. The victims of apartheid tended to expose and affirm the hidden realities of interacting identities as they converged daily in the drama of economics. But until recently they lacked the capacity to turn this tendency into a strategic advantage. This is what seems to be happening now: The real possibilities of South Africa seem to lie in our ability to face the full implications of our move towards interaction, away from the past of artificial separation.

Perhaps our tale, and the different forms it takes as its characters wear different masks, enables us to take stock of the extent of social anxiety in South Africa. For example, there is the fear that magnanimity has not only been misunderstood for weakness, but that it has, in fact, become weakness. There is the fear that the perception of a loss of face may restore old feelings of inferiority, or rage, in proportion to the increasing levels of confidence amongst those who lost very little else besides political power. There is the fear that right and constitutionality, for which the magnanimous fought long and hard, are being used to frustrate redress, to insult and to denigrate. There is the fear that the demands of a modern state, itself subject to powerful global forces, might overwhelm the project of emancipation.

However, all the rabbits that have left the cave to the lion realise that they have to return to it. At what cost? Exactly what do they stand to lose or gain? They are not sure what the lion really thinks, but they know that he is in power. They feel guilty about what they have done to the lion in the past, but pride will not allow them to acknowledge the feeling. They may resort to the Constitution and the Bill of Rights to assert themselves, but many may feel that doing so does not really enable them to push their anxieties away. What is to be done?

The story is told that, in the run-up to the historic elections of 27 April 1994, a solution had to be found to the increasing conflict between the ANC and a white right that could be mobilised effectively into an army of resistance. We are told that a series of meetings took place between the ANC and the generals of the white right. It is reported that the first meeting turned out to be one of the defining moments on the road towards freedom and reconciliation:

'If you want to go to war,' Mandela told the generals, 'I must be honest and admit that we cannot stand up to you on the battlefield. We don't have the resources. It will be a long and bitter struggle, many people will die and the country may be reduced to ashes. But you must remember two things. You cannot win because of our numbers: you cannot kill us all. And you cannot win because of the international community. They will rally to our support and they will stand with us.' General Viljoen was forced to agree. The two men looked at each other ... [and] faced the truth of their mutual dependency.[2]

It would appear that when the combatants recognised the balance of forces, a catastrophe that would have had an impact far beyond South Africa was avoided. This 'mutual dependency' that was recognised is, in fact, a central feature of South African history. Until that moment, this mutual dependency had been characterised as a range of binary relationships which defined apartheid: master–servant, oppressor–oppressed, superior–inferior, giver–receiver, taker–loser, urban–rural, white–black: the first pole positive, the second negative. In this pattern of relationships, only the claims of the positive pole were recognised as defining the South African national landscape, giving the only legitimate meaning to it. There was no balance. Power flowed mainly in one direction, defining the relationships as largely instrumental, as one sector of society serving another.

The new dependency is based on the recognition of an emergent balance, which hinges on a common awareness that the survival of South Africa is a common responsibility. It suggests a major shift in the flow of power and influence. A dependency once based on, and sustained by, the organising of oppression was reluctantly recognised as a condition of stability from which a new order could emerge. To make a new society possible, an apocalyptic disintegration of South Africa was perceived not to be in anyone's immediate or long-term interest. The preconditions for reconciliation were laid by acknowledging a common interest to preserve an imperfect zone of stability, in which the scale of morality was nevertheless seen to be tipped in favour of an emergent order.

There is another way in which the new binary relationship distinguishes itself from the old one. It is infinitely more interactive. Its character can be exemplified in the following questions which reflect many of the unresolved anxieties already mentioned: How can South Africans reconcile 'the black demand for majority rule [with] white concerns stemming from this demand'?[3] How can the redistribution of resources and opportunities occur without the destruction of the economy? How can South Africans protect the rights of its white citizens without entrenching the privileges of old? How can the cultural rights of groups be reconciled with a broader national project? How is equity possible in the face of continuing historical disparities in housing, education, income, media control, and in the broad cultural and linguistic dominance of a demographic minority? How is justice possible when perpetrators of terrible crimes and human rights abuses can walk away through amnesty?

These questions present us with formidable dilemmas, which demand to be addressed simultaneously. In doing so, we may need some working principles to guide our conduct. One of them is that it is important that we do not arrive at answers to problems too easily. Indeed, the difficulties faced in arriving at answers represent an investment towards the value of possible answers. This applies even when the solutions arrived at are later found to be unfeasible. The energies invested are of inestimable value in allowing parties a greater opportunity to fully establish their good faith. It is in the interactive struggle for the solutions that new relationships are forged between individuals, and within and between groups. The overriding challenge of governance is to provide and maintain public space for the resolution of difficult dilemmas to take place in a controlled, legitimate environment.

There is yet another principle. Our ability to shift into several identities in a multicultural society allows us the potential to locate ourselves within questions posed by others. Dwight Boyd has stated that 'anyone with an effective sense of democratic reciprocity will recognise that, as exactly the same claim can be made from the perspective of any of the differing cultures in question, any democratic collective answer to the question [of conflicting values, for example] must locate the speaker within the problem and must be affirmable from positions different from one's own'.[4]

The interactivity of our new binary relationship is a humanising space of immense complexity. It is infused with risk-taking, trust and suspicion, intrigue, transparency and obfuscation, real and imaginary boundaries, negotiation and imposition, honesty and dishonesty, concealment and discovery, alignments and realignments, shifting identities, the pains and horrors of lapses, loyalties and betrayals, idealism, greed, courage, doubts and certitudes, redeeming truths and insights leading to optimism and progress, and the excitement of infinite possibility. Interactivity releases energies that not only have the potential to render the inherited binary relationship inherently transient, but also threaten to explode into a multiplicity of relationships. The potential of an individual South African to establish relationships across inherited boundaries is a real feature of our national experience today. If there is any one thing the hearings of the Truth and Reconciliation Commission have done, it is to reveal the range of matters that lie at the centre of our interactive public space.

I will recall some elements of these matters very briefly. They range from the personal, through the experience of local communities, to issues that involve government and governance. In this way, the TRC attempted to take us through a wide spectrum of contemporary South African history in the period it was mandated to cover. It made a valiant attempt at an impossible task. But its reach, given the short life of the Commission, has been extensive.

The Report brings together the real extent of what the victims of apartheid have known all along: pervasive, state-organised violence, which permeated the entire fabric of South African society. It documents the pains and traumas of individual people. It shows us random invasions of homes, arrests of family members, often followed by their inexplicable disappearance. Some families would later witness exhumations of disappeared family members now painfully accounted for. It shows how communities of the oppressed, torn apart by fear, suspicion and mistrust, desperate to build and preserve unity, were led to hunt down people thought to be informers and collaborators. They met a gruesome fate at the hands of others who were convinced that they were working in the interests of the community.

Documented also is the history of 'bannings and banishment', a spate of judicial executions, 'the use of force on crowds and gatherings', 'torture and death in custody', infiltration, abductions, interrogations and gruesome assassinations. We see how law enforcement agencies had become corrupted by a culture of impunity as a result of laws that granted them sweeping powers. The TRC was able to capture vividly the history of perpetrator brutality. In some memorable incidents, former torturers demonstrated their methods of torture.

The homelands were another arena of gross violations of human rights. KwaZulu-Natal, the Ciskei, and KwaNdebele, in particular, are brought into close focus. These homelands, the Commission reports, suffered 'cyclical attacks and counter-attacks' in which 'the line between victims and perpetrators blurred, as comrades and vigilantes assumed both roles. The youth, relentlessly pursued by the *Imbokodo*[5] for months, initiated their own campaign against suspected vigilantes, frequently resulting in the most brutal of murders'.[6] In the townships, people experienced 'necklace killings', the burning of houses of suspected spies, and a reign of terror by groups acting in the name of liberation.

We are shown the war machinery of the apartheid state and how it wreaked havoc on neighbouring countries, violating their sovereignty in pursuit of South African citizens. The state intimidated and harassed civilians of those countries and bombed targets at will, turning the whole of southern Africa into a zone of insecurity.

We are also shown the agonies and ecstasies of waging a war of liberation. While the liberation movement was engaged in a just war, and there were many successful strikes against the apartheid state, there were also failures of judgement, particularly under threat of infiltration by the enemy. Fear and insecurity, resulting from a sense of being invaded from within, led to some gross violations of human rights in which comrades became enemies to be arrested, tortured and purged. Lapses in chains of command led to some 'unplanned military operations' with outcomes impossible to anticipate. The call for the country to be rendered ungovernable may have been a genuine strategy to incapacitate the state; but it also had unintended consequences.

The picture presented is broad, but incomplete. However, such incompleteness was to be expected. It was unavoidable in view of the limitations placed on the lifespan and activities of the TRC. Nevertheless, we do have sufficient material to enable us as South Africans not only to acknowledge the terrible aspects of our immediate past, but also to ponder the meaning of that past for the future. The TRC, its hearings, and its Report on their own cannot bring about reconciliation. It began a process that should continue.

We are in a position to make some observations based on our account so far. The anticipated disintegration of South Africa in a conflagration of violence did not take place. Prior to the elections of 1994, many South Africans saw threatening clouds of apocalyptic disintegration gathering in the sky. That the collapse did not occur has led to the peaceful transfer of power being called a miracle. But I believe that we do need to try to look for explanations. We may find, for example, that South Africans were more predisposed to co-operation than to fighting to the bitter end. If we take the farms of South Africa as a case study, based on the remarkable scholarship of Charles van Onselen,[7] we may find significant binding factors at play, which may explain better why the fear of disintegration may be less significant than a greater awareness of what Van Onselen called the 'nooks and crannies' of social life during the days of apartheid, wherein the daily intricate intimacies of co-operation between master and servant may have created reluctant bonds, particularly in the farming and sharecropping communities.

Coated over by layers of paternalism, authority flowed one way, resulting in various kinds of mutual accommodations, adjustments and readjustments. Such relationships may also have played themselves out on the factory floors, in business offices, in shops and in the civil service, albeit with increasing levels of conflict and rebellion over time. Indeed, the bonding that took place among the major political negotiators seems to me too remarkable to have had no historical or social grounding of some kind. The South Africans who sat together at the negotiating table were not total strangers to one another.

What has now happened is that power relations have changed radically, and relationships that were mediated by paternalism, largely unarticulated, have come into the open, the tensions being fully articulated. The verbalisation of pain and suffering through an official medium, recognised to be a result of change that was fought for, combined with the enforced revelation of the deeds of perpetrators, complicates relationships that were based on internalised assumptions. Articulation raises the social temperature, while it actually needs to be lowered. It is this temperature-lowering mechanism that demands our attention, for bringing down the temperature should translate neither into platitudes nor into buying time. Rather, it should translate into visible measures for improving the lives of the victims of the past, who, even though they are still at a severe disadvantage, ought not to experience themselves as victims any longer. The temperature-lowering mechanism is a direct matter of social policy.

Two other related factors may also have contributed to lessening any push towards disintegration. Firstly, the geographical boundaries that delineate South Africa enjoy a near-universal acceptance in the country, although subject to some low-intensity threats. For example, the Afrikaner far right wing entertains hopes for a mythical country of Afrikaners only. This demand is based on an elastic constitutional interpretation of the rights of cultural communities. Mandela's government, faced with the impossibility of meeting this demand, seems to have tried to find a way of living with this issue, rather than rejecting it out of hand, rather as if it were a recessive gene that will, from time to time, rear its head and then disappear again.

Secondly, an increasingly familiar commercial and industrial landscape has progressively drawn the population into a unifying pattern of economic activities. A uniform landscape of major commercial chains throughout the country has, over decades, become a feature of the country. Spatial familiarity of this sort renders the land familiar, less strange and more accommodating wherever you may be in the country. This kind of familiarity may have a binding effect, which cuts across the particularising tendencies of geographic and ethnic location. Linking the country is a complex network of communication systems that promises every citizen access to every part of the country. This sense of universal accessibility was seen as an achievement even before CODESA was under way. Later on, land restitution and economic empowerment emerged as attempts to translate optimism and potential into tangible gains.

These observations may lead us to ponder a little on the possibilities for democracy and reconciliation in an environment charged with both expectation and the counter-pressure of limitations we are called upon to accommodate.

Reflecting on its activities in Duduza, the TRC Report makes the observation that:

Reconciliation involves various stages of development and change. One essential step is dialogue between adversaries. The victim-oriented and perpetrator-oriented aspects of the Commission's work are broken into separate functions. Victims tell their stories in one forum and perpetrators in another. The interaction is thus often mediated purely by the media coverage of these events. While this may have been useful in providing safe space to engage them, or to maximise information gathering, the subsequent step of facilitating more direct dialogue still needs to be addressed.[8]

This view of reconciliation enables us to go well beyond the moral and religious connotations around it which have thus far dominated discourse. It pushes us towards the notion of reconciliation as a human project grounded in social process. The affective connotation of reconciliation as forgiveness often gains centre stage owing to our tendency to focus on its intended results rather than on the difficult process of working towards it. Reconciliation is something to be earned by South Africans. They will achieve it through facing the uncertainties and contradictions inherent in our transformation. To navigate through a great deal of human turbulence, the Constitution and the Bill of Rights provide a democratic framework within which the process of reconciliation can act itself out.

The Commission's Report is very clear on this point. Responding to 'erroneous notions of what reconciliation is about', the Chairperson of the Commission in his Foreword – on its own a remarkable document – asserts that reconciliation 'is not about being cosy; it is not about pretending that things were other than they were. Reconciliation based on falsehood, on not facing up to reality, is not true reconciliation and will not last'.[9] Later in the Report the point is made again: '[R]econciliation without cost and pain is cheap, shallow and must be spurned.'[10]

In fact, the more I read the Commission's Report, the more I became convinced that the predominance of religious connotation in the public discourse on reconciliation resulted from a tendency for many of us to focus on the Chairperson of the Commission as a man of God. The linking of reconciliation directly with forgiveness closed off many other angles of discussion. If reconciliation was a matter of confession and forgiveness (and there were not many white people confessing and asking for forgiveness), if things change while they remain the same, then it should not be surprising that there could be room for cynicism, disillusionment, and the feeling by many of having been fooled, of holding the roof. How do we avoid this kind of feeling?

Let us return to our tale. Rabbit has walked away. Maybe he wants to come back and talk. But he is too clever to put himself at risk. He fails to appreciate the extent to which his cleverness may create intractable problems for him, something that happens when his anxieties are hidden by his cleverness; when his instincts lead him to create and maintain the illusion of continual control. The best among the rabbits recognise the illusion for what it is. But to face it squarely, they will need the lion, who will constantly have to reassure the rabbit that he (the rabbit) will not be grabbed and eaten; that he has a role to fulfil in the social ecology. But Rabbit may find it difficult to make the move. Making the move is the primary responsibility of Lion. After all, it was the latter who embarked on the liberation struggle. And while doing so, he had told everyone what he learnt from Paulo Freire, who wrote thirty years ago that:

> [I]t is only the oppressed who, by freeing themselves, can free their oppressors. The latter, as an oppressive class can free neither others nor themselves. It is therefore essential that the oppressed wage the struggle to resolve the contradiction in which they are caught; and the contradiction will be resolved by the appearance of the new man: neither oppressor nor oppressed, but man in the process of liberation. If the goal of the oppressed is to become fully human, they will not achieve their goal by merely reversing the terms of the contradiction, by simply changing poles.[11]

Indeed, who is complaining today that the future is bleak? The results of a survey, which sought to find out how optimistic or pessimistic South Africans are about the future since the advent of democracy five years ago, were released a few months ago. It was found that those South Africans who lost very little in material wealth and general standard of living, whose rights were never really violated, were significantly pessimistic about the future, and were most unhappy with the current changes. Many are disgruntled and either want to leave, or are nostalgic about the past. Freire wrote perceptively about them:

> But even when the contradiction is resolved authentically by a new situation established by the liberated, the former oppressors do not feel liberated. On the contrary, they genuinely consider themselves to be oppressed. Conditioned by the experience of oppressing others, any situation other than their former seems to them like oppression. Formerly, they could eat, dress, wear shoes, be educated, travel, and hear Beethoven; while millions did not eat, had no clothes or shoes, neither studied nor travelled, much less listened to Beethoven. Any restriction on this way of life, in the name of the rights of the community appears to the former oppressors as a profound violation of their individual rights – although they had no respect for the millions who suffered and died of hunger, pain,

sorrow, and despair. For the oppressors, 'human beings' refers only to themselves; other people are 'things'. For the oppressors, there exists only one fight: their right to live in peace, over against the fight, not always even recognised, but simply conceded, of the oppressed to survival. And they make this concession only because the existence of the oppressed is necessary to their own existence.[12]

In contrast, those whose human rights were violated consistently by a racist state were hopeful about the future. They realise that they have gained something from the changes. They have far better access to water, electricity, telephones and houses than before. They experience a great deal more official responsiveness.

Lion is the maker of the future, he has the responsibility to take the initiative. It is not enough for him to read in the Commission's Report about Duduza that 'the Commission hearing was not attended by local whites' and then leave it at that. It would be even more worrisome if he saw a sign of racism in this. 'They are racists!' he may shout, not telling us anything new. Of course they did not attend; they were unlikely to attend, unless they had been somehow engaged on the matter. They are highly unlikely, in general, to come out and say they need help. And if Lion does not come forward and exercise responsibility, he will see a recurring situation in which there is more and more racism to condemn. Then Lion would be in real danger of reducing the enormous power of his position by retreating and voicing endless complaints about racism. What a disappointment it would be!

In the total scheme of things, the reason why millions of Africans in South Africa have a poor education is largely because of our history of institutional racism. But a question arises whether racism as causal explanation can provide us with all the tools necessary to find appropriate solutions. For example, we may find that certain aspects of the legitimate struggle for liberation may have compounded the problems of education. Looking for racists to blame will not improve the situation.

This question may suggest that in the new democracy with a black majority at its centre, white racism as a central category of analysis may lead to a distortion of the real issues of a post-apartheid society. It may condition us to focus on what we were denied in a time past, to which we cannot return, rather than on what we need to create for a future to be made. To clarify this matter, a further question may be asked: Is there a difference between resorting to race as an inherited category of social and political analysis on which to ground public policy, and resorting to race as a corrective tool to measure the progress of a policy of achieving equity, particularly in opportunity? In the former case, race carries the entire burden of explanation; in the latter, race is subsumed under a strategy of change.

One of the fundamental challenges in South Africa is whether the emancipated manage to avoid the conceptual trap of viewing white racism as the central problem of the country. We need to find appropriate development strategies – strategies that will ensure that the African majority ruling the country no longer feels the social and political pressures that resulted from being characterised as black; strategies that render such characterisation as ultimately irrelevant, because it is transcended by attainable emancipatory goals. This point does not want to deny that some continuing inequities are a result of a racist past. Rather, it illustrates how a subtle change in the point of departure can lead to significant new possibilities.

For many South Africans, the last five years have been a time of euphoria. New horizons came into view as people assumed new roles and new responsibilities. There have been many remarkable successes, but many fingers were cruelly burnt too. In the enthusiasm to serve, some tried to cut corners, perhaps unwittingly, resulting in painful reminders that public service is subject to systems and rules of accountability. Even more painful was the realisation that, although some of the systems and rules were an inheritance from a painful past, their legal force could not simply be pushed aside. There are, of course, others whose euphoria enabled them to see calculated opportunities for quick enrichment.

Whatever their nature, many actions were seen and experienced as the enactment of freedom. For example, new laws passed by Parliament over the last five years have been more significant as definitive acts of freedom than as instruments of regulation. The regulatory impact of these laws will become more pronounced as they are tested against the capacity of the new state, the people and their government to deal with all the problems unravelled by the TRC. The separation of law-making as an act of freedom and law-making as regulation is only beginning now. The question is at which point we will feel that the lingering effects of the former are sufficiently rooted in the national consciousness to be assumed to inform regulation and the maintenance of the state. When does social practice change from creativity to maintenance? In many areas of national life, that transition is still a long way off. But as we move along, we may wish to set up indicators to measure and trace the continuum of transition.

The real point is that as our new laws, which embody the emancipatory vision of the new democracy, are tested against the harsh realities of unsolved problems, such as those that will arise from the challenge of reconciliation, frustrations may result. Such frustrations may mistakenly be taken to indicate the failure of addressing the larger issues, while, in truth, these setbacks call for a redoubling of effort. That is the point at which danger lurks: when the lion is convinced that he has been duped.

The TRC was one mechanism for resolving difficult dilemmas. But by no stretch of the imagination did it offer a permanent solution. Rather, it allowed the country to cross a particular river of time and circumstance. Seen in this light, the negotiated settlement appears to have unexpectedly delivered a will to live with unresolved tensions, while seeking to ensure that the painful wound of tension does not fester. Instead, opposite poles can enter into controlled engagements in which fixed positions are gradually abandoned until a comfortable, if imperfect, solution is accepted as a *working position*. These working positions are crucial to ensuring that compromise is understood not as manipulation, but as offering substantial opportunities to the negotiating parties.

The TRC has yielded a potentially destabilising complex of dilemmas. The resulting tensions need to be handled with a high level of social skill, a rigorous intellectual disposition, and an inventive social imagination.

In conclusion, I offer a third and final frame of interpretation for the tale of Rabbit and Lion. Lion has to accomplish a mammoth task. He cannot afford to be distracted by the antics of a clever little fellow like Rabbit. Indeed, his task is to prop up the roof. The roof has not yet collapsed, and there is a meal to share in the cave. Hopefully, Rabbit will learn to make a humble request not only to share what is in the trap, but also to bring along a contribution.

Chapter Sixteen

The Rule of Law

Richard Goldstone

About ten years ago, the then United States Ambassador to South Africa, Ed Perkins, held a dinner to celebrate the two hundredth anniversary of the United States Constitution. I recall that at that dinner, his wife Lucy, who was Chinese, spoke of the occasion on which she became a United States citizen and attended a ceremony at a federal courthouse, where she took the oath that all new citizens are required to take by United States law. She said that she was surprised that she was not called upon to swear allegiance to the United States, or to the President, or even to the people of the country. Instead, she was required to take an oath of allegiance to the Constitution. As someone who came from Taiwan, she was shaken by the concept that one owed allegiance to a constitution.

South Africa has proudly joined the group of democratic nations that are governed by a supreme constitution and a Bill of Rights, which constrain all three branches of government. Certainly our Bill of Rights, expressly under our Constitution, constrains not only Parliament and the executive, but also the judiciary itself. All South Africans are subject to and constrained by the same provisions of our Constitution. We are still very much at the beginning of a learning process in respect of this entirely new system. We were not educated to understand it and even now very few of our school students or university students are being taught the effects and the consequences of being constrained by a constitution.

This lack of understanding emerged early in the life of our new Constitution, as a result of the opinion of the Constitutional Court in its very first case on the constitutionality of the death penalty. When the unanimous judgement came out, striking down the death penalty as being inconsistent with a number of provisions of the Bill of Rights, the National Party called for a referendum. They said that it was unacceptable that there was no death penalty in South Africa, and they were sure that the majority of South Africans would vote in favour of the death penalty. If they did, the Constitution should be amended to make allowance for the death penalty. Within a few hours, President Mandela responded on television, saying that he was surprised by this call for a referendum, as he thought that there had been agreement in the negotiations to a constitutional state, and to a Bill of Rights, which would bind all South Africans. Nevertheless, he said that if we wanted to rule by referendum, we should do so, as he did not have any great objection to it from a political point of view. He said, however, that he would add a second question to the first one on the death penalty. The second question would ask whether the majority of South Africans thought that white South Africans should be allowed to keep the property they had acquired over the past three hundred years.

His response was, of course, a wonderful lesson in the civics of a constitutional state, where the Bill of Rights is designed to constrain and keep within certain limits even the majority will represented in a democratically elected parliament. It is not an easy matter for the former disenfranchised majority in South Africa that was oppressed by a supreme parliament to accept that its will can now be thwarted by a provision in a supreme constitution.

The Truth and Reconciliation Commission has rendered an important service to our nation by graphically illustrating what happens in a country that operates under a repressive and undemocratic constitution – an aspect that has not been given sufficient attention. It has illustrated how the negation of the rule of law made possible the criminal violence perpetrated on so many victims by the state, and even from outside the government. The negation of the rule of law allowed for corruption, fraud and other illegal means of self-enrichment on the part of those whose duty it was to use the resources of the state for the benefit of all its people. There were many public scandals during the apartheid era: Muldergate; the prison conditions that, when reported in the *Rand Daily Mail*, resulted in criminal prosecution against the newspaper; and many instances of theft of public funds. All those scandals had one thing in common: They came to the attention of the public either through leaks by disgruntled insiders, or through the courageous work of investigative journalists. There was no constitutional mechanism that resulted in those scandals becoming public, and the public scandals that surfaced were unquestionably no more than the tip of the iceberg. The few remedies common law granted the victims of human rights abuses were whittled away by successive oppressive statutes, one after the other.

Let us now look to the present and the future, and at the system that has replaced the old order. We have our Constitution that enshrines the rule of law, and our Bill of Rights that is wider in its scope of protection than any other in the world. The provisions enabling people to approach the courts to protect their own and other people's rights are extremely wide. Virtually all persons and organisations now have the right to approach our courts to prevent the infringement of their rights. We have a host of independent officials and institutions, whose duty it is to protect the rights of citizens and to ensure that public servants do not abuse their positions, particularly through corruption. We have the Public Protector, the Auditor General, the Human Rights Commission, the Gender Commission, the Independent Complaints Directorate of the South African Police Services, and, of course, the Special Investigating Unit headed by Judge Willem Heath. The public scandals that have come to light since 1994 – and there have been no shortage of them – have been a result of the work of these public watchdogs. We no longer have to rely on leaks or investigative journalists, although I am not suggesting that they have no role to play. Even with the best will in the world, these officials and bodies cannot uncover everything that needs to be revealed.

These institutions may or may not have uncovered every scandal or instance of corruption, but I have no doubt that we are no longer looking merely at the tip of the iceberg. Their work is an effective deterrent: The likelihood of public scandals or police brutality, for example, going undetected has been significantly reduced. Such instances have not become non-existent, because there are criminal elements even in the best democracies; people break the law, and human rights are abused. However, the probability of criminal activity coming to light is obviously far greater in a democracy than in an oppressive society, and that is the important deterrent from which a constitutional state benefits.

The challenge facing us now is how to bring radical change to our skewed society relatively swiftly, within the discipline required by the Constitution. The fact that we will not achieve true reconciliation until we have a more evenly balanced society has been noted by Dumisa Ntsebeza and Albie Sachs. As long as we have a huge discrepancy between the 'haves' and the 'have-nots' – especially when the 'haves' are white, and the 'have-nots' are black – we cannot have a stable society. We shall remain in a state of instability. The question is how quickly we can transform the unstable, unfair, unjust situation that faces us every day of our lives. The removal of these inequities in ways that are consistent with the Constitution is the nettle we must grasp. Simply removing explicit racial or gender barriers does not produce an integrated, inclusive society that embraces members of historically excluded groups. As Harvard law professor Martha Minow has noted, colour-blindness leaves in place racialised thinking that benefits whites and seems rational because it is so familiar.[1] Yet at the same time we must recognise that there are obvious dangers inherent to racial classifications.

Taking into account the needs and the dangers to which I have referred, we need to consider the very carefully worded provisions of section 9(2) of our

Constitution. Section 9 is the equality clause, and section 9(2) deals with what is called affirmative action in the United States. Section 9 provides that equality includes the full and equal enjoyment of all rights and freedoms, and provides for the promotion of 'the achievement of equality, legislative and other measures designed to protect or advance persons, or categories of persons, disadvantaged by unfair discrimination'.[2] Legislative measures may be taken at all levels of government to protect or advance persons who were previously disadvantaged. The section contains its own death sentence, as it were, because as fewer South Africans are disadvantaged, as more South Africans are given the benefit of equal education and equal employment possibilities, so it will become more difficult for affirmative action to pass constitutional muster, and that is the huge advantage of dealing with the ills of an oppressed majority. We will recover – although I do not wish to underestimate how much time it will take – and we will achieve the benefits of these sorts of policies far quicker than they will be achieved in countries like the United States.

While appreciating that we face a daunting task, the implementation of a Constitution – a radical change from the past – is a wonderful start. The new institutions of our Constitution are doing their work and their progress is there for all to see. We should not forget that only ten years ago Nelson Mandela and many of his comrades were still in prison. Parliament and the government have quickly learnt to live with a system that requires action subject to constitutional constraints.

The financial costs of democracy are high, and I doubt whether we considered the financial implications of democracy. It is far cheaper to police by way of detention without trial and third-degree methods of torture than to police under the constraints of a Bill of Rights. It is far cheaper not to have constitutional jurisdiction in all our courts, and far cheaper not to have to finance the myriad of required constitutional bodies. But I am convinced that it is the best form of government, and acceptance thereof is growing around the world. I was amused, a few weeks ago, when I visited the European Court of Human Rights in Strasbourg, which is located in a magnificent new building. The European Court has state-of-the-art facilities and yet the judges were complaining that they were short of funds for many luxuries to which they felt entitled. I thought to myself how we would give anything to have, in our courts, a mere ten per cent of the facilities that are available to the judges in their new, magnificent building in Strasbourg.

There is a tendency in our country to blame the Constitution for many of the ills of our society. It is admittedly more difficult, as well as more expensive, to solve crimes without paid informers and the other trappings of an oppressive society. We should not forget, however, that the oppressive system that we have left behind did not succeed in preventing crime. It did succeed, more or less, in keeping crime from predominantly white communities, but at immeasurable cost to the moral fibre of our society. It is folly to contemplate abandoning or diluting the values enshrined in our Constitution. We have to find solutions to our problems by means that are consistent with the rule of law. I have no doubt that we can do so – we have done so thus far, and we shall continue to do so.

People are more likely to act decently and morally in a decent and moral environment. Let me give you one practical example. In 1992, my fellow Commissioners and I on the Goldstone Commission decided that we needed investigative units. We needed our own investigators to use the powers given to us, particularly the power to search and seize. If we had not had our own investigators, we would not have been able to raid Military Intelligence in November 1992. We certainly would not have been able to investigate the information we got from Chappies Klopper, which led to further information about Vlakplaas and the activities of Eugene de Kock. The question was whom we could approach to serve as investigators. Clearly our only option was the South African Police. With the approval of the Cabinet, I requested the Commissioner of Police to second fifteen appropriate South African policemen to the Commission. To ensure that they were indeed suitable, we published their names in every newspaper in South Africa, asking any South African to advise us if they possessed information that made those policemen unfit to serve with an independent commission. That, of course, placed a huge constraint on the Commissioner of Police, because he knew that any South African meant *any* South African, and that we would take into account any representations we received. We published the names of the fifteen policemen, and we received objections from the Eastern Cape to one of the policemen who had been recommended. The complaints appeared to be with merit, so this person was not appointed. Another was nominated, against whom there were no complaints. As an additional method of protection, we decided to appoint senior policemen who had been seconded to us by the European Union to act with each of the five units that were established. Furthermore, senior South African lawyers were made available by the Law Society to work with the investigative units. These units performed a magnificent service, enabling the Commission's investigators to investigate the criminal activities of their own police colleagues, since they were still members of the South African Police. The same people who would have thought nothing of following an order to commit a criminal offence given by their superiors in the police force, behaved magnificently in a different environment, and were very willing and happy to be doing so. People are malleable, and all of us are largely influenced by the traditions, the laws and the morality that infuses the institutions in which we work.

Achieving true equality and engendering compliance with the rule of law are two challenges we face. We cannot afford to fail. If we fail in our democracy, we will have to resort to some of the methods that the Truth Commission laid bare. If we fail, we shall be failing not only our own country, but also our continent, for the eyes of the African continent are set on us. Most Africans want us to succeed, because they realise that if we succeed, then there is hope for democracy elsewhere in Africa. I also believe that the eyes of many countries outside our continent are on us. If we do not succeed in our democracy, there is little hope for democracy in other parts of the developing world.

Chapter Seventeen

Fighting Corruption

Willem Heath

Corruption in a developing democracy such as South Africa constitutes a violation of the most basic of human rights. Corruption deprives people of housing, education, medical treatment and their basic human needs. This is the unfortunate reality that faces our country.

On numerous occasions, through the work of the Special Investigating Unit and its predecessor in the Eastern Cape, the Heath Commission, I have seen the human rights of people being violated by corrupt government officials, by corrupt and greedy businessmen and by people who have no concept of pain and suffering. Perpetrators of corruption are unscrupulous people who are intent on enriching themselves.

Democracy exists only when basic fundamental rights are protected, and if corruption makes that protection impossible, there is no true democracy. Present and past corruption must therefore be mercilessly uncovered and people must pay the price for their corrupt actions. Not only does the Special Investigating Unit do exactly that, but we publicise our actions so that those guilty of corruption know exactly where we stand.

South Africa has made much progress, and the fight for equality and freedom for all has been won on many fronts. However, the issues of law, corruption and morality still demand our attention. During its infancy and in the course of its many hearings around the country, the Truth and Reconciliation Commission faced heavy criticism from all quarters. Yet it managed to maintain an objective approach and to rise above the obstacles that were placed in its way.

In the Chairperson's Foreword to the TRC Report, Archbishop Desmond Tutu said: 'A venerable tradition holds that those who use force to overthrow or even to oppose an unjust system occupy the moral high ground over those who use force to sustain that same system … This does not mean that those who hold the moral high ground have *carte blanche* to the methods they use.'[1]

This unfortunately holds true for the corruption that was committed during the apartheid era and the corruption that is being committed now. Often the very people who occupy the 'moral high ground' are involved in defrauding the government and ultimately the people of this country. It seems that the *carte blanche* that Tutu referred to has somehow spilt over from the previous era into this one. Such people show no loyalty towards the rule of law or commitment to the eradication of corruption.

It is commendable that the TRC, during its many months of hard and committed work, dealt with gross human rights violations in the form of killings, torture, disappearance of family members and other matters that touched the hearts of many South Africans. Family members could now face the past, after many tears were shed and much was revealed. However, behind the acts of the perpetrators were the lies, the deceptions and the corruption of a system that was doomed to fail from the start. This was a system that was rotten to the very core, that allowed many people to become millionaires, while depriving many others of access to the resources that could have provided for their basic needs. Billions of rands were spent every year to support an apartheid system that was rejected by the majority of first-world countries. This, to me, constitutes the ultimate corrupt act.

The money that was squandered could have been used to upgrade schools, to provide better education, to supply qualified staff and medicine to rural clinics and hospitals, to curb crime, and to uplift the underprivileged and disadvantaged of our country. The following questions must be asked: Who will be held responsible for these acts of corruption? Who will be held responsible for the decay and chaos that took place over all those years? Will we allow this to continue with simply a change in role players?

Members of the public and the media frequently ask me whether corruption is as serious now as it was during the apartheid era, or whether it is worse. The answer is very simple. South Africa now has a free press, and we have structures in place to deal decisively with corruption. Thus the corruption that does exist has become more evident than it ever was in the past. We may never know the extent of the corruption that was committed in the past – I am sure that the files and the evidence have been buried very deeply, if not destroyed. Although the Special Investigating Unit's mandate includes investigating corruption as far back as 1976, I have my reservations as to whether the Unit will be able to recover a fraction of the billions of rands that were misused to the advantage of the apartheid system.

The statement that 'those with the most power to abuse must carry the heaviest responsibility'[2] rings true for the corruption that was committed during the period 1960 to 1994. To illustrate this I would like to quote some examples from the TRC Report.

The Special Investigation into Secret State Funding concluded that:[3]

> [t]he need clearly exists for the President to appoint an appropriate committee to enquire further into funding – not least with a view to ensuring that, where possible, funds in covert accounts were paid back to the treasury. Where such funding continues to be absolutely necessary, clear guidelines need to be put in place and the nature and extent of such funding reported to Parliament on a regular basis. This requires an evaluation of existing structures and regulations governing the use of secret funds.[4]

It is well known that the so-called 'slush funds' used by the various security bodies were abused and that this led to huge financial losses to the state during the apartheid years. The use of these funds to establish private companies, to pay for expensive cars and homes and to live a good life was commonplace amongst many operatives. This was corruption in its purest form, which has deprived thousands of South Africans of the basic services they needed and still desperately need.

In the chapter on the Institutional Hearing into the Legal Community the Commission records its disappointment that the judiciary failed to appear before the Commission:[5]

> The Commission finds that an appearance before the Commission … would have demonstrated accountability and would not have compromised the independence of the judiciary. History will judge the judiciary harshly. Its response to the hearing has again placed the questions of what accountability and dependence mean in a constitutional democracy in the public domain for debate.[6]

The Commission also expressed a strong view on the 'almost complete failure of the magistracy to respond to [its] invitation … the more so considering the previous lack of formal independence of magistrates and their dismal record as servants of the apartheid state in the past'.[7]

It is unfortunate that the judiciary has not escaped the clutches of corruption either. It is furthermore disheartening to learn that the judiciary declined an invitation to appear before the TRC to account for its actions during the period under review. I firmly believe that judges and magistrates are accountable for their judgements.

However, one must bear in mind that the independence of the judiciary was curtailed by the actions of the state. The objectivity of the members of the legal profession had been seriously warped by the manner in which the arms of the state had been acting in order to address the 'rooi gevaar' ('red danger'). In many cases the facts presented to the courts were so far from the truth, so distorted, and so far removed from the appropriate context that the presiding officer had no choice but to find in favour of the State and impose harsh sentences.

Reconciliation can only take place if the offenders admit their crimes and those who were wronged are given the opportunity to express their grievances and come face to face with those who did them wrong.

The corruption of a society will inevitably lead to a breakdown in morality and ultimately a breakdown in the law. The corruption of the apartheid system led to a situation in which both sides had to adopt a corrupt attitude in order to fight for what they believed in and for what they were struggling. It is unfortunate that these corrupt practices led to a morally depraved society, placing us in a position of having to rebuild our nation and re-configure our attitudes, not only towards each other but also towards the systems and the injustices of the past.

On numerous occasions President Thabo Mbeki has called for a moral regeneration of our country. He has a vision of an African Dream achieved through an African Renaissance – something we should all strive for and something that we can achieve.

In conclusion, let me quote Archbishop Tutu's words from the TRC Report:

Having looked the beast of the past in the eye, having asked and received forgiveness and having made amendments, let us shut the door on the past – not in order to forget it but in order not to allow it to imprison us. Let us move into the glorious future of a new kind of society where people count, not because of biological irrelevancies or other extraneous attributes, but because they are persons of infinite worth created in the image of God.[8]

Chapter Eighteen

The TRC and the Building of a Moral Culture

John de Gruchy

Democratic transformation can only be achieved in a society committed to the development of a moral culture, a society striving to uphold moral values and constantly seeking to achieve, elusive as it is, an ever broadening moral consensus. The painful dissecting of apartheid during the hearings of the Truth and Reconciliation Commission has not only helped us to understand better what 'crimes against humanity' mean, but it has given us vivid intimations of the kind of society we should strive for: a society that cares, cares about the truth, cares about justice, cares about victims, cares about the healing of its wounds and the flourishing of human life. Such values are embodied in our remarkable Constitution. But alongside that clinical text, the TRC has now set an inevitably messy, sometimes deeply passionate, but always very human testimony to what happens when a society disregards moral values, a testimony to the potential of moral values when vindicated and treasured. What happens when a society loses its moral sensitivity, its sense of shame, its moral indignation, has been documented. What might happen when it regains moral sensitivity, is ashamed by its failures, and becomes angry when human rights are trampled on, is the challenge we now face. The success or failure of the TRC is closely linked to whether we succeed in taking its work seriously.

While much of what the TRC unearthed was previously known, both to victims and perpetrators, knowledge was both selective and partial. Now we have the dramatic images of television coverage and five volumes of raw data etched into our common consciousness and conscience. No court of law could possibly have provided us with such vivid images and painful stories, such agonising debates and torturous confessions as became the stock-in-trade of the TRC. These images have already begun to reshape the discourse on moral formation and transformation in democratic transition, not only in South Africa but further afield, as can be seen in the plethora of articles, dissertations and books already published or forthcoming. Whatever our eventual conclusions about the achievements of the TRC, we can surely agree that it has opened up a debate that has reinforced our awareness of the urgent need to build a moral culture and strive for moral consensus for the sake of our future. In this way the TRC, if taken seriously, could save us from reducing the debate to platitudinous theory, the substance of shelved theses and reports.

The social history of South Africa since colonial times has been shaped by sectarian moral values, which have served the interests of some sections of society to the detriment and disadvantage of others. There has never been a shared set of moral values that has bound South Africans together. There has been little sense of the common good amongst those who have been our moral pontiffs and guardians, or amongst those who have followed their lead and example. Christianity, as a moral foundation for society, has been severely compromised by the way in which it was abused to legitimate colonial and apartheid ideology and power. The broadly Christian ethos that emerged in the late nineteenth century, which played a formative role in the development of the ANC, and which in many ways informed the liberation struggle, has partially redeemed Christianity as an important resource for the building of a moral culture. Yet it cannot be the sole basis for such a culture or for the development of moral consensus, given the pluralistic nature of our society. Indeed, the extent to which Christian norms and values shaped the work of the TRC has not been unproblematic.[1] This discovery was in itself part of a learning experience in our search for moral consensus that is more comprehensive and inclusive.

In the parry and thrust of the TRC hearings we were, time and again, made aware of classical moral ambiguities. The most difficult of all was probably that of moral symmetry. Can one equate the violations of human rights by the perpetrators of oppression with those of the oppressed who were engaged in a struggle for liberation? What does 'fairness' mean under such circumstances? These questions highlight the problem of giving moral principles absolute value irrespective of historical context. Can any moral principle be applied without taking context into account? I do not believe so, although I realise that this raises the issue of moral relativism and the danger of manipulating moral values so that they lose significance or authority. In seeking to adjudicate between moral absolutes and context it became necessary for the TRC to take cognisance of a range of other issues. Was an act legitimately political? What were the consequences of the deed? It is only as a society engages seriously in debating such issues within its particular historical framework that it begins to shape and sharpen its moral critical consciousness. I shall refer to and briefly comment on three of the moral issues lying at the heart of the debate that has been engendered by the TRC. There are, of course, others that could be discussed.

Telling the truth is better than living a lie, but telling the truth is not an end in itself

The TRC's mandate was to uncover the truth about our apartheid past in order to facilitate the process of national reconciliation. As one of the founding documents of the TRC put it: 'Once we know the truth, we can begin to put the past behind us and move with hope into a peaceful future.' There were good social and psychological reasons for assuming that uncovering the truth could help achieve this goal, but there was also an argument against such an assumption – one that claimed that uncovering the truth was a sure recipe for keeping alive past hatreds and inviting acts of revenge. This argument was seriously flawed, not necessarily on political or pragmatic grounds, but because it failed to recognise that over and above the demands of a negotiated settlement, there was the imperative to reconstruct South Africa on a moral foundation. It failed to understand the purpose of telling the truth.

The uncovering of truth on its own cannot achieve reconciliation, unless those who seek to know the truth are committed to such a goal. That is why hiding the truth, or even telling a lie for the sake of preserving life, can sometimes be of greater moral value than telling the truth. Torture was and remains a means of finding the truth, often leading to the arrest or murder of the victim's comrades. The consequences of telling the truth must be taken into account in any moral reckoning. But that was not the TRC's purpose for seeking the truth – quite the contrary: its purpose was to build a humane, just, caring, reconciling society. This was the moral justification for seeking to know the truth. It is only this kind of truth telling that sets us free to be truly human, that lays the foundation for a truly reconciled nation. If we are to build a moral culture, we need to know the truth about our past, that is, about ourselves, because without such knowledge we remain captive to our past. But what we do with the truth is the real moral test.

Victims have a prior moral claim on society, but their claim must not be reduced to political rhetoric

Whether or not all the victims of apartheid have been, or will be, satisfied by the outcome of the TRC – surely an impossibility under even the best of circumstances? – there can be little doubt that one of the motivating factors that led to the establishment of the TRC was a concern for the victims of apartheid. The struggle against apartheid was motivated by a moral commitment to its victims, which was continually strengthened by moral outrage at acts of victimisation and state terror; the TRC process was motivated by the need to provide a voice to those who had previously been silenced. However one may evaluate all the details of the victims' narrative, there can be no doubt that the

TRC was declaring in a loud voice that the victims of apartheid had a greater moral claim on society than anyone else.

Yet it is too easy for us to pay lip service to the rights and moral claims of the victims of a society without honouring that claim. This has always been a ploy on the part of those seeking to give their cause moral justification. The American Civil War and the South African War were morally justified, liberating slaves in the one case, and defending the rights of blacks in the other. Such hypocrisy abuses moral claims and undermines moral values. If the TRC's recommendations on reparation are not taken seriously, we shall be guilty of something similar and the victims will remain victims. This will inevitably undermine the building of a moral culture. If we are to build a moral culture, we need to demonstrate that we care, and care adequately, for those who are the victims of injustice and violence, or natural disaster. A moral society is a caring society. That is why in South Africa today it is of the utmost importance to ensure that the rights of the most vulnerable are protected and acted upon, for victims in our society are not simply those of the apartheid era; people become victims every day.

Forgiveness does not negate moral accountability but it has greater transformative power than vengeance

The TRC demonstrated the moral and transformative potential of truth telling as well as forgiveness. The need to elicit forgiveness was not part of its mandate, but by virtue of its importance it became a central feature in the TRC's attempt to deal with the truth and promote reconciliation. Yet forgiveness became one of the most hotly contested values during the course of the TRC's work. Can anyone demand or even expect those who have been wronged to forgive those who have been the cause of their suffering? Does forgiveness not short-circuit the cause of justice and undermine the rule of law? Is there not a place for unforgiving moral indignation and perhaps even vengeance in seeking to redress the injustices of the past and establishing a moral culture?

Properly understood, forgiveness does not mean excusing those who oppress and victimise. Forgiveness understood can never replace justice. The TRC demonstrated that forgiveness requires the perpetrators of evil to acknowledge what they have done, to take responsibility for their actions. In other words, forgiveness does not exclude the need for moral accountability. Perpetrators of crimes are accountable both to their victims and to the rule of law, and no one has the moral right to demand forgiveness; this prerogative remains with the victims alone.

Forgiveness cannot replace justice – it goes beyond justice. This is its moral courage, this is its moral power. If the perpetrators of crimes get away with what they did, then the rule of law is undermined. Yet if their punishment has no redemptive possibility, it deepens the divisions in society, increases enmity and resentment, prevents reconciliation and encourages vengeance. Forgiveness seeks to prevent the perpetuation of the cycle of violence, which inevitably leads to the undermining of the rule of law. It seeks the establishment of a just moral order that builds community and restores humanity. Telling the truth about the past alone does not heal; it might lead, in fact, to acts of violent vengeance. Remembering then becomes a fanning of the embers of a dying fire so that it bursts into flame again and devours us. The only way to redeem the past, to break the cycle of violence, is not to take revenge, but to have the moral courage to forgive.

The TRC, then, has set in motion a debate about moral values and the building of a moral culture which needs to be kept alive and taken forward and, above all, needs to find expression in very practical terms. For morality is not about theory, it is about what we do for the sake of the common good. What the TRC has done is to open up the debate and provide the raw material for the task. The critical question is how we are to take the debate further and process the memory of our corporate past that the TRC has set before us. What we do with these memories will, in large measure, shape the moral contours of the future South Africa. Our past will either be redeemed, or our future will be cursed, depending on our response. In other words, we do not only have the task of remembering, but of remembering rightly. And remembering rightly is a moral act, which builds the foundations for a moral culture

Law, Corruption and Morality

Mamphela Ramphele

Allegiance to the Constitution is an important foundation for our democracy. This, the first point I wish to make, raises the question of how one nurtures a culture that promotes such allegiance. There is a need for this culture to be inculcated from the highest offices of our land to the vigilantes in the backwaters. How are we going to ensure that a culture of allegiance to the Constitution is engendered and remains alive in the people of South Africa?

A further issue that needs to be raised is why there is such a gap between the values and rights enshrined in our Constitution, and the reality of the continuing violations of those rights. Why are our watchdog institutions not having the desired effect on our society? South Africa has become the crime hub of the world. What are the impediments to the success of these institutions? I contend that we are very good at sending mixed messages, and that these mixed messages come from the highest offices in the land, to the heads of institutions, and right down to the heads of households.

There is growing criticism that the Constitution is part of the problem. The argument is that crime is rampant because too much freedom is enshrined in the Constitution. This perception will continue, particularly in those who see themselves as victims, and who remain unprotected by the Constitution. They see criminals earning money to buy protection – through the 'proper' interpretation of the Constitution. I believe that we have a major problem with our criminal justice system, the members of which need to be educated in applying the Constitution. The gap between the protection of rights of victims and those of criminals must be closed, thus diminishing the perception that only criminals benefit from the Constitution.

As Judge Willem Heath has noted, corruption is indeed a violation of the fundamental rights of those deprived of the benefits of being citizens of a democracy. Many people will argue that corruption is universal. This is true, but corruption is unaffordable in South Africa – for a number of important reasons: We cannot build an allegiance to the Constitution for as long as there is such rampant corruption. Corruption threatens our very democracy. The United States might be able to afford corruption, because its democracy has been entrenched, but ours is still a very fragile democracy. In particular, corruption undermines citizens who are materially deprived, as it presents a threat to the possibility of meeting their socio-economic rights.

At the heart of the fire of corruption that continues to burn in South Africa are those who believe that they occupy the moral high ground. Particularly since the 1980s, a culture of entitlement has emerged and continues today. There is an essentialist view of the oppressed – the romantic view that if one is oppressed, there must be something good about one. It is a view that oppression in a sense almost creates saints out of people. This view is in part a response to the tendency of conservatives to blame victims of oppression. As a result of this romantic view, South Africans have failed to examine themselves closely, and to look at the effect of oppression on people, and on their approach to moral issues and human relationships. The Truth and Reconciliation Commission has provided a partial picture of what happened to the oppressors, but we also need to look at what happened to the oppressed. The same process that degraded the morality of the oppressors has had an impact on those who were oppressed. We tend to justify the acts of those who are oppressed. The survival culture during the struggle spawned a particular approach to life that undermines the building of a culture of rights *and* responsibilities. Unless we acknowledge the extent to which that past continues to shape the future, we will not be able to address this issue.

This brings me to the issue of the moral morass that John de Gruchy mentions. If you have had a society that criminalised normal behaviour, and normalised criminal behaviour, it will not be easy to change that society simply on the basis of an excellent Constitution, watchdog institutions and people who affirm their commitment to a democracy. It will require the focused building of a culture that recognises the very faulty foundations of our society. Unless we confront the implications of criminalising normal behaviour and normalising criminal behaviour, we will continue to experience problems in realising the dreams and aspirations of our Constitution.

I want to mention a few impediments to the building of a moral culture in South Africa. The first obstacle is that the ghosts from the past refuse to lie down. The ghost of continuing and growing inequality between 'haves' and 'have-nots' is haunting our society. These 'haves' and 'have-nots' are mainly white and black, respectively, but there is a growing group of 'haves' who are black, and who display the same approach to material possessions as their white counterparts.

Then there is the ghost of perpetrators who seem to continue to benefit from the spoils of the past. This makes people wonder what the point of the whole TRC process is, and so they try to reap some undeserved benefits too. Furthermore, the perception is that too little has been done to address reparation and the needs of victims. These ghosts need to be exorcised from our society, or we will continue to experience problems.

The second set of impediments relates to an issue that we find difficult to speak about: the continuing division between black and white South Africans. We can talk about the Rainbow Nation as loudly as we like, but we need to confront the implications and the consequences of the fact that a large group of South Africans were made to feel subhuman. Voting in 1994 and again in 1999 did not remove those scars of humiliation, particularly as the majority of people continue to live in squalor, are unemployed and without hope. This inferiority complex is a reality of most peoples' lives. Until and unless we confront it, we will not succeed. In the same vein, the superiority complex amongst white people needs to be confronted. I was fortunate enough to have had the opportunity to confront the inferiority complex of being black much earlier on, when I was still a student, otherwise I would not have survived my stay as Vice-Chancellor at UCT. The insults directed at me by some UCT alumni soon after my appointment were unbelievable. They felt that I did not have the right to be the head of their institution. My being a black person would, in their view, only mean problems (my brain being a little small!), and as for being a woman – well, I'd be so emotional, I wouldn't be able to think.

These realities continue to shape our social relationships and we cannot talk about a shared moral foundation for our society unless we confront them. One of the consequences of ignoring these issues is that, particularly on the side of the new black elite, we are beginning to see the troubling tendency of using racist labels to silence criticism. This will continue to happen, because we are not talking about the problem, we are walking around the problem.

I conclude by referring to John de Gruchy's point about the failure to do enough about the truth that we have spoken and uncovered. This failure is a real threat to the opportunity South Africa has to build a new moral order. Until there is an intense focus on reparation – not only on material reparation to those who were deprived, but also on addressing the psychological and spiritual needs of those who were dehumanised, we will not achieve the kind of society that we yearn for. If we find the courage to look at ourselves in the mirror, and stop pretending that we can simply talk ourselves into being a Rainbow Nation or into being a true democracy, we can develop into the kind of society we want to be. I am very optimistic, because we have the energy and the willingness to do it. But we must get down to work.

Part V:
Building the Assets
of the Nation

Addressing Poverty
and Inequality

Francis Wilson

In this essay we shall look at building the assets of the nation with a particular focus on addressing the issues of poverty and inequality. Other contributions in this book have discussed the limitations of the Truth and Reconciliation Commission, which flowed from a political process that was a consequence of enormous compromise and the product of the reform initiative made possible by the unstable equilibrium of the late 1980s. This critique of the TRC is important and necessary, but we do ourselves a disservice if we fail to acknowledge the massive achievement of a process that has unquestionably raised public consciousness of some of the things that were done. This process is helping us to clear out some of the rubble of our past in order to build anew. Others far more qualified than I have debated the extent to which the Commission succeeded in fulfilling its brief. Our task now is to start to move beyond the Commission, beyond the debate about human rights abuses in the past few decades, beyond the torture and the murder, even beyond the politics of reconciliation or the miracle of the negotiated shift from legalised racism to constitutional democracy.

The issue of economic justice is at the top of the political agenda. It is difficult to enforce respect for the Constitution and for constitutionality when enormous inequality remains a feature of our society. Raymond Aron made this point very succinctly when he said in effect that human community is impossible in a society with too great a degree of inequality.[1] This is the reality with which we now have to grapple.

I hardly need to repeat the long litany of facts about poverty and inequality in South Africa, but for the record and as a touchstone, let us remind ourselves of a few of the most salient. In terms of the Gini coefficient, South Africa is one of the most unequal countries in the world, lying somewhere .58 and .65 in statistical terms, placing us in the same range as Guatemala and Brazil. Much greater inequality exists in South Africa than in countries such as India or the Russian Federation.[2] To be a little more specific, in 1993, when the top 10 per cent of this country's population earned half the national income, the poorest 10 per cent earned 0.4 per cent. Indeed, the poorest half of South Africa, the bottom 50 per cent, almost all of whom are black, earned 8.9 per cent of the total income in 1993.[3] This degree of inequality implies massive poverty. In 1993, 45 per cent of the population earned less than the widely agreed minimum living level, with 21 per cent below the international rule of thumb of a dollar per person per day, which is a very rough measure. But it gives us some idea of the huge poverty built on massive inequality in our country. South Africa's average per capita Gross National Product places it in the upper-middle income range, eighty countries or more from the bottom of the world scale. On average, ours is not a poor country, but in reality it is, for many people.[4]

If we deconstruct these numbers, we can see that the inequality average has further components to it, the main one being race. The median household incomes for 1995 were:

Black African	R12 400
Coloured	R19 400
Indian	R40 500
White	R60 000

Source: J. May, p. 27

If we look at those who are poor in South Africa, 95 per cent are black, less than 1 per cent are white, less than 1 per cent are Indian, and about 5 per cent are coloured.

Then there is an urban–rural dichotomy: 71 per cent of the rural population is poor, while only 29 per cent of the urban population is poor. There is also a gender perspective: 31 per cent of households headed by men are poor, while 60 per cent of households headed by women are poor. Furthermore, there is an age perspective. Approximately 60 per cent of children live in poor households, where stress levels are high, and widespread abuse is evident. There is mounting evidence that children suffer unduly from poverty and its consequences.

The figures for unemployment throw into sharp relief the contours of poverty sketched above. In 1993 the unemployment figures were:

Black African	39%
White	5%
Rural areas	40%
Urban areas	22–26%
Women	35%
Men	26%
Youth under 25 who are not at school or university and who want to work	53%
Between 55 and 64	15%

Source: Project for Statistics on Living Standards and Development:
South Africans Rich and Poor: Baseline Household Statistics
(Cape Town, 1994), pp. 141–3

When these categories overlap, inequality is reinforced. For example, the combination of race and age, taking no account of geography or gender, shows that unemployment for young blacks under the age of 25 runs to 65 per cent. For older whites between 55 and 64, the unemployment figure lies at 2 per cent. People in South Africa clearly live in different universes.

In South Africa, despite all the quite extraordinary achievements of the past ten years on which we can build, we have to be aware – particularly those of us who live at the rich end of this universe – that people are living worlds apart. In South Africa, there is, as the World Bank never tires of reminding us, a real problem of economic growth. In the first half of the 1960s, the growth rate was about 6 per cent per annum. From the mid-eighties it went into reverse. The figures for per capita Gross National Product, allowing for population growth and other factors, show that there was negative growth in South Africa for the ten years following 1982. This is part of what our present government has inherited and did not make matters any easier for a new government having to deal with the issues of poverty and inequality.

Economic growth, as we know only too well from South African history, is not a sufficient condition for eradicating poverty, but it is a necessary one. Underlying the failure of economic growth were factors such as the decline in public investment by parastatals in 1985, the lack of consumer business and confidence, and unnecessary capital-intensive investment in apartheid policies. We need to be aware of the decisions that were made about investment in this country from the 1950s to the 1980s, as these decisions reverberated into the 1990s and into the new millennium.

There was also the failure of human capital investment, which to my mind is one of the most serious and one of the most difficult to deal with. Let us consider some basic information on human capital in South Africa in 1993:

Those over the age of 13 who had completed Standard 8 or more:	
All	55%
White	90%
Black African	46%
Those over the age of 15 who had completed Standard 8 or more:	
All	38%
White	83%
Black African	27%
Those over the age of 17 who had completed Standard 10 or more:	
All	20%
White	61%
Black African	11%

Source: Project for Statistics on Living Standards and Development: South Africans Rich and Poor: Baseline Household Statistics (Cape Town, 1994), pp. 141–3

Considering the education needed in a modern information society, and the fact that two thirds of whites have completed Standard 10 or more, a figure of only one tenth for Africans having completed Standard 10 or more is alarming. There is a close correlation between income and education or human capital. Redressing the bias in human capital investment should be one of our most urgent priorities.

If we look for deeper reasons for this imbalance, we have to go back to the labour and land issues in South Africa. We do need to recognise the consequences of slavery, the pass laws, and the migrant labour system. While the migrant labour system generated wealth in South Africa, it also generated poverty, largely in the rural areas, in the old homelands. Similarly, the process of conquest meant that the land went into the hands of a particular group, along with the right to obtain minerals and water. Because of riparian rights, he (and it was he) who controlled the land, also controlled the water. Thus the political economy of land and water in South Africa is part of our inheritance.

We need to be conscious of the constraints facing the new government. Just as the TRC faced constraints as a result of its mandate that was the result of a political process, so the government's economic policies are subject to constraints too. One of these constraints is the fact that in terms of the Constitution, the restitution of property taken from individuals or communities as a result of past racially discriminatory laws or practices applies only to land taken after 19 June 1913.[5] This was a necessary compromise – an acceptance that the land pattern of 1913 is part of our inheritance. At the same time we need to recognise that, because of the process of urbanisation, land is no longer the important asset it was when South Africa had a largely rural economy. Today, many assets are urban-based, but we still have to pay close attention to rural development.

Another constraint the government faced in terms of policy was job security – certainly for the first five years – of the old civil service. There was the issue of the loyalty of a civil service that continued work after 1994, and there are other circumstances after 1994 that need to be briefly considered.

One circumstance was that the economy had become static at the end of a century of extraordinary economic development, at one level. It was racist and unequal, but in terms of the growth in Gross National Product, it was an extraordinary period. But the very fact that the economy had come to a grinding halt helped to bring about the political transition. So there was an ambiguity at the very heart of what was happening between 1990 and 1994.

At another level, there was the global macro-environment, which was post-Thatcher, post-Reagan, but sternly anti-inflationary and strictly limited in its tolerance of budget deficits. We need to recognise that global wisdom at the moment is based on the horrors of macro-economic populism in Latin America, and the destruction of good changes by runaway inflation. There is the real concern of the managers of any modern economy about inflation getting out of hand. The danger of macro-economic populism is enormous. By 1994, when the new government came to power, the global consensus about the enormous importance of controlling inflation was there. I was very intrigued to read a comment made by Chris Stals, former Governor of the Reserve Bank, upon his retirement: '[A]s a central banker my primary concern was inflation. If I'd been a macro-economist, I would perhaps have worried more about unemployment.'

The other constraint is globalisation, which is not a new phenomenon, as it really developed very rapidly in the nineteenth century. Globalisation does seem to be associated with the building of global inequality, with the whole process of globalisation placing enormous constraints on what the South African government can do in terms of policy.

What then did the Mandela government do when it came to power in 1994? Firstly, a very public commitment was made to dealing with the issues of poverty and inequality. This was almost the first statement the Government of National Unity made, and it has been constantly reiterated. There have been a number of strands to the macro-economic policy designed to stimulate growth and redistribution in favour of the poor. This, of course, is an issue that continues to be debated and economists will continue arguing about 'the optimum policy'.

Secondly, strategies for generating employment by means of appropriate macro-economic growth policies and public works programmes were put in place. Thirdly, there was a focus on human development by means of better education, better health facilities, better nutrition and so forth. Fourthly, there was an expansion of infrastructural services, water and electricity, as well as institutional reform for the more effective management and the strengthening of the social security net.

Looking back, one can argue that the central theme of the new government's economic policy was to address the issues of poverty and inequality. And although it cannot be faulted on its attempts, we need to assess those attempts. In 1988, a report commissioned by the government itself was produced, trying to take stock of how well it had done, and where it had failed.[6] This poverty and inequality report should be considered by those who want to move beyond the TRC to deal with the central issue of economic justice.

My view is that the very process of compiling such a report and then ensuring that its findings are discussed publicly is itself a major contribution to the fight against poverty. But as far as assessing the government's performance is concerned, the report is mixed. In terms of commitment to tackling the problems of poverty and in terms of changing the overall political environment to one that encourages anti-poverty programmes, the new democratic government has done exceptionally well. Specific programmes such as 'Working for Water' (the Department of Water Affairs' attempt to supply water to the rural areas), electrification and other development initiatives have achieved a great deal. Yet everyone agrees, not least the departments themselves, that we still have a very long way to go, and that we are severely handicapped by a lack of funds. The feeling is that we have not achieved as much as we could have, or should have, but I think it is fair to say it is not for want of trying.

I now want to identify some of the components of good governance that we must focus on as we move ahead. There has to be leadership and commitment, and this call needs to be seen partly in the light of a public debate on the recommendations of the TRC. It is part of moving towards greater justice – restorative justice, economic justice. There have to be sound, yet creative, macro-economic policies. Perhaps, now that we have a macro-economist rather than a central banker at the Reserve Bank, there will be a greater emphasis on the unemployment problem and less on inflation. But the balance is very difficult to maintain.

We need infrastructural investment in poor communities and poor areas. This has been neglected, and a great deal more should be done. If we consider how poverty was generated by the structures of racism long before 1948, we have to think very carefully about how we can redress this historical imbalance. There is a need for some fundamental public debate about employment generation in rural areas, particularly in areas like the Eastern Cape. Encouraging people to move to Cape Town and Johannesburg will not solve the problem.

Then there is the issue of education and training. We already operate in a knowledge-based economy. At the same time, we have to overcome the appalling legacy of the apartheid government – the development of Bantu Education, which destroyed the education system that was in place. In my view this destruction of old education systems and the failure to let systems develop naturally was one of the very worst sins of the previous regime.

One of the questions we could ask ourselves is why our schools are not functioning. Then we need to consider what we can do right now to ensure that, for example, all the primary schools of our particular town are functioning as proper schools. We will be reaping the proverbial whirlwind if we move into the twenty-first century with the kind of education that so many of our youngsters are receiving, or not receiving, at school. We have to deal with this at a micro-level and it seems to me, as an economist, as a human being, as a citizen, that the initiative for improving primary school education in every nook and cranny of the country should be one of the major priorities.

We need a legal framework that encourages initiatives by private individuals. We need effective constraints against the growth of corruption. We need competent management and organisational capacity. We need the capacity to enforce the law and prevent crime effectively.

Mamphela Ramphele referred to the ghosts that refuse to lie down: poverty and inequality. Dealing with those ghosts within a sustainable environment is the challenge for the twenty-first century. The challenge is how to build a new solidarity not only within South Africa, but also between nations. The statistics that are currently emerging about global inequality are horrendous. The wealthiest 20 per cent of the world's population as a ratio to the poorest 20 per cent was about 3:1 in 1817. It had risen to 30:1 by 1960, by 1990 it was 60:1, and by 1998 it was 85:1. That is the state of the global economy.[7]

We are stretched on the rack, because we have workers who are on a par with those in Mozambique and Lesotho, or unemployed, and we have people at the other end of the spectrum who are saying that we have to compete with world rates. We need to build a new solidarity beyond race, although the shadow of race is right there, making the situation explosive. The challenge for the twenty-first century is to build this new solidarity, to find ways of constructing bridges across the great divide.

The first evil that we had to deal with in South Africa was apartheid. Many people – many generations – gave their lives, and countless people were imprisoned for many long years. Finally, against all odds, we overcame this evil. We have had the euphoria and a space of five years to enjoy that success.

Now we have to recognise that there is a second evil – the evil of poverty based on huge and growing inequalities. How do we restructure our world; how do we restructure our country? South Africa is where it is all happening, and we have to find a way forward. I believe that we can be more optimistic now than we could be in the past, because in those times we could see no way forward; we operated on pure faith. Now we know that the dragons can be slain. But it will only happen if we get down to work.

Chapter Twenty-one

Educating the Nation

Grace Naledi Pandor

In this essay I shall look at the challenge of educating the nation, of building our assets based on the opportunities created by the Truth and Reconciliation Commission. Any reflection on the TRC or on issues arising from the process has to begin with an acknowledgement that the TRC process is one of the most significant processes in a society grappling with the challenge of defining itself in a new and transformed mode. It is difficult for those of us who are primarily outside the detailed process to comment with accuracy on the TRC. Although it was a very visible part of our lives for many months, there was a sense of being somewhat excluded if you were not right in the middle of it. I am not voicing a criticism here; I am merely acknowledging this sense of a perceived mystique that I am convinced many of us had – a mystique that seemed to surround the Commission.

My contribution constitutes an appreciation of the TRC's role in making South Africans reflect on themselves, on their progress, and on the introduction of a new set of values and norms for all our people. I shall consider the TRC's educational lessons: Did it provide any for us, and can these lessons be incorporated into our education system and policy? In my view a focus on education is necessary and important, particularly given our aim of ensuring that every young person enjoys the right to education.

The importance of the focus on education was confirmed for me by a newspaper article written in 1983, which sought to assess the role of the private sector in education in the turbulent late 1970s and 1980s. The article quotes another 1983 newspaper report that reflected on deliberations in the committee of the Anglo American Chairman's Fund. In that particular meeting in 1983, the Chairman's Fund stated that '[t]he shortcomings in black education strain South Africa's social fabric more than any other factor in society'. Any attempt to measure the educational significance of South Africa's momentous enterprise of seeking truth and reconciliation must confront and reckon with this straining of the social fabric. The Fund's committee was speaking sixteen years ago, but we know that the straining of the social fabric continues unabated for many communities in our country.

As a first step in preparing this contribution, I attempted to read those volumes of the TRC Report that focus on education. It was difficult to trace a direct institutional focus. The Commission held institutional hearings on the following sectors: the media, business, prisons, the faith community, the legal system and the health system. Immediately, the question that arose was why the Commission had chosen not to include the education sector. Surely it would have been an obvious choice, given that one of the most lasting imprints on South African society will be the unravelling of the social fabric that is the result of apartheid education? When I asked these questions, colleagues responded by saying that the TRC's brief was to focus on gross violations of human rights, and that the denial of education to people was not a gross violation of human rights.

It is difficult for me to frame an adequate response to such comments, particularly whilst I have not made a sufficiently detailed study of the TRC Report. My contribution seeks to build on these preceding comments by briefly stating what, in my view, might have been tabled in education hearings. I shall then outline some of the educational challenges that we have to respond to if the TRC process is to have any lasting impact on our society.

Comments tentatively suggest that apartheid education and the inequality arising from that framework of injustice constitute gross violations of human rights. These statements arise particularly from the observation that apartheid education is guilty of the high crime of having conferred a stubborn and lasting status of inferiority on the previously oppressed. In addition, it also created a means of perpetuating dominance and of the wholesale transmission of oppressive structures in our society. When we consider the economy, issues of corruption and issues of rural development, we discover that all these are directly linked to the issue of education. The notion of whites as masters and blacks as subordinates was portrayed consistently at all levels of education under apartheid. The values of the dominant class were promoted as superior values, and the supposed superiority of whites was considered inviolate.

My experience at a recent dinner confirmed to a certain extent this view of an inequality of values. I was sitting next to someone who turned the conversation to the TRC. After a few minutes of discussion, she looked directly at me and said, 'You know, you people amaze me. I really admire you to just come along and forgive like that – I mean Mandela after all his suffering, I would never have reacted like you people – I would not forgive.' I was not quite sure, from the look on her face, whether I was in fact admired by her or despised for my mildness in forgiving. A number of fellow blacks have experienced such comments, which, I suspect, reflect this teaching of superiority in values that our education system conveyed in the past.

Advantage in education went beyond values and opportunities. It also served as a vehicle for entrenching racial and ethnic divisions. Interestingly, several women speaking at a hearing of victims held by the *Ilitha Labanthu* organisation called for the state to make reparation to them, purely by supporting the education of their children. They asked for nothing else. They recognised that education might be the one vehicle that offers a positive outcome to their offspring.

Apartheid education taught white learners to see themselves as part of a larger world, while black learners were taught to accept the confines of their racial and ethnic enclaves. The curriculum and content of education reinforced the stereotype of white ascendancy, while confirming the inadequacy of black entrants to education. The history, traditions, norms and values of those excluded from the levers of power did not feature at all in the curricula of the past. Even language, usually a tool for education, became a tool of oppression rather than empowerment. The advantaged in South Africa benefited from a positive focus on their history, their traditions and their culture – a focus that once more reinforced a supposed inherent belief in superior values. School facilities, teacher quality, teacher motivation, resources for learning, and state financial and development support all served to reinforce advantage.

It would be useful to begin our consideration of education's potential role in building our nation by reflecting on what might have been tabled if we had held hearings on educational apartheid. Would an expression of the apartheid education crimes have helped to lay the foundations for a process of redress that would directly challenge the residue of this policy? Would the voices of education victims have helped to create an understanding of why education became the enemy to many black people, of why black success in black schooling came to be seen as reactionary? Would senior academics have come before the TRC to confess their duplicity in producing mediocre books for black learning, in propping up apartheid's tertiary institutions that were designed to support the myth of black incompetence? Would those who burned down classrooms and schools have come forward to help us understand this particular crime against humanity?

We all heard of the gruesome experiences of the victims of apartheid crime, and the horrifyingly cold confessions of many perpetrators. Perhaps apartheid educational administrators would have come forward and told us why they established schools without toilets, without electricity, without water, without teachers or books. They would have clarified the intentions of such educational provision. While evidence of several perpetrators in the hearings on other sectors has clearly outlined the methods of domination, control and destruction that were systematically utilised, the silence that has been permitted on education as a form of violation is, in my view, stunning in its intensity.

Readings on apartheid education concretely show us that there was a method in past education provision and policy. Let us consider for a moment the design and history of our tertiary institutions. White institutions are located in cities and major towns, buttressed by a firm economic base and a cultural milieu that can stimulate pride in learning. Critical faculties such as engineering, medicine, science and technology are located in such institutions. Students are drawn from a background that allows conformity and one that confirms the fit through successful outcomes. It is all so neat and natural. In contrast, black institutions were seen as a channel for producing black graduates to feed into the 'homelands'. Fields of study were limited to the arts, social sciences and education. These institutions were staffed mainly by academics who lacked a senior academic background. They served to perpetuate the already accepted myth of black incompetence and poor ability.

If education hearings had been held, they would have included submissions by black teachers and black academics. I believe that they have much to tell about the role they played in providing an educational challenge to the apartheid educational design. Currently, in this post-transition phase, are they supporting and promoting educational empowerment? Fortunately, we do have a number of education studies and reports which show that there were many courageous black educators who resisted the apartheid design and actively made a difference. There have been reports of rural schools that have produced a high level of matriculation exemptions, and of departments in black tertiary institutions that have produced exceptional graduates. If we had held hearings, we might have heard of and learnt from these heroic examples.

These reflections on what might have been said provide clear evidence of areas that must be addressed in South Africa if we are to utilise education successfully as a vehicle for building our nation. The TRC Report states that admitting the truth restores one's dignity and identity, confirms experience as real and not illusory, and affirms one's sense of self. The Report encourages South Africans not to seek amnesia as a means of confronting the past, because the past refuses to lie down quietly. It has the uncanny habit of returning to haunt us. I believe that South Africa has begun the process of putting ointment on its educational wounds. But I also believe that we have to face the question of whether we are healing the most serious and damaging wound or, as some people suspect, whether we are ignoring it, in the hope that it will eventually heal.

Let us revisit for a moment the notions of superiority reinforced throughout the past decade. In our schools, in our universities, in our technikons, we have clearly just begun to touch on the eradication of this particular myth. Building schools and providing proper resources is but one step; a clear focus on the content of the classroom and the lecture hall is urgently required. The active input of parents and communities in shaping schools and their progress is also critical. If it is true that schooling at all levels transmits, overtly or covertly, certain values, then surely education is South Africa's main hope for creating a new South Africa, for building its assets. All South Africans are aware that, despite all the ills of education, the majority of parents in our country and most of our youth strongly desire educational opportunities. Just as the TRC will be able to build on South Africa's strong desire for peace and reconciliation, so could this desire for education be used to build education as an effective vehicle for transforming communities and our society.

The most potent force for a desirable outcome lies with teachers. Teachers should be alerted to their role in enhancing educational success. We tend to speak of teachers as though they are delinquents. Maybe some of them are, perhaps a large number of them are, but we need to start making them aware that they can play a new role, and that society insists that they play that role. So rather than focusing on the delinquency of teachers, we need to focus on the contribution they can make towards building the assets of our country.

I referred to education as a means of teaching and learning values. The plans announced by the Minister of Education, Kader Asmal, to improve teacher development and to support teachers in schools are a welcome indication of this new and necessary focus. Our former system clearly promoted negative values. Our new curriculum makes references to the positive values that should be inculcated in schools: democracy, an appreciation of human rights, problem-solving, tolerance, respect for diversity, non-sexism and non-racism. Schools are faced with the challenge of implementing reading materials that reflect these values, and teachers have to learn how to promote them. What is perhaps absent from the new curriculum is a need to learn that violence is not an effective tool for resolving problems. Our current record suggests that we need to give attention to this.

If we were to spend a few days visiting some schools, would we find that the objectives of learning about non-racism and non-sexism are present in our classrooms? I suspect that we would not. These difficult topics, and discussions about them, appear to be taboo in most of our schools. It seems that our teachers avoid them, perhaps because they have not been provided with the skills for addressing them, leaving learners to cope with new contexts and challenges by themselves. I wonder what some of our top matriculants would say of the TRC lessons and about building the nation. Do they know about the TRC? Are the introductions to the various volumes of the TRC part of the reading material we could use in school discussions? Is the TRC Report a means of conveying valuable lessons, or is the TRC Report a subject to be avoided? What kind of South Africa are we building if our youth are not aware of our history, and do not realise that we should build positive values, which challenge the history that we have inherited?

Educational practitioners owe it to South Africans to engage all of us in a concerted effort to review our educational truth with a view to leading us towards a fundamental transformation, which could shape our future positively. If, as the TRC Report urges us to do, we use our past to give better shape to the future, we may finally come to realise that memories can provide unbelievable opportunities for creating a more democratic history. In my view, a realistic assessment of the truth of apartheid education could help us come to terms with the enormous challenges facing South Africa in reconstructing and transforming education. Once we confront these challenges we can begin the process of building our nation.

In conclusion, I would like to refer to some further sources regarding the content of our classroom processes. The Institute for Democracy in South Africa (Idasa) conducted a study on South African attitudes towards sustaining democracy.[1] The initial phase of the study found that large numbers of South Africans did not appreciate the need to sustain democracy, but the second phase of the study reflected a greater appreciation of this need. Is our youth being imbued with an appreciation of democracy in schools and universities? A European Union study on awareness of rights in South Africa indicates that South Africans generally seem to know that there is something called a Bill of Rights – they're not quite sure what it is, but it's a phrase they quote now and then. We urgently need to educate people about their rights, so that our society can commit itself to ensuring that these rights become a practical reality in our country.

I believe that one of the TRC's lessons for the new millennium is that a new set of values and norms can and must offer different outcomes through education. We should actively address the values and norms we convey in our schools in order to entrench a positive educational framework in South Africa.

Chapter Twenty-two

The Second Republic

Jeffrey Lever and Wilmot James

South Africa belongs to a class of societies that are products of the wave of expansion unleashed in Western Europe from the fifteenth century onwards. It has interesting population diversity, immigrants from all continents and a dynamic urban, industrial life. The majority of the South African indigenous population did not succumb to the combination of force of arms and an army of germs under colonialism, but survived and flourished; today they are in large majority indigenous.[1] By the end of the twentieth century a sophisticated modern economy had brought millions of people of diverse origin into the closest of contact and after much suffering had created the most highly developed industrial democracy on the African continent.

South Africa has a history of hardening white supremacy that endured into the twentieth century.[2] After years of apartheid, it only gave way to democratic government in 1994. A liberation struggle, bolstered by increasing levels of international support in the 1980s, led to the undoing of white supremacy in government and public affairs, leaving first Nelson Mandela and his government between 1994 and 1999, and now Thabo Mbeki and his government, elected on 2 June 1999, with the task of building a decent society from a history where the progress of a white minority depended on the deliberate regression of a black majority.

The difficulties and challenges of this historical undertaking are born of the unusual combination – for Africa and southern Africa – of having democratic institutions and strong elements of an advanced technical base resting upon very uncertain social foundations. The benefits of economic and scientific advance have spread only to the minority. An urban industrial society has arisen, which resembles nineteenth-century Dickensian England in its squalor. As in the England of that time, there is talk of 'two nations': one rich, one poor.[3] Unlike

England, each nation bears the badge of its economic status on its outward appearance, for the rich nation is white and the poor nation black – in crude outline, that is.

The material extremes pose what is called the problem of 'democratic sustainability' in some quarters, which has in part to do with the extent to which a recently developed democratic regime of rights can contain, absorb and deflect the potentially destabilising forces for mass-based political mobilisation. It is, of course, a problem of political management, of how to find the balance between democracy and stability in a highly unequal transitional society. Comparatively speaking, South Africa is, of course, not alone with this problem.

Racism and Democracy

With the abolition of most racially based laws in 1991, racism in South Africa was officially de-institutionalised. What remains is the phenomenon that some scholars have referred to as 'modern racism': sporadic, everyday incidents and rearguard actions in associational and community life.[4] Just how pervasive this racism may be is hard to ascertain, given its protean and now furtive existence in a formally non-racial state. At the public level there is an ideological consensus on the untenability of racial discrimination. Even the white right wing (except for its most die-hard remnants) concedes that its former dreams of an orderly white paradise in which blacks appear only as docile work-hands were both impractical and illegitimate. It would, of course, be naïve to conclude that racism (construed as objectionable treatment on grounds of one's 'racial' membership) and racial hostility have disappeared. Formal juridical equality has in some ways inflamed grass-roots 'racial' consciousness under circumstances of continued material inequity and new forms of resource competition. Affirmative action policies necessarily drive home the relevance of ethnic background, particularly for those, mainly the 'minorities', who feel aggrieved by them.

In view of the country's history, what is perhaps most remarkable is the absence of sustained mass-based racial conflict. The symbolism of a united non-racial population so keenly projected since 1994 by the country's first democratically elected President, Nelson Mandela, has worn more than a little thin recently, but retains its basic ascendancy. Amongst the most visible incidents of what might be called communal racism on the part of the formerly dominant white population have been clashes at a small number of high schools, mostly in the smaller towns or in the poorer, lower-middle-class suburbs of the major cities.[5] Here racist resistance has often been interwoven with issues of the language of tuition (with black pupils preferring English to Afrikaans), the ability to pay school fees and adolescent peer friction. Likewise, a number of tertiary campuses have experienced racial flare-ups as white students have ranged themselves against campaigns mounted by black entrants over such matters as fees. The latter, however, had also been features of campus life at the almost exclusively black tertiary institutions, suggesting that race as such is not the central motif.

It seems fair to suggest that consciousness of race remains high, but that overt racism has declined considerably. Nevertheless, there are continuing reports of rather anomic outbreaks of inter-personal violence, such as the shooting of a black child by a white farmer early in 1998 and a recent bus shooting in Pretoria. The former has to be viewed against a spate of killings of white farm occupants that took on worrying dimensions in 1997. It is an open question to what extent the high levels of crime (as in the farm killings) are in some sense racially based or at least racially justified in the minds of perpetrators. Similarly, the extent to which the economically dominant white section practices informal racial exclusion of an odious kind is not easy to gauge.

Democracy has brought to the fore perhaps the most dangerous potential communal cleavage of a racial kind that may shape future South African society in disturbing ways. This division is constituted by the political, cultural and economic realities that divide the majority African section from the three minority groups, the white, coloured and Indian segments. Public opinion surveys consistently reveal an almost stable pattern of differences on social and political matters.[6] The two most prosperous sections – whites and Indians – have increasingly convergent (and conservative) political views, with coloured people in a middle position. The issue is exacerbated by one of the least debated but most consequential social inequalities: the problem of language. Under the constitutional camouflage for equal treatment of the country's eleven official languages, the reality is that those with high English-language competence are at a definite advantage in education and business. In this regard, many – perhaps most – mother-tongue speakers of one of the other nine African languages, in other words the African majority, suffer an almost automatic handicap, which the country's poor schooling system seems unlikely to eliminate in the medium term.

The historic compromise forged in the pre-1994 negotiations has thus resulted in both a cultural and economic accommodation of the prevailing contours set by generations of white dominance. In the economic sphere the decision to accept pro tem the pattern of asset ownership – forswearing the ANC's well-known pledge in its key visionary document, the Freedom Charter of 1955, to nationalise the country's 'monopoly industries' – meant that the new regime has had to make a shift in its fundamental strategy of socio-economic transformation. If assets could not be transferred to the people at one fell swoop, then other means had to be devised to undo racial inequalities. Since 1994, the efforts of the new government in this regard have largely crystallised around four major goals: poverty alleviation, a steady move to the equalisation of state social spending, and, perhaps most importantly, the state-supported restructuring of the occupational and ownership structure of the economy. Given the limited public funds available, the scope for dramatic changes in the profile of racial inequality by way of the first two is limited.

By 1994, the ANC had replaced its former quasi-socialist rhetoric with more endearing phrases for both international and local business elites: the Reconstruction and Development Programme (RDP) and Affirmative Action. Conceived as a kind of super-ministry of development co-ordination, the RDP as institution has suffered the fate of similar ventures elsewhere. The RDP Ministry closed down in 1996 and the RDP has all but disappeared as an overarching blueprint of socio-economic transformation.[7] Nevertheless, the reform process in the economic arena is far from dead, although transmuted into a host of business plans, the nature of which does lend itself to high-profile political marketing.

By mid-1998 the most compelling slogans with more than symbolic import for the continued siege on white economic dominance were those of affirmative action and black empowerment. Affirmative action had early on been adopted by the ANC policy-makers as a useful concept to promote its goals of black advancement while appearing as less than militant revolutionists. In 1994 Albie Sachs lucidly sketched the policy dilemmas facing the ANC prior to its assumption of power. A middle way had to be found between a mere political transition to universal franchise and the strategy of a revolutionary confiscation of white-owned assets in a post-apartheid South Africa.

> The solution we chose was that of affirmative action. The phrase had no Cold War associations. It was sufficiently open to take on a specific South African content and meaning, and yet concrete enough to have an unmistakable thrust in favour of the oppressed. Whatever form might emerge or whatever definition be given, everyone knew what the essence of affirmative action was: it meant taking special measures to ensure that black people and women and other groups who had been unfairly discriminated against in the past, would have real chances in life.[8]

The idea of affirmative action was, of course, not new to South Africa. Many companies had been paying at least lip service to such a policy since the 1980s, in a form of 'anticipatory socialisation'.[9] Particular emphasis had been placed on the rapid creation of a black managerial stratum through various company training and advancement programmes. The success of these ventures had been very limited, as a penetrating analysis of the 1980s by sociologist Blade Nzimande (elected in 1998 as General Secretary of the South African Communist Party) demonstrated.[10] Progress in the 1990s was not markedly better, and a survey in 1997 claimed that 'in the three-year period to 1997, the number of black senior managers increased by only 2.3 per cent, with a paltry 1.6 per cent increase among middle managers'.[11]

Sceptical of the capacity of the normal hiring and promotion processes to move towards demographic representativeness, and with data to back up its beliefs, the ANC-dominated government has thus of late increasingly focused on how to engineer black occupational advancement through affirmative action policies. Matters will doubtlessly be more easily arranged in the public sector. A recent White Paper on Affirmative Action in the Public Service envisages affirmative action programmes for all civil service departments that will mandate affirmative action plans, including numeric targets for the increased employment of the 'historically disadvantaged groups'.[12]

More controversial is a similar scheme to be implemented in the private sector through the provisions of an Employment Equity Act. Described as the 'first major piece of race-based legislation to enter the statute books since our country became democratic',[13] the measure seeks to achieve 'employment equity' for 'designated groups' (blacks, women and physically challenged people) in all private enterprises employing more than forty-nine workers. Employers will be required to submit employee profiles together with plans to increase representation of the designated groups at all levels to the Ministry of Labour, which will have wide powers to monitor and induce compliance. No specific quotas are stipulated, but employee representatives such as trade unions will have the right to negotiate and register complaints on the process.[14]

On paper a measure of major import, the Employment Equity Act may of course fall far short of its goals in a system in which governmental ambition outreaches its current capacity. In any case, black economic advancement that rests upon jobs alone cannot be considered in any sense adequate in a modern industrial society. The ownership structure of private property, and especially of productive assets, cannot be sustained in the long run if it is largely monopolised by whites. Few deny the necessity of change; the question remains as to who will pay the price, and how. Land reform will contribute to this transformation, but only to a limited extent; for an increasingly urbanised population the demand is for the widening of human and economic capital in the nation's cities and towns.

Dramatically higher rates of black participation in the nation's modern business sector have thus emerged as a priority much more clearly than ever before. The means to this goal are at hand, the promotion of black entrepreneurial investment in the equity market being the most publicised one. Since 1994, black-owned or controlled enterprises have increased their share in the capitalisation of the Johannesburg Stock Exchange from about 1 per cent to some 5 per cent.[15] The growth of black business will benefit greatly from the new form of the state: 'affirmative procurement' means that black-owned firms receive preference from the state regarding tenders, procurements and licences. White-owned firms are encouraged to seek black partnerships, while government policy induces the private sector to look to the use of black sub-contractors where possible.

To what extent these new developments will lead to the fulfilment of the economic aspirations of the emerging black elites is by no means clear. It is unlikely, for example, that the leading black business pressure group, the National African Chamber of Commerce, will see its '3-4-5-6' formula – 30 per cent black representation in directorships, 40 per cent black equity ownership, 50 per cent black external procurement and 60 per cent black representation in management – fulfilled by its target year of 2000.[16] The progress registered by black business firms on the Johannesburg Stock Exchange must be qualified by the fact that '[m]ost black economic empowerment deals are little more than investment syndicates taking small equity in firms, only a handful of which are start-ups'.[17] Black participation is most evident in the media and publishing sector, but lacking in major manufacturing. The operational capacity of black-owned firms remains heavily dependent on white management, and much of the money made by empowerment deals has ended up enriching white advisers and brokers. In short, a numerically significant black entrepreneurial stratum outside of the small business sector has yet to consolidate.

South Africa has entered the new millennium with its profile of racial inequality, which was built up over three centuries of white domination, largely intact on a material level. But the relative success in installing a modern urban industrial economy – for Africa – has meant that the floor on which this inequality rests is subject to shifts over time. Significant segments of the wider black population have moved upwards and the political transition of 1994 has accelerated this trend. Politically, the white minority is now for the first time a true minority group, and economic transformation is now more feasible under a regime of juridical equality and a broad integrative social thrust.

In the medium term, much depends on the ability of the economy to grow and create jobs, which remains an uncertain possibility. South Africa's growth in Gross Domestic Product was 3 per cent in 1996/7 and 1,5 per cent in 1997/8.[18] While these growth figures are considerably higher than those achieved in the early 1990s, they fall well below the figures required by the Growth, Employment and Redistribution (GEAR) macro-economic framework accepted by the government and the trade unions as the guiding light of economic and fiscal policy. It is a matter of debate for economists why it is that South Africa is under-performing, and why even modest growth is being accompanied by a loss and not a growth in jobs.[19]

Much too depends upon the relative stability of political and social life, at present subject to a battering by crime, an economic downturn and the material discontent of broad layers of the population. Short of a mass exodus of the dominant white group, a sharp and sudden reversal of racial inequality was always an unrealistic prospect. The issue remains to what extent the system can generate the business optimism and economic competence that will attract investment and increase growth. If in the process the state can pursue its current reforms while maintaining a reasonable measure of efficiency, then the diminution of racial inequality becomes feasible.

The Second Republic

When the Government of National Unity came into power in 1994, it embarked on a massive and ambitious agenda of social change. In simple terms, one part of the agenda was aimed at creating and entrenching – by constitutional and other means – the protection of individual citizens' rights, while the other part was intended to deal with the socio-economic inequality bequeathed by apartheid. On balance, the first period of democratic government was necessarily devoted more to the protection of rights, although these noble and important checks against the abuses of apartheid came increasingly under fire as government struggled to enforce a human rights policy in the face of a seeming explosion of criminal conduct, much of it rooted in apartheid's other legacy: black poverty.

Nelson Mandela's leadership gave additional impetus to reconciliation between the 'racial groups', and he appeared particularly concerned about Afrikaners and their place in the new democratic order. The extreme expression of Afrikaner anxiety was the demand for a *Volkstaat*, made both by an extra-parliamentary paramilitary group by the name of the Afrikaner Weerstandsbeweging (Afrikaner Resistance Movement) and the parliamentary Freedom Front, though the latter was willing to wait a hundred or so years to achieve its goal. A less extreme view was to seek some form of 'group' protection through the recognition of minority language and cultural rights.

Though Mandela in his presidential conduct made many – some say too many – overtures to the Afrikaner community, he and his government were insistent that every South African was juridically equal and that no concessions on a group basis were to be made. The presumption of jurisprudence was that strong and enforceable protection of individual rights was enough of a check against potential abuse of a group, particularly one that was seen to be historically responsible for the abuses of apartheid. But the insistence on individual rights also required a reading of South African history based on individual and not group responsibility.

The Truth and Reconciliation Commission was established by Nelson Mandela's government in 1994 to find individual causes for egregious human rights abuses committed during apartheid. Its origins were rooted in two important conferences organised under the auspices of Idasa and the thinking of some members of the ANC, in particular that of Kader Asmal, Dullah Omar, Johnny de Lange and Albie Sachs.[20] South Africa's Interim Constitution contained a clause negotiated at Kempton Park, which allowed for the granting of amnesty to those who committed serious human rights abuses on both sides of the struggle. A law passed in 1994 established the Commission and defined its brief, and the final constitution passed in 1995 confirmed its role as one of the many commissions established to support democratic consolidation in the country.

While the TRC was one of many rights institutions – others are the Electoral, Gender, Human Rights and Youth commissions – its work dominated South African public life until 1998, when its voluminous Report was submitted to then President Nelson Mandela.[21] Over a period of four years South Africa heard evidence of many victims of apartheid's atrocities (much less was heard from victims of the ANC, PAC and the other liberation organisations' war against apartheid) and the confessions of the perpetrators, again mostly from the apartheid security machinery side.[22] The premise of the TRC's work was that amnesty was to be granted on the basis of individual responsibility and truth telling, which is why the cause of blanket amnesty was rejected. However, by virtue of South African history, most of the perpetrators were Afrikaners, leading some commentators to proclaim that the TRC was an Afrikaner witch-hunt, alienating some leading members of the Afrikaner establishment.

The point of the TRC was to establish individual culpability and so to confirm a central principle of the rule of law. It was also to collate a South African memory and so to present and cultivate new values, showing what was to be tolerated as proper and decent public and private conduct among citizens and officials of the state. Beyond that, the TRC was part of a larger set of initiatives designed to promote democratic values and practices, the observance of human rights and the rights of women, and the establishment of properly functioning democratic institutions. More than anything else, these initiatives were the mark of Mandela's presidency, the creation and consolidation of what is sometimes called the democratic 'software'. These initiatives were doubly reinforced by Mandela's concern with reconciliation between the former enemies and the peaceful co-existence of South Africa's main population groups.

As we have seen, the TRC is not without its critics. While we might dismiss the self-interested and boisterous critique of the right, we cannot but observe that the victims of apartheid abuse received shabby administrative treatment from the government; that there was mismanagement in the politics of securing measures for reparation; and that many important things, such as the publication of an annotated list of those who died or disappeared, were left undone. Van Zyl Slabbert's penetrating observations have cast a dark shadow of doubt on whether the TRC would ever have discovered the truth. Courts, he argues, are the only device for doing so.[23]

Barely under the surface lurks, now seen, now unseen, the question of the political economy of racial inequality. The issue clearly and increasingly occupied the mind of South Africa's Deputy-President Thabo Mbeki who, in becoming South Africa's second democratically elected president, made it a recurring theme of public policy. On becoming president he elevated the delivery of social and public service to a position of pre-eminence; he linked black poverty to white wealth; and he stated his belief that social and political stability cannot be achieved other than by growth. Finally, he insisted that South Africa's future is part of a putative Renaissance of the African continent.[24]

Mbeki's challenge is to find political stability in a democratic framework that is subject to domestic and global tensions. He has to invoke some major and painful changes in the economy in order to live up to a presidency of delivery and poverty-reduction on the one hand, while rendering South Africa globally competitive on the other. In his address at the Opening of Parliament in February 2000 he appeared ready to tackle the issue of entrenched labour and trade union rights, which many argue are responsible for an inflexible, stagnating labour market and the slow growth of small black business. In 1999, his government successfully faced down the public sector unions on the issue of salary increases. Limits and restrictions on free trade, investments and currency flows are being eased considerably, though carefully managed by the Finance Ministry and the Reserve Bank in a manner that aims not to become inflationary.

The consequence of opening the economy more and more to global competition in an environment that is shedding jobs at an alarming rate is, of course, potentially dangerous and could damage political relations between the various constituencies of the ANC, COSATU and the Communist Party. Van Zyl Slabbert suggests that Mbeki's main task is to control the public policy agenda and the ANC, both of which he has strategically mastered. By a skilful combination of co-optation and patronage, both COSATU and the Communist Party are under ANC hegemony. The public policy agenda is being strategically shaped by some key individuals in the much-enlarged President's Office. The key question remains whether he can retain COSATU and the Communist Party's loyalty when the going gets tough, when jobs are increasingly at risk. Mbeki's success depends in large measure on his ability to deliver better social services and a better life for the African majority under circumstances in which the most realistic prospects are a largely white-owned and controlled economy, an increasingly black middle class of professionals and entrepreneurs, and an underclass of black Africans trapped in the townships and squatter camps of the cities.

The balance between the democratic values promoted by the TRC and the challenges of our political economy is, of course, a matter of political leadership. We search for the new South Africans, neither white nor black, democratic by inclination, capable of transcending the divides of culture, language and geography. The TRC provides us with the memories of the unjust and the values of the just. Herein lie the foundations of the moral character of the new South African.

Endnotes

Introduction

1 We are grateful to two academic colleagues of Wilmot James who, about fifteen years ago, played with this metaphor as a possible title for a book that was unfortunately never written.

2 See, for example, G. Bizos, *No-one to Blame? In Pursuit of Justice in South Africa* (Cape Town, 1998); E. de Kok, *A Long Night's Damage: Working for the Apartheid State* (Saxonwold, 1998); A. Krog, *Country of My Skull* (Johannesburg, 1998); J. Pauw, *Into the Heart of Darkness: Confessions of Apartheid's Assassins* (Johannesburg, 1997); G. Slovo, *Every Secret Thing: My Family, My Country* (London, 1997); A. Wolpe, *The Long Way Home* (Cape Town, 1994); S. Williamson's photographic work entitled *Truth Games; Faultlines* Exhibition, Castle of Good Hope, Cape Town, June 1996.

3 *Truth and Reconciliation Commission of South Africa Report* (5 vols., Cape Town, 1998).

4 G.J. Gerwel, 'National Reconciliation: Holy Grail or Secular Pact?', in C. Villa-Vicencio and W. Verwoerd (eds.), *Looking Back/Reaching Forward: Reflections on the Truth and Reconciliation Commission of South Africa* (Cape Town and London, 2000), pp. 277–86.

5 C. van Onselen, *The Seed is Mine: The Life of Kas Maine, a South African Sharecropper, 1894 to 1985* (Cape Town, 1996).

6 See also M. Minow, *Between Vengeance and Forgiveness: Facing History after Genocide and Mass Violence* (Boston, 1998).

7 See K. Asmal, L. Asmal and R. Roberts, *Reconciliation through Truth: A Reckoning of Apartheid's Criminal Governance* (Cape Town and New York, 1997).

8 Some commentators have argued that where a state-sponsored amnesty is in operation, the state also bears the responsibility for ensuring that victims/survivors are compensated. See, for example, C. Villa-Vicencio, 'Why Perpetrators Should Not Always Be Prosecuted: Where the International Criminal Court and Truth Admissions Meet', *Emory Law Journal*, vol. 49, 2000, pp. 101–118, at p. 113.

9 Anthea Jeffery's myopic treatment of the TRC unsurprisingly fails to grasp this point. See A. Jeffery, *The Truth about the Truth Commission* (Johannesburg, 1999).

10 D. Tutu, *No Future Without Forgiveness* (New York, 1999).

Chapter One

1 G. Simpson, 'A Brief Evaluation of South Africa's TRC: Some Lessons for Societies in Transition', paper presented at conference 'The TRC: Commissioning the Past' at the University of the Witwatersrand, Johannesburg, June 1999, p. 27.

2 H. Wolpe, *Race, Class and the Apartheid State* (London, Addis Ababa, Paris, 1988), p. 103.

3 P.W. Botha: Prime Minister of South Africa from 1978 to 1984, and State President from 1984 to 1989.

4 H. Marais, *South Africa: Limits to Change: The Political Economy of Transformation* (London and Cape Town, 1998), p. 89.

5 Cited in Marais, *Limits to Change*, p. 90.

6 Marais, *Limits to Change*, p. 93.

7 Simpson, 'A Brief Evaluation', p. 4.

8 Simpson, 'A Brief Evaluation', p. 5.

9 Simpson, 'A Brief Evaluation', p. 19.

10 *Truth and Reconciliation Commission of South Africa Report* (5 vols., Cape Town, 1998), vol. 1, ch. 4, para. 31(a).

11 D. Posel, 'The TRC Report: What Kind of History? What Kind of Truth?', paper presented at conference 'The TRC: Commissioning the Past', p. 10.

12 *TRC Report*, vol. 1, p. 4.

13 *TRC Report*, vol. 1, pp. 2, 18.

14 Posel, 'The TRC Report', p. 12.

15 Posel, 'The TRC Report', p. 14.

16 *TRC Report*, vol. 1, ch. 6, para. 37.

17 This and the preceding paragraph are based on Posel, 'The TRC Report', pp. 15–18; quotation on p. 18.

18 J. Derrida, *Archive Fever: A Freudian Impression* (Chicago and London, 1996), p. 10, cited in B. Harris, 'The Archive, Public History and the Essential Truth: The TRC Reading the Past', paper presented at seminar series 'Refiguring the Archive', University of the Witwatersrand, 1998, p. 7.

19 *TRC Report*, vol. 1, 'Chairperson's Report', p. 22, para. 91.

20 Harris, 'The Archive', p. 3.

21 *TRC Report*, vol. 1, p. 7, para. 27.

22 *TRC Report*, vol. 1, pp. 201–43. See also V. Harris, ' "They should have destroyed more": The Destruction of Public Records by the South African State in the Final Years of Apartheid', paper presented at conference 'The TRC: Commissioning the Past'.

23 A. du Toit, 'The Product and the Process: On the Impact of the TRC Report', paper presented at conference 'The TRC: Commissioning the Past', p. 2.

24 L. Buur, 'Monumental History: Visibility and Invisibility in the Work of the South African TRC', paper presented at conference 'The TRC: Commissioning the Past'.

25 *TRC Report*, vol. 1 pp. 62–64, paras. 51, 53, 58.

26 Posel, 'The TRC Report', p. 10.

27 *TRC Report*, vol. 2, pp. 194–97.

28 M. Hunter, *Reaction to Conquest*, 2nd ed. (London, 1961), p. 470.

29 *Report of the Police Commission of Inquiry, 1937*, UG 50, 1937, cited in H. J. Simons, 'The Law and its Administration', in Ellen Hellman (ed.), *Handbook on Race Relations in South Africa* (Cape Town, 1949), pp. 41–108, at p. 75.

30 H.J. Simons, 'The Law and its Administration', p. 76. (Simons, incidentally, footnoted this evidence to a 1936 publication.)

31 S. Marks and N. Andersson, 'The Epidemiology and Culture of Violence', in A. du Toit and N. C. Manganyi (eds.), *Political Violence and the Struggle in South Africa* (London, 1990), p. 32.

32 Cited in J. Pauw, 'Terrifyingly Normal', *Siyaya!*, no. 3 (Spring 1998), p. 32.

33 M. Mamdani, 'A Diminished Truth', chapter 5 of this publication.

34 G. Davis, 'Overview', *Siyaya!*, no. 3 (Spring 1998), p. 8.

35 P. Connerton, *How Societies Remember* (Cambridge, 1989), p. 1.

36 P. Connerton, *How Societies Remember*, p. 2.

37 H. Marais, *Limits to Change*, p. 239.

Chapter Two

1 See N. Ascherson, 'You Don't Have to be Clever to Run a Country: But It Helps', *Guardian and Observer*, 20 June 1999.

2 N. Ascherson, 'You Don't Have to be Clever to Run a Country'.

3 *Truth and Reconciliation Commission of South Africa Report* (5 vols., Cape Town, 1998), vols. 1, 2.

4 Quoted in Bundy, 'The TRC Report: What Kind of History? What Kind of Truth?', paper presented at conference 'The TRC: Commissioning the Past', at the University of the Witwatersrand, Johannesburg, June 1999.

5 A. Jeffery, *The Truth about The Truth Commission* (Johannesburg, 1999).

6 In his address to the 29th Provincial Synod of the Church of the Province of Southern Africa, Durban, 16 July 1999.

7 *Cape Argus*, 7 August 1999.

8 S. Ellis, 'The Truth and Reconciliation Commission of South Africa', in *Critique Internationale*, October 1999.

9 Cited in J. Cherry, 'Historical Truth and the Truth and Reconciliation Commission', in C. Villa-Vicencio and W. Verwoerd (eds.), *Looking Back/Reaching Forward: Reflections of the South African Truth and Reconciliation Commission* (Cape Town and London, 2000).

10 Human Rights Violations Committee hearing, Cape Town, 22 April 1996.

11 Pamela Reynolds, Inaugural Lecture (University of Cape Town), 20 August 1997.

12 A. Jeffery, *The Truth about the Truth Commission.*

13 G. Simpson, 'A Brief Evaluation of South Africa's TRC: Some Lessons for Societies in Transition', paper presented at conference 'The TRC: Commissioning the Past', p. 19.

14 See also C. Villa-Vicencio and W. Verwoerd, 'Constructing a Report: Writing Up "the Truth"' in R. Rotberg (ed.), *Truth versus Justice* (Princeton, 2000).

15 A. Neier, 'Truth Commission of South Africa Report (Cape Town, South Africa, 1998) and *Country of My Skull* by Antjie Krog (Johannesburg: Random House, 1998)', in *The New York Review of Books,* 1999.

16 See *TRC Report*, vol. 1, ch. 6.

17 A. Krog, *Country of My Skull* (Johannesburg, 1998).

18 J. Thompson, *Ideology and Modern Culture: Critical Social Theory in the Era of Mass Communication* (Stanford, 1990).

19 'Truth Trickle Becomes a Flood', *Mail and Guardian*, 1–7 November 1996.

20 *Eugene de Kock*: Former commanding officer of the Vlakplaas unit outside Pretoria, a division of the South African Police's Security Branch.

21 *Jeffrey Benzien*: A former security policeman who confessed to the torture (by the so-called wet-bag method) and killing of political activists in the 1980s.

22 D.W. Shriver, *An Ethic for Enemies: Forgiveness in Politics* (New York, Oxford, 1995), p. 230.

23 *TRC Report*, vol. 1, pp. 24–43.

24 M. Mamdani, 'A Diminished Truth', chapter 5 of this publication.

25 A. Sachs, public lecture on the TRC, 4th D.T. Lakdawala Memorial Lecture, 18 December 1998, New Delhi.

26 A. du Toit, 'Perpetrator Findings as Artificial Even-Handedness? The TRC's Contested Judgements of Moral and Political Accountability for Gross Human Rights Violations', paper presented at conference 'The TRC: Commissioning the Past'.

27 A. du Toit, 'Perpetrator Findings as Artificial Even-Handedness?'.

28 Skweyiya Commission Report, 1992. Included in the ANC's submission to the TRC, August 1996.

29 L. Jaworski, *After Fifteen Years* (Houston, 1961).

30 J. Garlinski, *Fighting Auschwitz* (London, 1994), p. 139.

31 Personal conversation.

32 *TRC Report*, vol. 5, ch. 7.

33 T. Garton Ash, 'The Truth about Dictatorship', in *The New York Review of Books*, 19 February 1998, p. 40.

Chapter Three

1 I. Buruma, 'The Joys and Perils of Victimhood', in *The New York Review of Books*, 8 April 1999, pp. 4–9.

2 N. Frei, *Vergangenheitspolitik: Die Anfänge der Bundesrepublik und die NS-Vergangenheit* (Munich, 1996), p. 405.

3 H. Dubiel, *Niemand ist frei von der Geschichte* (Munich, 1999), p. 276.

4 P. Reichel, *Politik mit der Erinnerung. Gedächtnisorte im Streit um die nationalsozialistische Vergangenheit* (Frankfurt, 1999); M. Cullen (ed.), *Das Holocaust-Mahnmal. Dokumentation einer Debatte* (Zürich, 1999); M. Jeismann (ed.), *Mahnmahl Mitte* (Cologne, 1999).

5 A. Neier, *War Crimes: Brutality, Genocide, Terror, and the Struggle for Justice* (New York, 1998), p. 228.

6 I. Buruma, 'The Joys and Perils of Victimhood'.

7 M. Ignatieff, *The Warrior's Honour: Ethnic War and the Modern Conscience* (Toronto, 1998), p. 170.

8 M. Ignatieff, *The Warrior's Honour*, p. 185.

9 A. Neier, *War Crimes*, p. 213.

10 J. Habermas in *Die Zeit*, 15 May 1999.

11 S. Karstedt, 'Coming to Terms with the Past in Germany after 1945 and 1989: Public Judgements on Procedures and Justice', *Law and Policy*, vol. 20:1, January 1998, pp. 15–56.

12 S. Karstedt, 'Coming to Terms with the Past', pp. 15–56.

13 C. Goschler, 'Offene Fragen der Wiedergutmachung', *Leviathan*, vol. 18, 1998, pp. 38–52; quotation on p. 49.

14 Personal conversation, 7 February 1999.

15 M. Minow, *Between Vengeance and Forgiveness* (Boston, 1998), p. 132.

16 M. Mamdani, 'A Diminished Truth', chapter 5 of this publication.

17 M. Minow, *Between Vengeance and Forgiveness*, p. 127.

18 G. Schwan, *Politik und Schuld* (Frankfurt, 1997), p. 245.

19 *Dirk Coetzee*: Eugene de Kock's predecessor as commander of Vlakplaas, who in 1989 revealed the existence of a 'hit-squad' at the Vlakplaas police base.

20 E. de Kock, *A Long Night's Damage: Working for the Apartheid State* (Saxonwold, 1998).

21 J. Pauw, *Into the Heart of Darkness: Confessions of Apartheid's Assassins* (Johannesburg, 1997).

22 *Winnie Madikizela-Mandela*: Together with the Mandela United Football Club (a gang of youths which acted as her unofficial bodyguards) she was implicated in several human rights violations cases dating back to the 1980s.

23 M. Ignatieff, *The Warrior's Honour*, p. 176.

24 M. Ignatieff, *The Warrior's Honour*, p. 173.

Chapter Four

1 This is a revised version of an article entitled 'Must the victims always wait?', *Siyaya!*, no. 3 (Spring 1998).

2 As in the case of Argentina.

3 As in the case of El Salvador and its famous 'death squads'.

4 Although Chile held free elections, former President Pinochet still holds his 'vitalicio' seat in the Senate.

5 At the time of the El Salvador Truth Commission's work, the Defence Minister was known to be responsible for the killings of Jesuit priests in 1990.

6 The El Salvador Truth Commission was the only one to disseminate the names of those who, according to the results of its investigations, were the authors of terrible crimes. In Chile, names were never disclosed; in Argentina, the names were presented only to the President. This information swiftly fell into the hands of the press and prompted the start of legal proceedings.

7 The Chilean Truth and Reconciliation Commission, also known as the Rettigg Commission, after the name of its chairperson.

8 This refers to the Latin American countries in particular.

9 This is an understanding of public policy as a set of articulated measures oriented towards a specific end. To reach this end a policy has to have its resources, rely on political support and be based on an analysis that allows it to determine the viability of those measures.

10 By looking at the difficulties transitional governments have to face in their efforts to meet the state's obligation to provide justice and truth, the international community has created other mechanisms, such as the International Criminal Tribunals for the former Yugoslavia and Rwanda, and more recently, the proposed International Criminal Court.

Chapter Five

1 This essay was originally published in *Siyaya!*, no. 3 (Spring 1998).

Chapter Six

1 This essay originally appeared as Chapter 8 in the English translation of F. Van Zyl Slabbert, *Afrikaner Afrikaan: Anekdotes en Analise* (Cape Town, 2000).

2 *Carel Boshoff*: Leader of the Freedom Front in the Northern Cape, who is firmly committed to the ideal of an Afrikaner 'Volkstaat'.

3 *Constand Viljoen*: National leader of the Freedom Front, a political party that favours Afrikaner self-determination.

4 *Eugene Terre'Blanche*: Former leader of the Afrikaner Weerstandsbeweging (Afrikaner Resistance Movement), an extra-parliamentary paramilitary group.

5 *Mangosuthu Buthelezi*: Leader of the Inkatha Freedom Party, also Minister of Home Affairs in the Government of National Unity.

6 *B.J. (John) Vorster*: Prime Minister of South Africa from 1966 to 1978.

7 *Betsie Verwoerd*: Widow of H.F. Verwoerd, Prime Minister of South Africa from 1958 to 1966, who was assassinated by Dimitri Tsafendas in September 1966.

8 A. Krog, *Country of My Skull* (Johannesburg, 1998); J. Pauw, *Prime Evil*, SABC 1 documentary, 1996; M. du Preez's television programme, *TRC Special Report*, SABC 3, 1998.

Chapter Seven

1 *New York Times*, 3 November 1998.
2 *New York Times*, 5 November 1998.
3 *New York Times*, 1 November 1998.
4 G.J. Gerwel, 'Reconciliation: Holy Grail or Secular Pact?', in C. Villa-Vicencio and W. Verwoerd (eds.), *Looking Back/Reaching Forward: Reflections of the South African Truth and Reconciliation Commission* (Cape Town and London, 2000), pp. 277–86.
5 G.J. Gerwel, 'Reconciliation: Holy Grail or Secular Pact?'.
6 Statement by Deputy President Thabo Mbeki at the opening of the debate on 'Reconciliation and Nation-Building', National Assembly of the Parliament of South Africa, 29 May 1998.
7 Statement by Deputy President Thabo Mbeki at the opening of the debate on 'Reconciliation and Nation-Building'.
8 Statement by Deputy President Thabo Mbeki at the opening of the debate on 'Reconciliation and Nation-Building'.
9 *Business Day*, 17 June 1999.
10 J. Zalaquett, 'Balancing Ethical Imperatives and Political Constraints: The Dilemma of New Democracies Confronting Past Human Rights Violations', in N. J. Kritz, *Transitional Justice* (3 vols., Washington, D.C., 1995), vol. 2, pp. 495–96.
11 H. Arendt, *The Human Condition: A Study of the Central Conditions Facing Modern Man* (Garden City, NY, 1959), p. 214.
12 K. Jaspers, *The Question of German Guilt* (New York, 1947), p. 31.
13 Quoted in W. Niemöller, *Neuanfang 1945: Zur Biographie Martin Niemöller* (Frankfurt, 1976).
14 Media statement issued on 8 May 1997.
15 A. Krog, in A. Boraine and J. Levy (eds.), *The Healing of a Nation?* (Cape Town, 1994), pp. 112–119.
16 Interim Constitution of the Republic of South Africa, Act No. 200 of 1993.
17 *Azanian People's Organisation (AZAPO) and Others v President of the Republic of South Africa and Others*, 1996 (8) BCLR 1015 (CC).
18 *Siyaya!*, no. 3 (Spring 1998), p. 60.
19 A. Michnik, in A. Boraine and J. Levy (eds.), *Dealing with the Past* (Cape Town, 1994), p. 16.
20 M. Ignatieff, *Index on Censorship: Wounded Nations, Broken Lives*, vol. 5, 1996, p. 122.

Chapter Nine

1 M. Twala, *Mbokodo: Inside MK: Mwezi Twala, a Soldier's Story* (Johannesburg, 1994).
2 Max du Preez's television programme, *TRC Special Report*, SABC 3, 1998.

Chapter Ten

1 *Goldstone Commission*: The Commission of Inquiry Regarding Public Violence and Intimidation (which became known as the Goldstone Commission, after its chairperson, Richard Goldstone) was established by government in 1991 to investigate the causes of the political violence and intimidation occurring in the 1980s and early 1990s.

2 A. Jeffery, *The Truth about the Truth Commission* (Johannesburg, 1999).

3 *Albert Luthuli* was President of the ANC from 1952 to 1967; he was awarded the 1960 Nobel Peace Prize. *Oliver Tambo* was acting President of the ANC from 1967 to 1977 and President of the ANC from 1977 to 1990; he lived in exile from 1960 to 1990.

4 Three anti-apartheid activists who lived for many years as exiles in Mozambique.

Chapter Eleven

1 The Elliot Four are a case in point. The relatives of these four persons expressed satisfaction at the success of locating and exhuming the bodies of the deceased, who had been missing since 1981. Even evidence suggesting that they may have been criminally executed before they were buried has not prompted the families to press charges. They had come to terms with the truth because they knew where their sons or brothers were buried.

2 See the Human Rights Violations Committee hearing, Case No. JB0289/013ERKWA at http://www.truth.org.za/hrvtrans/duduza/molok.htm, accessed on 15 May 2000.

3 See the Human Rights Violations Committee hearing, Case No. EC0051/96 at http://www.truth.org.za/hrvtrans/hrvel1/savage.htm, accessed on 15 May 2000.

4 The transcript of the proceedings of this Forum can be found at http://www.truth.org.za/debate/economic.htm, accessed on 15 May 2000.

5 A women's group for victims and survivors of apartheid atrocities, associated with the Centre for the Study of Violence and Reconciliation.

6 See the Amnesty Committee hearing, Case No. 3918/96 at http://www.truth.org.za/amntrans/pe1/snyman.htm, accessed on 15 May 2000.

7 All these experiences and divergent views were thoroughly explored by the TRC and have been painstakingly reflected in vol. 5, ch.1 of the TRC Report.

8 A. Jeffery, *The Truth about the Truth Commission* (Johannesburg, 1999).

9 In this I agree with André du Toit, who has suggested that it will take about fifty years before the impact of the TRC can be fully appreciated.

10 See the decision of the Amnesty Committee: AC/96/0011 at http://www.truth.org.za/decisions/1996/961209Mitchell.htm, accessed on 15 May 2000.

Chapter Thirteen

1 The research for this paper was conducted as part of the 'Project on Public Pasts' (POPP), funded by the National Research Foundation.

2   *Reader's Digest Illustrated Guides to Southern Africa, Southern and Eastern Cape* (Cape Town, 1983), p. 48.

3   J. Watson, *The Urban Trail: A Walk Through the Urban Heritage of East London's Central Business District and Older Suburbs* (East London, 1989), pp. 13–14.

4   'What's on in East London', East London Publicity Association (pamphlet), January 1994, p. 16.

5   D. Beresford, 'Theatre of Pain and Catharsis', *Mail and Guardian*, 19–25 April 1996.

6   D. Beresford, 'Theatre of Pain and Catharsis'.

7   D. Beresford, 'Theatre of Pain and Catharsis'.

8   M. Gevisser, 'The Ultimate Test of Faith', *Mail and Guardian*, 12–18 April 1996.

9   See S. Laufer, 'Television Needs to Bring Grief of Truth Hearings to the Nation', *Business Day*, 6 May 1996, for a discussion of the TRC, history and television. See also C. Braude, 'SA's Hearings Are Not Nuremberg, But Expediency Must Not Fudge the Truth', *The Sunday Independent*, 26 May 1996. However, both Laufer and Braude fail to distinguish between 'visibility' and 'visuality' in their arguments. For an examination of these issues see G. Minkley, C. Rassool and L. Witz, 'Thresholds, Gateways and Spectacles: Journeying through South African Hidden Pasts and Histories in the Last Decade of the Twentieth Century', paper presented at conference 'The Future of the Past: The Production of History in a Changing South Africa', University of the Western Cape, 10–12 July 1996.

10 Promotion of National Unity and Reconciliation, Act No. 34 of 1995.

11 'A Summary of Reparation and Rehabilitation Policy, including Proposals to be Considered by the President', Truth and Reconciliation Commission (1998), pp. 6–8.

12 *TRC Report*, vol. 5, ch. 9.

13 P. Steyn, 'Tutu Onsteld oor Leemte in Begroting', *Die Burger*, 28 February 2000; *Cape Times*, 26 April 2000; *Weekend Saturday Argus*, 29/30 April 2000.

14 A. Koopman, 'ANC Wants Community Reparations', Independent Online, http://archive.iol.co.za/Archives/1999/9902/26/reparations.html, accessed on 16 March 2000.

15 'A Summary of Reparation and Rehabilitation Policy' (1998), p. 15; see 'Proposed Policy for UIR and Final Reparation: Discussion Document' (Truth and Reconciliation Commission National Consultation, 2 April 1997), especially Annexure A, for an earlier stage in the development of ideas on symbolic reparations, after a series of national consultations.

16 'The Portfolio of Legacy Projects: A Portfolio of Commemorations Acknowledging Neglected or Marginalised Heritage' (Discussion Document, January 1998), p. 5.

17 Transcript of session 'Unfinished Business' at conference 'After the Truth and Reconciliation Commission: Reconciliation in the New Millennium', University of Cape Town, 10–12 August 1999.

18 'Address by President Mandela – Heritage Day', *Ilifa Labantu*, vol. 1, no. 9 (October 1997), p. 3.

19 For an extensive discussion on displays at the McGregor Museum see L. Witz, C. Rassool and G. Minkley, 'The Boer War, Museums and Ratanga Junction, the

Wildest Place in Africa: Public History in South Africa in the 1990s', Basler Afrika Bibliographien Working Paper No. 2: 2000, presented in Basel, 10 February 2000.

20 Notice at entrance to *Faultlines* exhibition, Castle of Good Hope, Cape Town, June 1996.

21 J. Taylor, interviewed on SAFM, SABC Radio, 30 June 1996.

22 B. Atkinson, 'Review of *Truth Veils* at the Gertrude Posel and Market Theatre Galleries, 14 June–9 July 1999', ArtThrob (www.artthrob.co.za/99dec/reviews.html), accessed on 19 March 2000.

23 D. Hooks, 'Review of *Truth Veils* at the Gertrude Posel and Market Theatre Galleries, 14 June–9 July 1999', ArtThrob (www.atrthrob.co.za/99dec/reviews.html), accessed on 19 March 2000.

24 S. Williamson, '*Truth Games* – a Series of Interactive Pieces around the Hearings of the Truth and Reconciliation Commission of South Africa' (Cape Town, 1999) (brochure).

25 Notice of Sue Williamson's exhibition, *Can't Remember, Can't Forget*, ArtThrob (www.atrthrob.co.za/99dec/reviews.html), accessed on 19 March 2000.

26 S. Hermans, 'A quick creative buck', *The Argus*, 26 May 1993.

27 R. Friedman, 'Tutu Visits War Memorial'; '"White Bums" Missing from TRC Benches', *Cape Times*, 3 July 1996.

28 'The Portfolio of Legacy Projects', p. 1.

29 'Statement by Minister Mtshali on Legacy Projects' (1998).

30 'The Portfolio of Legacy Projects', pp. 10–11, 20–21, 28.

31 'The Portfolio of Legacy Projects', p. 19.

32 'The Portfolio of Legacy Projects', p. 27.

33 'A Summary of Reparation and Rehabilitation Policy'. This image of 'Nelson Mandela Rylaan' is most probably a picture of the main street in Umtata, which was renamed 'Nelson Mandela Drive' in honour of Mandela's 'commitment to peace and reconciliation'. The road was opened by Thabo Mbeki during a special ceremony held by the Umtata City Council on 18 January 1999. A commemorative monument to the renaming stands on Nelson Mandela Drive, Umtata.

34 B. Harris, '"Unearthing" the "Essential" Past: The Making of a Public "National" Memory Through the Truth and Reconciliation Commission, 1994–1998', unpublished MA mini-thesis, University of the Western Cape (1998), pp. 100–103.

35 P. Singh, 'Memorial to Honour "Trojan Horse" Dead', *Cape Times*, 17 March 2000.

36 Y. Kemp, 'Mayor Unveils Monument to Mark Fall of Guguletu Seven', *Cape Argus*, 21 March 2000.

37 These extracts from speeches are from notes taken by the authors at the unveiling of the Trojan Horse monument in Athlone, 21 March 2000.

38 P. Singh, 'Memorial to Honour "Trojan Horse" Dead', *Cape Times*, 17 March 2000.

39 Authors' notes at the unveiling of the Trojan Horse monument in Athlone, 21 March 2000.

40 *Cape Times*, 9 September 1997.

41 These heads are contained in the 'Peoples of Namibia Collection' at the Hunterian Museum at the University of the Witwatersrand Medical School and form part of the

George Elkin Collection. They are displayed to medical students in a cabinet across the floor from the Raymond Dart Gallery of African Faces. There are seven heads in the collection: Ovahimba, Nama, Bushman, Damara, Herero, Ovambo, as well as a sculpture of 'Oubaas', a 'Pituitary Midget' from Ghanzi in Botswana. For a discussion of anthropometric collections at the University of the Witwatersrand, see C. Rassool and P. Hayes, 'Science and the Spectacle:/Khanako's South Africa, 1936–7', in W. Woodward, P. Hayes and G. Minkley (eds.), *Deep Histories: Gender and Colonialism in Africa* (forthcoming).

42 City of Cape Town Bulletin, vol. 22, no. 4, April 2000, p. 2.

43 Y. Kamaldien, 'Guguletu Seven, Trojan Horse Dead Honoured', *Cape Times*, 22 March 2000.

44 B. Anderson, *Imagined Communities: Reflections on the Origin and Spread of Nationalism*, revised edition (London, 1991), p. 10.

45 *The Argus*, 28 June 1996.

46 *The Argus*, 17 April 1996.

47 *Weekend Argus*, 27–8 April 1996, quoting Archbishop Desmond Tutu.

48 *The Argus*, 17 April 1996.

49 *Cape Times*, 27 June 1996.

50 *Cape Times*, 3 April 1996.

51 *Sunday Times*, 5 May 1996.

52 *Business Day*, 6 May 1996.

53 *City Press*, 7 April 1996; *The Citizen*, 7 May 1996; *Business Day*, 10 May 1996, *Sunday Independent*, 5 May 1996.

54 There was a strong plea for a TRC archive to be established at the session 'Unfinished Business' at conference 'After the Truth and Reconciliation Commission: Reconciliation in the New Millennium', University of Cape Town, 10–12 August 1999.

55 B. Harris, '"Unearthing" the "Essential" Past', p. 2.

56 B. Harris, '"Unearthing" the "Essential" Past', p. 3.

57 J. Derrida, *Archive Fever: A Freudian Impression* (Chicago and London, 1996), pp. 7–11, quoted in B. Harris, '"Unearthing" the "Essential" Past', p. 8.

Chapter Fourteen

1 The comments and suggestions of Professor Tom Bennett and Dr Charles Villa-Vicencio in respect of this essay are gratefully acknowledged.

2 See the *Truth and Reconciliation Commission of South Africa Report* (5 vols., Cape Town, 1998), vol. 5, ch. 3, para. 3. While the remainder of the TRC was suspended on 31 October 1998, the lifespan of the Amnesty Committee was extended to allow it to attend to outstanding amnesty applications.

3 *TRC Report*, vol. 1, ch. 10.

4 B. Hamber, 'Living with the Legacy of Impunity: Lessons for South Africa about Truth, Justice and Crime in Brazil', in *Latin American Report*, vol. 13, no. 2, July–December 1997, at http://www.wits.ac.za/csvr/papbraz.htm, p. 6 (accessed on 4 April 2000).

5   *TRC Report*, vol. 1, ch. 1, p. 12.

6   Promotion of National Unity and Reconciliation Act, No. 34 of 1995, section 3.

7   G. Simpson, 'Tell No Lies, Claim No Easy Victories: A Brief Evaluation of South Africa's Truth and Reconciliation Commission', paper delivered at conference 'Dealing with Apartheid and the Holocaust – A Comparative Perspective', Yale Law School, March 1998, at http://www.wits.ac.za/csvr/artrcyal.htm, pp. 3–4 (accessed on 4 April 2000).

8   *Azanian People's Organisation (AZAPO) and Others v President of the Republic of South Africa and Others*, 1996 (8) BCLR 1015 (CC).

9   AZAPO case, pp. 1027–1028.

10 AZAPO case, p. 1030.

11 AZAPO case, p. 1031.

12 AZAPO case, p. 1032.

13 AZAPO case, p. 1032.

14 'Don't Shut Out the World (Again) – Serjeant at the Bar', *Mail & Guardian*, 23 August 1996.

15 A. O'Shea, 'Constitutional Court Judgment "Not Thorough"', *Mail & Guardian*, 20 September 1996; P. van Zyl, 'Justice Without Punishment: Guaranteeing Human Rights in Transitional Societies', in C. Villa-Vicencio and W. Verwoerd (eds.), *Looking Back/Reaching Forward* (Cape Town and London, 2000), pp. 42–57, at pp. 48–9.

16 M. C. Bassiouni, *Crimes Against Humanity in International Criminal Law* (Dordrecht, 1992), p. 37.

17 M. C. Bassiouni, *Crimes Against Humanity*, p. 38.

18 D. Orentlicher, 'Settling Accounts: The Duty to Prosecute Human Rights Violations of a Prior Regime', *Yale Law Journal*, vol. 100, 1991, pp. 2537–2615, at p. 2541.

19 D. Orentlicher, 'Settling Accounts', p. 2593.

20 D. Orentlicher, 'Settling Accounts', p. 2595.

21 D. Orentlicher, 'Settling Accounts', pp. 2595–6.

22 C. Nino, 'The Duty to Punish Past Abuses of Human Rights Put into Context: The Case of Argentina', *Yale Law Journal*, vol. 100, 1991, pp. 2619–40.

23 C. Nino, 'The Duty to Punish Past Abuses', p. 2637.

24 C. Nino, 'The Duty to Punish Past Abuses', p. 2638.

25 A. Cassese, 'Is There a Need for International Criminal Justice?', Distinguished Lecture at the Summer Session of the Academy of European Law, European University Institute, Florence, 7 July 1997.

26 Quoted in A. Cassese, 'Is There a Need for International Criminal Justice?', p. 5.

27 A. Cassese, 'Is There a Need for International Criminal Justice?', pp. 5–6.

28 M. Minow, *Between Vengeance and Forgiveness: Facing History after Genocide and Mass Violence* (Boston, 1998), pp. 133–35.

29 P. van Zyl, 'Justice Without Punishment', pp. 43–4.

30 P. van Zyl, 'Justice Without Punishment', pp. 51–4.

31 C. Villa-Vicencio, 'Why Perpetrators Should Not Always Be Prosecuted: Where the International Criminal Court and Truth Commissions Meet', *Emory Law Journal*, vol. 49, 2000, pp. 101–118, at p. 113.

32 C. Villa-Vicencio, 'Why Perpetrators Should Not Always Be Prosecuted', p. 102.

33 *TRC Report*, vol. 1, ch. 5, para. 82.

34 *TRC Report*, vol. 1, ch. 5, para. 82.

35 *TRC Report*, vol. 1, ch. 5, para. 98.

36 Quoted in the *TRC Report*, vol. 1, ch. 5, para. 98.

37 C. Villa-Vicencio, 'Why Perpetrators Should Not Always Be Prosecuted', p. 110.

38 C. Villa-Vicencio, 'Why Perpetrators Should Not Always Be Prosecuted', p. 111.

39 R. Slye, 'Justice and Amnesty', in C. Villa-Vicencio and W. Verwoerd (eds.), *Looking Back/Reaching Forward*, pp. 174–83, at p. 179.

40 See decision of the Amnesty Committee: AC/99/0172. (Decisions of the Amnesty Committee can be found on the TRC's website at http://www.truth.org.za.)

41 'What the Hani Judgment Said', *Mail & Guardian*, 9 April 1999.

42 'What the Hani Judgment Said', *Mail & Guardian*, 9 April 1999.

43 See decision of the Amnesty Committee: AC/98/0030.

44 See decision of the Amnesty Committee: AC/98/0030.

45 Statement of Judge A. Wilson, quoted in G. Davis, 'Past Flashes By in Death of a Golden Girl', *Mail & Guardian*, 11 July 1997.

46 Statement of R. Brink, the TRC's lawyer, quoted in G. Davis, 'Past Flashes By'.

47 G. Davis, 'Past Flashes By'.

48 R. Lyster, 'Amnesty: The Burden of Victims' in C. Villa-Vicencio and W. Verwoerd (eds.), *Looking Back/Reaching Forward*, pp. 184–92, at p. 189.

49 R. Lyster, 'Amnesty', p. 189.

50 R. Slye, 'Justice and Amnesty', p. 182.

51 B. Hamber, 'Living with the Legacy of Impunity', p. 7.

52 B. Hamber, 'Living with the Legacy of Impunity', p. 12.

53 T. Mtshali, 'Truth about Dlomo Made His Mother's Grief Unbearable', *Mail & Guardian*, 19 March 1999.

Chapter Fifteen

1 *Masakhane*: 'Let us build together' (Pay your electricity and rates campaign); *Bambanani*: 'Hold each other' (Pay your TV licence campaign); *Zama Zama*: 'Try' (Scratch-card competition).

2 A. Sparks, *Tomorrow is Another Country: The Inside Story of South Africa's Negotiated Revolution* (Johannesburg, 1994), p. 204.

3 A. Sparks, *Tomorrow is Another Country*, p. 53.

4 D. Boyd, 'Dominance Concealed through Diversity: Implications of Inadequate Perspectives on Cultural Pluralism', *Harvard Educational Review*, vol. 55, no. 3 (Fall 1996).

5 *Imbokodo* means 'the grinding stone' – a vigilante organisation in KwaNdebele that carried out brutal attacks in which hundreds of ordinary residents were viciously assaulted (*TRC Report*, vol. 2, ch. 5, p. 479, para. 293).

6 *Truth and Reconciliation Commission of South Africa Report* (5 vols., Cape Town, 1998), vol. 2, ch. 5, p. 491, para. 333.

7 C. van Onselen, *The Seed is Mine: The Life of Kas Maine, a South African Sharecropper, 1894 to 1985* (Cape Town, 1996).
8 *TRC Report*, vol. 5, ch. 9, p. 429, para. 130.
9 *TRC Report*, vol. 1, ch. 1, p. 17, para. 69.
10 *TRC Report*, vol. 5, ch. 8, p. 307, para. 12.
11 P. Freire, *Pedagogy of the Oppressed* (New York, 1968), p. 42.
12 P. Freire, *Pedagogy of the Oppressed*, p. 43.

Chapter Sixteen

1 M. Minow, *Making All the Difference: Inclusion, Exclusion, and American Law* (Ithaca, 1990), pp. 20–1, 70–2, 375–6.
2 Constitution of the Republic of South Africa, Act No. 108 of 1996.

Chapter Seventeen

1 *Truth and Reconciliation Commission of South Africa Report* (5 vols., Cape Town, 1998), vol. 1, ch. 1, p. 13, para. 54.
2 *TRC Report*, vol. 1, ch. 4, p. 70, para. 80.
3 *TRC Report*, vol. 2, ch. 6.
4 *TRC Report*, vol. 2, ch. 6, p. 525, para. 4.
5 *TRC Report*, vol. 4, ch. 4.
6 *TRC Report*, vol. 4, ch. 4, p. 107, para. 46.
7 *TRC Report*, vol. 4, ch. 4, p. 108, para. 48.
8 *TRC Report*, vol. 1, ch. 1, p. 22, para. 91.

Chapter Eighteen

1 J. Cochrane, J. de Gruchy and S. Martin (eds.), *Facing the Truth: South African Faith Communities and the Truth and Reconciliation Commission* (Cape Town, 1999).

Chapter Twenty

1 R. Aron, *Eighteen Lectures on Industrial Society* (London, 1967), p. 42.
2 *World Development Report*, Washington Annual.
3 A. Whiteford, D. Posel and T. Kelatwang, *A Profile of Poverty, Inequality and Human Development* (Pretoria, 1995), p. 13.
4 J. May (ed.), *Poverty and Inequality in South Africa* (Cape Town, 2000), p. 30.
5 Constitution of the Republic of South Africa, Act No. 108 of 1996.
6 J. May (ed.), 'Poverty and Inequality in South Africa', report prepared for the office of the Executive Deputy President and the Inter-Ministerial Committee for Poverty and Inequality (May 1998).
7 *World Development Report*, Washington Annual.

Chapter Twenty-one

1 R. Mattes, H. Thiel and H. Taylor, 'Citizens' Commitment to Democracy', in W. James and M. Levy (eds.), *Pulse: Passages in Democracy-Building: Assessing South Africa's Transition* (Cape Town, 1998), p. 93.

Chapter Twenty-two

1 J. Diamond, *Guns, Germs and Steel: The Fates of Human Societies* (New York, 1997).
2 A. Marx, *Making Race and Nation: A Comparison of South Africa, the United States, and Brazil* (New York, 1998).
3 T. Mbeki, *The Time Has Come* (Johannesburg, 1998).
4 Y. Fakier, *Grappling with Change* (Cape Town, 1998); W. James, 'Contours of a New Racism', *Siyaya!*, no. 2 (Winter 1998), pp. 60–61.
5 K. Odhav, M. Ndandani and K. Semuli, 'Critical Incidents of Schools and Legal Contestation Regarding Transformation: The Vryburg High School Crisis' (unpublished paper, University of the North-West, 1999).
6 R. Mattes, *The Election Book* (Cape Town, 1995).
7 I. Goldin and C. Heymans, 'Moulding a New Society: The RDP in Perspective' in G. Maharaj (ed.), *Between Unity and Diversity: Essays on Nation-Building in Post Apartheid South Africa* (Cape Town, 1999).
8 A. Sachs, 'Affirmative Action and the New Constitution' (African National Congress, 1994), p. 1.
9 K. Adam, 'The Politics of Redress: South African Style Affirmative Action', in *Journal of Modern African Studies*, vol. 5, no. 2 (1997), p. 231.
10 B. Nzimande, 'Black Advancement, White Resistance and the Politics of Class Reproduction' (University of Natal, unpublished Ph.D. dissertation, 1991).
11 Explanatory Memorandum to the Employment Equity Bill, *Government Gazette*, 1 December 1997.
12 White Paper on Affirmative Action in the Public Service, April 1998.
13 White Paper on Affirmative Action in the Public Service; M. Brassey, 'None So Silent as Those Afraid to Speak', *Sunday Times*, 12 July 1998.
14 Employment Equity Bill, *Government Gazette*, 1 December 1997.
15 S. Segal, 'Black Economic Empowerment', in W. James and M. Levy (eds.), *Pulse: Passages in Democracy-Building: Assessing South Africa's Transition* (Cape Town, 1998), p. 80.
16 M. Makanya, 'An Overview of Affirmative Action in South Africa', in A. van der Merwe (ed.), *Industrial Sociology: A South African Perspective* (Johannesburg, 1995), p. 162.
17 S. Segal, 'Black Economic Empowerment', p. 82.
18 Figures supplied by IDASA economist Warren Krafchik.
19 See R. Parsons, *The Mbeki Inheritance: South Africa's Economy, 1990–2004* (Johannesburg, 1999).

20 A. Boraine and J. Levy (eds.), *The Healing of a Nation?* (Cape Town, 1995); A. Boraine and J. Levy (eds.), *Dealing with the Past: Truth and Reconciliation in South Africa* (Cape Town, 1997); K. Asmal, L. Asmal and R. Roberts, *Reconciliation through Truth: A Reckoning of Apartheid's Criminal Governance* (Cape Town and New York, 1997).

21 *Truth and Reconciliation Commission of South Africa Report* (5 vols., Cape Town, 1998).

22 See the brilliantly written searing account of A. Krog, *Country of My Skull* (Johannesburg, 1998). See also: A. Krog, 'Truth and Reconciliation Commission', in W. James and M. Levy (eds.), *Pulse*, p. 42.

23 F. Van Zyl Slabbert, *Afrikaner Afrikaan: Anekdotes en Analise* (Cape Town, 1999).

24 T. Mbeki, *The Time Has Come.*

Bibliography

Books

H. Adam and K. Moodley, *The Opening of the Apartheid Mind* (Berkeley, 1993)

H. Adam, F. Van Zyl Slabbert, K. Moodley, *Comrades in Business: Post-Apartheid Politics in South Africa* (Utrecht, 1998)

B. Anderson, *Imagined Communities: Reflections on the Origin and Spread of Nationalism*, revised edition (London, 1991)

H. Arendt, *The Human Condition: A Study of the Central Conditions Facing Modern Man* (Garden City, NY, 1959)

R. Aron, *Eighteen Lectures on Industrial Society* (London, 1967)

K. Asmal, L. Asmal and R. Roberts, *Reconciliation through Truth: A Reckoning of Apartheid's Criminal Governance* (Cape Town and New York, 1997)

M.C. Bassiouni, *Crimes Against Humanity in International Criminal Law* (Dordrecht, 1992)

G. Bizos, *No-one to Blame? In Pursuit of Justice in South Africa* (Cape Town, 1998)

A. Boraine and J. Levy (eds.), *The Healing of a Nation?* (Cape Town, 1995)

A. Boraine and J. Levy (eds.), *Dealing with the Past: Truth and Reconciliation in South Africa* (Cape Town, 1997)

J. Cochrane, J. de Gruchy and S. Martin (eds.), *Facing the Truth: South African Faith Communities and the Truth and Reconciliation Commission* (Cape Town, 1999)

P. Connerton, *How Societies Remember* (Cambridge, 1989)

M. Cullen (ed.), *Das Holocaust-Mahnmal. Dokumentation einer Debatte* (Zürich, 1999)

E. de Kok, *A Long Night's Damage: Working for the Apartheid State* (Saxonwold, 1998)

J. Derrida, *Archive Fever: A Freudian Impression* (Chicago and London, 1996)

J. Diamond, *Guns, Germs and Steel: The Fates of Human Societies* (New York, 1997)

H. Dubiel, *Niemand ist fre von der Geschichte* (Munich, 1999)

Y. Fakier, *Grappling with Change* (Cape Town, 1998)

N. Frei, *Vergangenheitspolitik: Die Anfange der Bundesrepublik und die NS-Vergangenheit* (Munich, 1996)

P. Freire, *Pedagogy of the Oppressed* (New York, 1968)

J. Garlinski, *Fighting Auschwitz* (London, 1994)

M. Hunter, *Reaction to Conquest*, 2nd ed. (London, 1961)

M. Ignatieff, *The Warrior's Honour: Ethnic War and the Modern Conscience* (Toronto, 1998)

W. James and M. Levy (eds.), *Pulse: Passages in Democracy-Building: Assessing South Africa's Transition* (Cape Town, 1998)

K. Jaspers, *The Question of German Guilt* (New York, 1947)

L. Jaworski, *After Fifteen Years* (Houston, 1961)

A. Jeffery, *The Truth about the Truth Commission* (Johannesburg, 1999).

M. Jeismann (ed.), *Mahnmahl Mitte* (Cologne, 1999)

A. Krog, *Country of My Skull* (Johannesburg, 1998).

H. Marais, *South Africa: Limits to Change: The Political Economy of Transformation* (London and Cape Town, 1998)

A. Marx, *Making Race and Nation: A Comparison of South Africa, the United States, and Brazil* (New York, 1998)

R. Mattes, *The Election Book* (Cape Town, 1995)

J. May (ed.), *Poverty and Inequality in South Africa* (Cape Town, 2000)

T. Mbeki, *The Time Has Come* (Johannesburg, 1998)

M. Minow, *Between Vengeance and Forgiveness: Facing History after Genocide and Mass Violence* (Boston, 1998).

M. Minow, *Making All The Difference: Inclusion, Exclusion, and American Law* (Ithaca, 1990)

A. Neier, *War Crimes: Brutality, Genocide, Terror, and the Struggle for Justice* (New York, 1998)

W. Niemoller, *Neuenfang 1945: Zur Biographie Martin Niemoller* (Frankfurt, 1976)

R. Parsons, *The Mbeki Inheritance: South Africa's Economy, 1990–2004* (Johannesburg, 1999)

J. Pauw, *Into the Heart of Darkness: Confessions of Apartheid's Assassins* (Johannesburg, 1997)

P. Reichel, *Politik mit der Erinnerung. Gedächtnisorte im Streit um die nationalsozialistische Vergangenheit* (Frankfurt, 1999)

G. Schwan, *Politik und Schuld* (Frankfurt, 1997)

D.W. Shriver, *An Ethic for Enemies: Forgiveness in Politics* (New York, Oxford, 1995)

G. Slovo, *Every Secret Thing: My Family, My Country* (London, 1997)

A. Sparks, *Tomorrow is Another Country: The Inside Story of South Africa's Negotiated Revolution* (Johannesburg, 1994)

J. Thompson, *Ideology and Modern Culture: Critical Social Theory in the Era of Mass Communication* (Stanford, 1990)

Truth and Reconciliation Commission of South Africa Report (5 vols., Cape Town, 1998)

D. Tutu, *No Future Without Forgiveness* (New York, 1999)

M. Twala, *Mbokodo: Inside MK: Mwezi Twala, a Soldier's Story* (Johannesburg, 1994)

C. van Onselen, *The Seed is Mine: The Life of Kas Maine, a South African Sharecropper, 1894 to 1985* (Cape Town, 1996)

F. Van Zyl Slabbert, *Afrikaner Afrikaan* (Cape Town, 1999)

C. Villa-Vicencio and W. Verwoerd (eds.), *Looking Back/Reaching Forward: Reflections on the Truth and Reconciliation Commission of South Africa* (Cape Town and London, 2000)

A. Wolpe, *A Long Way Home* (Cape Town, 1994)

H. Wolpe, *Race, Class and the Apartheid State* (London, Addis Ababa, Paris, 1988)

C h a p t e r s   i n   B o o k s

I. Goldin and C. Heymans, 'Moulding a New Society: The RDP in Perspective', in G. Maharaj (ed.), *Between Unity and Diversity: Essays on Nation-Building in Post-Apartheid South Africa* (Cape Town, 1999)

M. Makanya, 'An Overview of Affirmative Action in South Africa', in A. van der Merwe (ed.), *Industrial Sociology: A South African Perspective* (Johannesburg, 1995), p. 162

S. Marks and N. Andersson, 'The Epidemiology and Culture of Violence', in A. du Toit and N. C. Manganyi (eds.), *Political Violence and the Struggle in South Africa* (London, 1990), p. 32

C. Rassool and P. Hayes, 'Science and the Spectacle: /Khanako's South Africa, 1936–7', in W. Woodward, P. Hayes and G. Minkley (eds.), *Deep Histories: Gender and Colonialism in Africa* (forthcoming)

H. J. Simons, 'The Law and its Administration', in Ellen Hellman (ed.), *Handbook on Race Relations in South Africa* (Cape Town, 1949), pp. 41–108

C. Villa-Vicencio and W. Verwoerd, 'Constructing a Report: Writing Up "the Truth"' in R. Rotberg (ed.), *Truth vs Justice* (Princeton, 2000)

J. Zalaquett, 'Balancing Ethical Imperatives and Political Constraints: The Dilemma of New Democracies Confronting Past Human Rights Violations', in N.J. Kritz, *Transitional Justice* (3 vols., Washington DC, 1995), vol. 2, pp. 495–96

J o u r n a l   A r t i c l e s

H. Adam, 'Widersprüche der Befreiung: Wahrheit, Gerechtigkeit und Versöhnung in Südafrika', *Leviathan*, vol. 18, 1998, pp. 350–70

K. Adam, 'The Politics of Redress: South African Style Affirmative Action', *Journal of Modern African Studies,* vol. 5, no. 2 (1997) p. 231

W. Bergmann, 'Kommunikationslatenz und Vergangenheitsbewältigung', *Leviathan*, vol. 18, 1998, pp. 393–408

D. Boyd, 'Dominance Concealed through Diversity: Implications of Inadequate Perspectives on Cultural Pluralism', *Harvard Educational Review*, vol. 55, no. 3, Fall 1996

I. Buruma, 'The Joys and Perils of Victimhood', *The New York Review of Books*, 8 April 1999, pp. 4–9

S. Ellis, 'The Truth and Reconciliation Commission of South Africa', *Critique Internationale*, October 1999

T. Garton Ash, 'The Truth About Dictatorship', *The New York Review of Books*, 19 February 1998, p. 40

C. Goschler, 'Offene Fragen der Wiedergutmachung', *Leviathan*, vol. 18, 1998, pp. 38–52

B. Hamber, 'Living with the Legacy of Impunity: Lessons for South Africa about Truth, Justice and Crime in Brazil', *Latin American Report*, vol. 13, no. 2, July–December 1997, at http://www.wits.ac.za/csvr/papbraz.htm

M. Ignatieff, *Index on Censorship: Wounded Nations, Broken Lives*, vol. 5, 1996, p. 122

W. James, 'Contours of a new racism', *Siyaya*, Issue 2, Winter 1998, pp. 60–61

S. Karstedt, 'Coming to Terms with the Past in Germany after 1945 and 1989: Public Judgements on Procedures and Justice', *Law & Policy*, volume 20:1, January 1998, pp. 15–56

H. König, et al. (eds.), 'Vergangenheitsbewältigung am Ende des zwanzigsten Jahrhunderts', *Leviathan*, vol. 18, 1998

'Address by President Mandela – Heritage Day', *Ilifa Labantu*, vol. 1, no. 9 (October 1997), p. 3

A. Neier, 'Truth Commission of South Africa Report (Cape Town, South Africa, 1998) and *Country of My Skull* by Antjie Krog (Johannesburg: Random House, 1998)', *The New York Review of Books*, 1999

C. Nino, 'The Duty to Punish Past Abuses of Human Rights Put into Context: The Case of Argentina', *Yale Law Journal*, vol. 100, 1991, p. 2619

D. Orentlicher, 'Settling Accounts: The Duty to Prosecute Human Rights Violations of a Prior Regime', *Yale Law Journal*, vol. 100, 1991, p. 2537

Siyaya!, no. 3 (Spring 1998)

C. Villa-Vicencio, 'Why Perpetrators Should Not Always be Prosecuted: Where the International Criminal Court and Truth Commissions meet', *Emory Law Journal*, vol. 49, 2000, p. 113

Conference Papers / Lectures

C. Bundy, 'The TRC Report: What Kind of History? What Kind of Truth?', a paper delivered at a conference organised by the Wits History Workshop and the Centre for the Study of Violence and Reconciliation, *TRC: Commissioning the Past*, June 1999

L. Buur 'Monumental History: Visibility and Invisibility in the Work of the South African TRC', paper delivered at a conference organised by the Wits History Workshop and the Centre for the Study of Violence and Reconciliation, *TRC: Commissioning the Past*, June 1999

A. Cassese, 'Is There a Need for International Criminal Justice?' Distinguished Lecture at the Summer Session of the Academy of European Law, European University Institute, Florence, 7 July 1997

A. du Toit, 'Perpetrator Findings as Artificial Even-Handedness? The TRC's Contested Judgements of Moral and Political Accountability for Gross Human Rights Violations', a paper delivered at a conference organised by the Wits History Workshop and the Centre for the Study of Violence and Reconciliation, *TRC: Commissioning the Past*, June 1999

A. du Toit, 'The Product and the Process: On the Impact of the TRC Report', a paper delivered at a conference organised by the Wits History Workshop and the Centre for the Study of Violence and Reconciliation, *TRC: Commissioning the Past*, June 1999

B. Harris, 'The Archive, Public History and the Essential Truth: The TRC Reading the Past', paper in *Refiguring the Archive* seminar series, University of the Witwatersrand, 1998

V. Harris, ' "They should have destroyed more": The Destruction of Public Records by the South African State in the Final Years of Apartheid', a paper delivered at a conference organised by the Wits History Workshop and the Centre for the Study of Violence and Reconciliation, *TRC: Commissioning the Past*, June 1999

G. Minkley, C. Rassool and L. Witz, 'Thresholds, Gateways and Spectacles: Journeying through South African Hidden Pasts and Histories in the Last Decade of the Twentieth Century', a paper presented at the conference *The Future of the Past: The Production of History in a Changing South Africa*, University of the Western Cape, 10–12 July 1996.

D. Posel, 'The TRC Report: What Kind of History? What Kind of Truth?', a paper delivered at a conference organised by the Wits History Workshop and the Centre for the Study of Violence and Reconciliation, *TRC: Commissioning the Past*, June 1999

P. Reynolds, Inaugural Lecture, UCT, 20 August 1997

A. Sachs, Public lecture on the TRC, 4th D.T. Lakdawala Memorial Lecture, 18 December 1998, New Delhi

G. Simpson, 'A Brief Evaluation of South Africa's TRC: Some Lessons for Societies in Transition', a paper delivered at a conference organised by the Wits History Workshop and the Centre for the Study of Violence and Reconciliation, *TRC: Commissioning the Past*, June 1999

G. Simpson, 'Tell No Lies, Claim No Easy Victories: A Brief Evaluation of South Africa's Truth and Reconciliation Commission', presentation at conference on *Dealing with Apartheid and the Holocaust – A Comparative Perspective*, Yale Law School, March 1998, at http://www.wits.ac.za/csvr/artrcyal.htm

C. Villa-Vicencio, 'Living in the Wake of the Truth and Reconciliation Commission: A Retroactive Reflection', paper presented in Siena, Italy, 16–19 March 2000

L. Witz, C. Rassool and G. Minkley, 'The Boer War, Museums and Ratanga Junction, the Wildest Place in Africa: Public History in South Africa in the 1990s', Basler Afrika Bibliographien Working Paper No 2: 2000, presented in Basel, 10 February 2000

<h2 style="text-align:center">Newspaper Articles</h2>

N. Ascherson, 'You Don't Have to be Clever to Run a Country: But It Helps', *Guardian and Observer*, Sunday, 20 June 1999

B. Atkinson, 'Review of Truth Veils at the Gertrude Posel and Market Theatre Galleries, 14 June–9 July 1999', ArtThrob (www.artthrob.co.za/99dec/reviews.html)

D. Beresford, 'Theatre of Pain and Catharsis', *Mail and Guardian*, 19–25 April 1996

M. Brassey, 'None So Silent as Those Afraid to Speak', *Sunday Times*, 12 July 1998

C. Braude, 'SA's Hearings Are Not Nuremberg, But Expediency Must Not Fudge the Truth', *The Sunday Independent*, 26 May 1996

G. Davis, 'Past Flashes By in Death of a Golden Girl', *Mail & Guardian*, 11 July 1997

R. Friedman, 'Tutu Visits War Memorial'; ' "White Bums" Missing from TRC Benches', *Cape Times*, 3 July 1996

M. Gevisser, 'The Ultimate Test of Faith', *Mail and Guardian*, 12–18 April 1996

J. Habermas, in *Die Zeit*, 15 May 1999

S. Hermans, 'A Quick Creative Buck', *The Argus*, 26 May 1993

D. Hooks, 'Review of Truth Veils at the Gertrude Posel and Market Theatre Galleries, 14 June–9 July 1999', ArtThrob (www.atrthrob.co.za/99dec/reviews.html)

Y. Kamaldien, 'Gugulethu 7, Trojan Horse Dead Honoured', *Cape Times*, 22 March 2000

Y. Kemp, 'Mayor Unveils Monument to Mark Fall of Guguletu 7', *Cape Argus*, 21 March 2000

A. Koopman, 'ANC Wants Community Reparations', Independent Online, at http://archive.iol.co.za/Archives/1999/9902/26/reparations.html

S. Laufer, 'Television Needs to Bring Grief of Truth Hearings to the Nation', *Business Day*, 6 May 1996

T. Mtshali, 'Truth about Dlomo Made His Mother's Grief Unbearable', *Mail & Guardian*, 19 March 1999

A. O'Shea, 'Constitutional Court Judgment "Not Thorough" ', *Mail & Guardian*, 20 September 1996

P. Singh, 'Memorial to Honour "Trojan Horse" Dead', *Cape Times*, 17 March 2000

P. Steyn, 'Tutu Onsteld oor Leemte in Begroting', *Die Burger*, 28 February 2000; *Cape Times*, 26 April 2000; *Weekend Saturday Argus*, 29/30 April 2000

'Don't Shut Out the World (Again) – Serjeant at the Bar', *Mail & Guardian*, 23 August 1996

'Truth Trickle Becomes a Flood', *Mail and Guardian*, 1–7 November 1996

'What the Hani Judgment Said', *Mail & Guardian*, 9 April 1999

Legislation/Policy Documents/ Case Law

Azanian People's Organisation (AZAPO) and Others v President of the Republic of South Africa and Others, 1996, (8) BCLR 1015 (CC)

Constitution of the Republic of South Africa, Act No. 108 of 1996

Employment Equity Bill, *Government Gazette* (1 December 1997)

Interim Constitution of the Republic of South Africa, Act No. 200 of 1993

J. May (ed.), 'Poverty and Inequality in South Africa', report prepared for the office of the Executive Deputy President and the Inter-Ministerial Committee for Poverty and Inequality (May 1998)

Promotion of National Unity and Reconciliation Act, No. 34 of 1995

'The Portfolio of Legacy Projects: A Portfolio of Commemorations Acknowledging Neglected or Marginalised Heritage' (Discussion Document, January 1998)

White Paper on Affirmative Action in the Public Service (April 1998)

Miscellaneous

B. Harris, ' "Unearthing" the "Essential" Past: The Making of a Public "National" Memory Through the Truth and Reconciliation Commission, 1994–1998', unpublished MA mini-thesis, University of the Western Cape (1998)

B. Nzimande, 'Black Advancement, White Resistance and the Politics of Class Reproduction' (University of Natal, unpublished Ph.D. dissertation, 1991)

K. Odhav, M. Ndandani and K. Semuli, 'Critical Incidents of Schools and Legal Contestation Regarding Transformation: The Vryburg High School Crisis', unpublished paper, University of the North-West (1999)

A. Sachs, 'Affirmative Action and the New Constitution' (1994, African National Congress)

Website of the South African Truth and Reconciliation Commission: http://www.truth.org.za

Index

AIDS 4

accountability 37, 56, 63, 65, 67–8, 70, 111, 136, 155, 165, 170

Acts of Parliament 132; Employment Equity Act 195; Group Areas Act 41, 60, 66, 95; Interim Constitution Act, No. 200 of 1993, Postamble of the 101; Promotion of National Unity and Reconciliation Act, No. 34 of 1995 (TRC Act) 16, 19, 24, 27, 41, 43, 45, 68, 73, 101, 104–5, 110, 116, 128–9, 131, 138

affirmative action 63, 160, 192, 194–5

affirmative procurement 196

African National Congress (ANC) 41, 45, 67, 70, 88, 193–4, 199; and affirmative action 195; and gross violations of human rights 28–9, 44, 89–90; and reparation 116–17; and the IFP 12, 63; and the negotiation process 11–12, 90, 146–7; and the TRC 44, 72, 74, 91–2, 198; Freedom Charter (1995) 193

Afrikaner Weerstandsbeweging 197

Alfonsin, Raul 133–4

amnesia 33–4, 36–7, 134, 188; in Germany 33–6

amnesty 3, 37, 63, 70, 131, 133–5, 198; and justice 99, 136; and reconciliation 130, 133; and the ANC 11–12, 72, 88–9; and the TRC 24, 43, 53–5, 58, 90, 101, 105, 109–10, 128, 138; and truth 130–1, 138–9, 198; blanket 130, 132, 135, 198; in Latin America 70, 130, 132–4; legal requirements in South Africa for 128–9, 138

Amnesty International 89

Anglo American Chairman's Fund 185–6

Anglo–Boer War 78–9, 121–2

apartheid 28, 46, 66, 146–7, 149, 179, 184, 198; aim of 84; and corruption 164, 166; and education 104, 183, 185–8; and the UN 133; dismantling of 67; monuments 121–2; moral claims of victims of 169–70; the truth about 59–60, 167

Appollis, Tyrone 124–5

archives 15, 25, 127

Arendt, Hannah 18–19, 60, 77

Argentina 51, 54, 57, 79–80, 131–4

art exhibitions 118–20

Ash, Timothy Garton 21, 24, 30

Asmal, Kader 29, 189, 198

Australia 39–40

Azanian People's Liberation Army (APLA) 137

Azanian People's Organisation (AZAPO) 89–91, 130–2

Benzien, Jeffrey 25, 69, 98

Biehl, Amy 76, 137–8

Biko, Nkosinathi 103

Biko, Steve 69, 103, 124–5

black business 195–6

black empowerment 194, 196

Boraine, Alex 68, 70

Boshoff, Carel 63, 206

Botha, P.W. 66, 69, 92, 202

Brandt, Willy 78

Bundy, Colin 21–2, 25, 27, 30–1, 95

Burundi 82, 84–7
Buthelezi, Mangosuthu 63, 78, 206

Canada 39–40
Cassese, Antonio 134
Central African Great Lakes Region 85
Chile 37, 45, 54–5, 57, 70, 73, 77, 131–2
Citizens' Army for Multi–Party Politics
    (CAMP) (Uganda) 86
Civil Co–operation Bureau (CCB) 16
CODESA *see* Convention for a Democratic
    South Africa (CODESA)
Coetzee, Dirk 43, 126, 205
Commission for Gender Equality 3
confession 65–9, 71, 79, 152
Congress of South African Trade Unions
    (COSATU) 199
Constitutional Court 130–2, 157
constitutionality 157–8, 177
Convention for a Democratic South Africa
    (CODESA) 151
corruption 57, 158–9, 163–6, 173, 186; as a
    violation of human rights 163, 172–3;
    commitment to eradication of 4, 164,
    183; public watchdogs 159, 164, 172

de Gruchy, John 173–4
de Klerk, F.W. 11, 45, 62–7, 69–70, 78, 93
de Kock, Eugene 25, 43, 64–5, 69, 94,
    96, 161
de Lange, Johnny 198
death penalty 157–8
dehumanisation 84–5, 96, 139
democracy 3, 26–7, 56–7, 162, 200; and
    stability 192; as threatened by corruption
    173; constitutional 165; emerging 37,
    137, 151, 163; financial cost of 160;
    sustainability of 190, 192
Democratic Republic of Congo 84, 87
Department of Arts and Culture, Science and
    Technology (DACST) 117
Derby-Lewis, Clive 137–8
Derrida, Jacques 15, 127
Douglas Commission 89
du Preez, Max 70–1, 92

Economic Community of West African States
    Monitoring Group (Ecomog)
    (Sierra Leone) 86
economic growth 179, 181–2, 196–7, 199

education 183, 185, 187, 189; and nation-
    building 187–9; effect of apartheid on 4,
    104, 154, 180, 183, 185–8; inequality of
    180, 186–7; transformation of 189–90
Eisenmann monument 35, 42–3
El Salvador 131–2
entitlement, culture of 173
equality 159–60, 162–3, 192, 196–7;
    see also affirmative action; inequality
ethnicity 45, 84, 86, 192

fairness 168
forced removals 59–60
forgiveness 63–5, 77–8, 101–3, 106, 109,
    166, 170–1, 186–7; reconciliation as 152
Freedom Front 197
Freire, Paulo 153–4
Frente de Libertação Moçambique
    (Frelimo) 85

Gandhi, Mohandas 97, 122–3
Germany 33–4; and reconciliation 82;
    guilt 77–8; lustration in 39;
    memorialising in 33–5; negotiated
    restitution and compensation 40–1;
    political re–education 42–3
Gerwel, Jakes 74–5
globalisation 181
Gobodo-Madikizela, Phumla 96, 103
Goldstone Commission 94, 161, 208
government; constraints facing it 181; under
    Mandela 3, 151, 182, 191, 198; under
    Mbeki 3, 191
Government of National Unity (GNU)
    11–12, 63, 182, 197
Growth, Employment and Redistribution
    (GEAR) 196
guilt 39, 69–70, 77, 80; and accountability
    70; collective 37, 42, 71, 82–3, 134;
    individual 37; or lack thereof 43–4

Habyarimana, *President* 83
Hani, Chris 137–8
Harris, Brent 15, 25
Heath, Willem 159, 172–3
heritage 116–18, 122–4, 127
historical injustice 40, 47
homelands 149, 180, 188
human rights 3, 28, 38, 57, 197;
    international law on 132